Occasional Papers in the Study of Islam, No. 8 (2019)

AYESHA'S SISTERS

Some Perspectives on Women in Islam

Editor

Ruth J Nicholls

The Arthur Jeffery Centre for the Study of Islam
Melbourne School of Theology

An affiliated college of the Australian College of Theology

mst press
Melbourne School of Theology

Arthur Jeffery Centre for the Study of Islam Occasional Papers, No 8.
(2019)
Ayesha's Sisters: Some Perspectives on Women in Islam

ISSN 1836 – 9782
ISBN: 978-0-9876401-1-6

Editor
Ruth Nicholls

Series Editor
Peter Riddell

Production and Cover Design
Ho-yuin Chan

Publishing Services
Thanks to Richard Shumack for his publishing services
Published by Melbourne School of Theology Press

Arthur Jeffery Centre for the Study of Islam

Melbourne School of Theology
5 Burwood Highway, Wantirna, Victoria 3152, Australia.
PO Box 6257, Vermont Sth., Victoria 3133, Australia
Ph: +61 3 9881 7800, Fax: +61 3 9800 0121
info@jefferycentre.mst.edu.au

People involved in the field of Christian engagement with Islam are welcome to submit related items to the Editor for consideration for publishing in the Arthur Jeffery Centre for the Study of Islam Occasional Papers.

ARTHUR JEFFERY CENTRE FOR THE STUDY OF ISLAM,
Melbourne School of Theology, Australia

Formerly known as the Centre for the Study of Islam and Other Faiths it was renamed the Arthur Jeffery Centre for the Study of Islam in 2016. Arthur Jeffery was an Australian Methodist missionary who first went to India and ultimately developed proficiency in 19 languages. A contemporary of Samuel Zwemer, Jeffery was invited to join the staff of the American University in Cairo, also becoming a recognized scholar of Islam. His book, "The Foreign Vocabulary of the Qur'an" which was first printed in 1938, still stands as the standard text in the field.

The Arthur Jeffery Centre for the Study of Islam is the only such Centre in Australia. Through its team of expert scholars and teachers of Islam it provides a variety of resources at both academic and public levels for those involved in or desiring to be involved in loving and meaningful engagement with Muslims.

The Centre is responsible for designing, preparing and teaching subjects approved by the Australian College of Theology at undergraduate and postgraduate levels relating to Islam. The Centre also aims for academic excellence through its publications which include not only scholarly works but also information for those who desire to increase their understanding of Islam. As part of its public engagement the Centre also holds open seminars and events, often joining with others sharing a similar vision and ethos. Staff are also available to speak at public programs.

In 2018 the Centre celebrated 10 years of operation and has established itself as a major centre for postgraduate studies in Islam.

For further information about the Centre and its activities, as well as opportunities to study Islam in a Christian context at both undergraduate and postgraduate levels, email info@JefferyCentre.mst.edu.au

TABLE OF CONTENTS

Editorial

Celebrating, honouring and respecting women is the aim of this edition of the Arthur Jeffery Centre for the Study of Islam Occasional Papers. Indeed, since women constitute some 50% of the human population it is fitting that they receive focused attention. As expressions of God's unique creation, they have their own distinctives and bring their own special giftings and abilities to life. So not surprisingly, all the contributors to this particular volume are women, who in turn reflect their own special understandings of the topic under consideration.

However, this volume has a particular nuance, for the specific angle being taken is more limited and specific. It is attempting to focus on those women living in an Islamic context, hence the title *Ayesha's Sisters: Some Perspectives on Women in Islam*. Since the Arthur Jeffery Centre for the Study of Islam area of expertise is Islam, surely it is not surprising that one of its volumes should focus on a significant group within that context – women. Such a choice, even in this day, could be considered by some not only to be controversial but also polemical. Some may even consider it to be demeaning while for others it is an opportunity to give the honour and respect which is felt to be due to women for whom for many years it has been denied. Even part of the title, *Women in Islam*, can be misconstrued to mean that women in Islam are a monolithic, undifferentiated, static group, living and experiencing Islam in the same way wherever they are. The truth, however, is very different. Muslim women live in a variety of geographical locations, influenced by underlying cultural distinctives that have been overlain by Islam, experiencing great diversity of economic and social conditions. As a result, each Muslim woman lives her own story, experiences Islam in her own way and grapples with the reality of her Islamic faith within her own personal context. While recognising this vibrant diversity, because these women are Muslim believers, they do share a commonality which unites them across the globe.

At the same time, the subject *Women in Islam* is simply vast and this is but a small volume which by implication can only touch on a limited number of subjects – hence the rider *Some Perspectives*.

Yet, given the diversity of opinions relating to the topic, this volume attempts to graciously and thoughtfully tell the story of women as it is – and by so doing, it aims to give honour where it is due while at the same time recognising the limitations that for many Muslim women are very real. Nevertheless, this volume invites the reader to consider the issues raised and to explore them further.

Controversy over the status of women in an Islamic context has been evident even from earliest (Islamic) times. The early writings regarding women in Islam also suggest that the status of women in Islam itself gave rise to questions and queries that continue to trouble both women (and men) inside Islam and those looking in from outside. In talking about early feminine Islamic saints, Farid al-Din Attar, one of the greatest Sufi writers, chose to consider them as honorary males, while at the same time recognizing that two-thirds of the Islamic faith owed its origin to the Prophet's wife Ayesha.[1] Indeed, even prior to Attar's work, various hadith relating to women had been circulating from the time of the Prophet if the records of their transmission are correct. Even Ayesha, one of the prophet's wives and apparently the favourite so the reports go, transmitted the saying that women were *deficient in intelligence and religion* (Sahih Bukhari 1:6: 301 [cf. also 2:24:541]). Surely this raises the question, which voice speaks the loudest and the strongest, or which voice has greater authority: the Qur'an with its divine revelation or the later assembled collections of hadith, some of whose origin is questioned and debated?

In the West, even prior to the feminist movement of the 1960s, though the suffragette movement in England was active during the early 1900s, there were those that echoed these negatives impressions of the status of women in Islam. The foreword to Dr and Mrs Zwemer's book entitled *Moslem Women* is introduced with the words: 'the tragic story of women under the Moslem faith,' in terms of their need to know and understand about the Christian faith.[2] Further into the volume they write,

---

[1] Farid al-Din Attar, *Muslim Saints and Mystics: Episodes from the 'Tadhkirat al-Auliya' (Memorial of the Saints)*, trans. A. J. Arberry (London: Routledge, 1966), 40.

[2] Dr and Mrs Samuel M. Zwemer, *Moslem Women* (West Medford, MA: Centre Committee on the United Study of Foreign Missions, 1926), Foreword.

In Mecca Mohammed was born, and here the legislation which determined forever the lot of millions of mothers and girls for many centuries received its divine sanction.[3]

While these words emerge from the 1920's milieu with its overarching negative view towards Islam, even within Islam itself there are women today who are questioning the time-honoured male interpretation and enforcement of the traditional understanding of the ancient texts. Equally one might ask, who are these women? Firstly, many are educated women who have grown up in the arms of Islam and have been subject to the traditional interpretations and whose very actions and life have been governed by that understanding. Secondly, some of these women are themselves grappling with the very text of Islam, be it the Qur'an and/or the Hadith. In so doing they are taking up the challenge of being Islamic scholars in their own right with the ability to offer exegesis of the Qur'anic text itself. Not surprisingly, the results of their interactions with, and their exegesis and interpretation of, the texts, are differing views. Some have, to varying degrees, been influenced by the feminist movements which have been actively pursued in the West and so in turn are grappling with the time-honoured interpretations. Other women, though, have learnt to work the system operating within the confines that have bound them for centuries which for some mean that they are slowly impacting the Islamic edifice, like waves moulding a coastline. Still others, however, who have taken a more vocal position, even attempt public demonstrations, while for others this protest has been with their pens.

Within this volume we traverse the varied sands of an Islamic woman's world. The first part of our study looks at the 'texts'. These are the sources from which the attitudes and the current interpretations of a Muslim woman's world have emerged. Cathy Hine begins by taking us through the vexed question of an Islamic theology of women. This, for some, raises the question as to whether the issue is a valid avenue of study since both men and women are 'human', thus 'affirm[ing] their equality'.[4] Her paper highlights the unsettled and difficult-to-clarify nature of the controversy that is found within the Islamic world regarding the position of women, and the understanding of a woman's place and her role in particular. Hine

---

[3] Zwemer, 12.

[4] Ibid., 7.

3

also raises the issue of the insider and the outsider perspective, especially since both these perspectives are founded on ingrained worldviews with preconceived frames of reference and interpretations. Having identified this, she deliberately attempts to listen attentively to what Muslim women, *Muslima*, themselves are saying. Yet, at the same time, from the perspective of an outsider, Hine herself raises a number of very important issues in relation to a theology of women in Islam.

Central to any understanding of Women in Islam is a study of the portrayal of women within the Qur'an itself. Carol Walker skilfully analyses how the Qur'an itself depicts women and by using a table clearly indicates how much space in the Qur'an itself is given to women. Interestingly, she notes that Miriam (Mary, the mother of Jesus) is the only woman who is named. The many other women referred to in the Qur'an are usually mentioned in terms of their relationship to a male. Walker notes that the main *sura* in which the Prophet's wives are mentioned is Q33, while Q66 refers to a number of women. While this paper is limited in the extent to which it can consider the portrayal of women in the Qur'an, *sura* 66, to quote Walker, 'refer[s] to women from past periods of monotheism' and by so doing 'censur[es] the women of Muhammad's world who are not following their example.'

While the revelations of the Prophet have been recorded in the Qur'an, it is, however, the *sira* of the Prophet's life and the *hadith,* the collection of sayings attributed to the Prophet, that have also shaped and influenced much of Islamic life and culture. Tara MacArthur's paper "Mother's of the Faithful" details how these records of Muhammad's dealings with his wives and his relationships with them have not only shaped but have determined attitudes toward women, how they are treated, and how their lives as women have been shaped.

The second part of the volume looks at Women in Islam: Living as Muslim Women. Obviously, the emphasis is not on the 'theoretical' but on how women in Islam actually live out their understanding of their faith. In the first of the papers by Moyra Dale, she outlines the living practice of a Muslim woman and how this is shaped not only by the five pillars of Islam, but also the interpretations of Islam as have been handed down over the centuries. Dale also paints a picture of women who are active

4

participants in their faith even though they are also subject to the restrictions of being women. In her second article, Dale highlights the formal role of Muslim women in the mission of Islam not only in an attempt to spread Islam where it is not known but also to ensure that Muslim women understand and practice their own faith.

One might ask, are there models of faith that Muslim women can follow? The answer is yes and one of the most famous of these is one of the early Sufi woman saints, Rabi'a al-'Adawiyya, who it appears has also left a written record of her understanding in poetry. Ruth Nicholls outlines the major characteristics of this holy woman who not only rose to the level of a Sufi saint but who also, because of her knowledge, was acknowledged as a teacher and instructor. While this for her male counterparts 'raised her' to the status of a man, Rabi'a was a woman who became famous for serving God out of 'love'. However, Rabi'a al 'Adwayyia is not alone. There are written records of many women who have conscientiously lived out their faith. In so doing, they become models for the women who follow them.

In a second article by Nicholls, she looks at a very practical aspect of the life of a Muslim woman. Since neither the Qur'an nor Hadith, *sunna* or *sira* provide all the answers for living in obedience to Allah, a complex system of establishing what is acceptable has arisen. This has been formalised through the pronouncements of specially formed councils which issue formalised pronouncements known as *fatawa* (sing. *fatwa;* Engl. pl. fatwas) which determine much of the actual behaviours of both men and women. However, it certainly seems that these *fatawa* are far more detailed and explicit for women. Nicholls' article explores the role of the *fatawa* in determining the lived lives of women while at the same time showing how women, who understand *fatawa* together with their knowledge of Islamic *shari'a,* use both to their own advantage.

As was mentioned earlier, the world of Muslim women is incredibly diverse. Penelope Tan's article looks at the current place of women in Singapore. While 'the stereotype of women in Islam worldwide being oppressed and marginalised is a common perception among non-Muslims,'[5] she asks 'how equal can equal

---

[5] p169

5

get?"[6] suggesting that within the multi-cultural, multi-religious context of Singapore, a Muslim woman's legal position is a different story. In her conclusion she notes 'it is fair to conclude that these women enjoy an equality that is reasonable within the confines of moderate Islam'.[7] In turn, however, one needs to ask are there women in Singapore who are living within the context of a more conservative Islam? If there are, how do they fare? Does government legislation also work on their side? Those questions are left unanswered though there are hints that conservative Islam is alive and well in that nation.

Jane Wiseman's article, however, reflects on a very different situation – a situation so different that Baroness Cox, a human rights activist on behalf of abused Muslim women, was the instigator of an independent review into the application of *Shari'a* law especially as it related to *Shari'a* councils operating in the UK. The review noted that since there is no registry of married Muslim women they are in effect 'not married' under British law and are therefore at a disadvantage legally. The review made a number of recommendations while one of the commentators noted that, in truth, the change must come from within Islam itself.

The next article by Shirin Taber raises the very important question relating to the role of women in the economic development in a country. While the opportunities for economic gain by a roving woman in a desert environment is extremely limited, in countries where women play a significant role in economic development the status of women there is a significant difference in women's status and in attitudes towards them. In her study, Taber examines the role of Khadijah, the Prophet's wife in the life of her husband in a desert environment where trade played an important role. Taking Khadijah's life as instructive Taber asks why 'more Muslim women' are not following her example?[8] This leads Taber to ask questions about Islamic feminism and the interpretation of the Qur'an in today's world. From this Taber then considers that Quranic nature of God as well as religious freedom. Taber writes,

> ... the huge task of promoting women's rights in conjunction with religious freedom is not a venture that Muslims can

---

[6] p169
[7] p184
[8] p213

accomplish alone. The risks are too dangerous. ... Women are punished for speaking out or demanding their universal human rights. Some Muslim women are imprisoned and even killed.[9]

In her conclusion Taber challenges everyone everywhere to come alongside Muslim women. She claims that while Muslim women are striving for their rights and religious freedom they must be supported by those outside their world, so that they can 'fulfil their God-given purpose.'

Women in Islam – this small volume can provide but a glimpse, a brief foray into the world of a geographically, economically and socially diverse group of people, especially women who are united by the fact that they are adherents of Islam. Sadly, most of this volume has been written by outsiders looking in, though this was not the plan. Hopefully, the papers included here will encourage you to read further and more widely. Most importantly, though, I hope that it will also encourage you to listen to the voices of Muslim women themselves and so discover the rich variety of their experiences and their understandings of their world.

Ruth Nicholls

---

[9] p220

PART I

WOMEN IN ISLAM

LISTENING TO THE TEXTS

WHEN WOMEN SPEAK:

Listening to Muslima 'Theologies of Women'.

Cathie Hine[1]

For Muslim men and Muslim women, believing men and believing women, devout men and devout women, truthful men and truthful women, men and women who are patient and constant, men and women who are humble, men and women who give charity, men and women who fast, men and women who guard their private parts; men and women who remember God a lot, God has prepared forgiveness for them and a great reward (Q33:35).

I shall not lose sight of those (who work in my way) be it man or woman. You are members, one of another (Q3:195).

And he it is Who has brought you into being from a single being (Q6:98).

Whereas Asma Barlas contends that Muslims have not yet derived a theory of equality from the *Qur'an*, Nora Amath says, 'Islam views men and women as independent individuals, equal in the eyes of God' (n.d., 1). This view is further explicated by Muna Tatari as she asserts,

> The Qur'an contains a number of verses that deal with gender. These verses speak of an ontological equality between man and woman and call for equal standards of ethical behavior, ask-ing both sexes to participate in their community and their environ-ment as a manifestation of their God-given responsibility (2013, 157).

In recent times, Amina Wadud has been a leading voice in the call

---

[1] Cathy Hine is a practitioner scholar and the co-founder of the *When Women Speak* network, with interests in women, Islam, change and the gospel.

for reinterpretation of the *Qur'an* based on a view that the *Qur'an* does not differentiate between men and women, rather that it affirms their equality in creation, purpose and relationship to God (1999a).

These Muslim women's views are often dismissed as being marginal, the voices of a few, western-influenced, feminist scholars. While it is true that they are not voices at the centre of fundamentalist, orthodox Islam, they are nonetheless part of a growing movement of women (and men) seeking to engage their religious texts to address issues of equality and justice for women. Their works are marked by a determination that theology must be a lived reality, both concrete and relevant to the world in which they live.

Different voices read and interpret the texts differently. Verses such as the following from the *Qur'an*, in addition to others from the *Ahadith*, are used to theologise that women are less than men in creation, in ethics, in morality and in relationship with God, and therefore need to be contained and limited for the health of the community.

> Q33:53, *'O you who believe! Enter not the dwellings of the Prophet for a meal without waiting for its time to come, unless leave be granted you. But if you are invited, enter; and when you have eaten, disperse. Linger not, seeking discourse. Truly that would affront the Prophet, and he would shrink from telling you, but God shrinks not from the truth. And when you ask anything of [his wives], ask them from behind a veil [hijāb].'*

> Q24:31, *'And tell the believing women to lower their eyes and to guard their private parts, and to not display their adornment except that which is visible thereof. And let them draw their kerchiefs over their breasts, and not to display their adornment except to their husbands, or their fathers, or their husbands' fathers, or their sons, or their husbands' sons, or their brothers, or their brothers' sons, or their sisters' sons, or their women, or those whom their right hands possess, or male attendants free of desire, or children who are innocent of the private areas of women.'*

> Q4:34, *'Men are in charge of women by [right of] what Allah has given one over the other and what they spend [for maintenance] from their wealth. So righteous women are devoutly obedient, guarding in [the husband's] absence what Allah would have them guard. But those [wives] from whom you fear arrogance - [first] advise them;*

[then if they persist], forsake them in bed; and [finally], strike them.
But if they obey you [once more], seek no means against them.
Indeed, Allah is ever Exalted and Grand.'

On what basis do I, a Christian woman, speak about a Muslim Theology of women? I am a neighbour looking in. I read and interpret these texts of Islam, the *Qur'an* and the *Ahadith*, through my Western, Christian, feminist lens. There are preconceptions that I constantly struggle against in order to hear the voices of my Muslima neighbours.

Hence, the approach of this essay is to seek to listen to some of the voices of Muslima Theologies. I say 'seek' to listen because I acknowledge that overcoming preconceptions to truly hear is not easy, and without longer ongoing reflective conversations with my Muslima neighbours, my understanding of their ideas and thoughts has not been tested. 'Muslima' is used intentionally, reflecting the way women are articulating their own identity as women of faith (Aslan, 2013; Lamptey, 2018). Then, as women are speaking from their multiple locations, interrogating their religious texts to know who they are in relation to God and how they are to live that out so as to reflect the nature of God, there is not one single theology that emerges. The use of the 'theologies' acknowledges the many understandings, and articulations of those understandings, that shape Muslima lived faith.

This essay explores Muslima 'Theologies of women' through four thematic areas: the nature of God; contested interpretations on women's deficiency and *fitna*; the Prophet Muhammad as exemplar for Muslims; and community in the practices of ritual and leadership. It draws on a diverse range of Muslima voices in an effort to understand their efforts to reinterpret the religious texts. It explores fresh articulations of women in their identity and roles, and listens to their desire for justice for women founded on solid and coherent theologies. However, as we seek to listen to their voices, there is a question that is fundamentally problematic: why do we explore a 'theology of woman'?

The problematic of gendering the normative in theology

If we seek to trace the development of theologies of women, are we also pursuing theologies of men? Whatever our faith tradition, it seems perplexing that it is necessary to consider a 'theology of woman' as separate from a 'theology of man', especially since in my own Christian faith tradition 'man' is usually said to refer to mankind.[2] Is male the normative in developing theology and defining the fundamentals of religion? Do women receive different treatment from men in understanding the nature of relationship to God and a lived faith?

The problem is exacerbated by many of the assumptions underlying Christian articulations of the faith and life of Muslim women. The starting point is a male normative: male interpretations of religious texts, male legislation of acceptable limits around behaviour, male regulations imposed through *Shari'a*; male appropriation of religious space. Male becomes the base-line standard for articulating religious belief and practice, the measure by which we make deterministic decisions about what Islam says about women.

Muslima theologians have identified this issue. Quoting the work of Kecia Ali, Jerusha Tanner Lamptey says that significant issues are created for women when we fail to

> problematize the underlying patriarchal infrastructure of Islamic law, which assigns differing value and agency to men and women. As a result, they end up inadvertently reinforcing male normativity and male dominance (2018, 14).

Asma Lamrabet concurs:

> There is an explicit Islamic discourse that categorises women in a monolithic framework, that of the 'status or rights of women,' when it does not do the same with the masculine equivalent, or make a specific reference to the 'status or rights of men.' This inevitably forces the idea of an 'Islamic standard,' that is of an 'ideal man' who represents 'human nature' or the 'human being' in all of its totality and glory. Following this logic, the woman, in comparison, brings to mind only the image of a structurally subordinate, deficient, dependent, and eternally stigmatised being, given its inability to achieve the universal standard embodied by man (2018, 11).

---

[2] Ed. Note: However, with the rise of feminism the concept of 'man' as in 'mankind' has been strongly criticised and is often interpreted as referring to 'men' only.

Being cognisant of some of the problems inherited by starting with an androcentric norm, this essay seeks to hear Muslima voices as they work to shift the weight of normative interpretations within Islam to include feminist voices.

This essay also acknowledges that 'feminist' is a contested label in faith traditions, and is no less a challenge for Muslima women rearticulating theologies. The first wave of Muslima scholars seeking to reinterpret the *Qur'an* sought to distance themselves from the 'feminist' label or frame of reference in tackling the issues of women. More recent scholarship owns at least the influence of feminism, with some embracing it from within Islam.

Acknowledging these issues, I move now to hear from my Muslima neighbours, and their work to develop a theology of women.

The nature of God in formulating theologies of woman

Quoting Anne McGrew Bennet, Asma Barlas says:

> ... a culture's idea of divinity is central not only to that culture's religious life but also to its social, political, familial institutions and relationships," [so] how we define God has implications not only for patriarchies but also for a theology and hermeneutics of liberation (2002, 94).

Seeking to understand how women living under Islam understand God and the nature of their relationship with him is one step to grasping their concepts of women. Notions of identity are formed in the framework of an understanding of the nature of God. One place this is encapsulated for Muslims is in the *Shahada* and its declaration of the unique and incomparable being of God. Muslima interpreters of their religious texts argue that this One God is the source of liberation from all forms of oppression for humans. They seek to demonstrate that the *Shahada* bears witness to this and is a testimony to human equality and an expression of divine justice (Lamrabet, 2018, 28).

The idea is developed by Amina Wadud, Asma Barlas, Jerusha Tanner Lamptey, and Kecia Ali, among others, who build their understandings of women through their conceptualisation of *tawhid* and the ways they apply this to lived experiences. *Tawhid* describes the unicity, oneness, uniqueness of God. Wadud says:

> '...tawhid relates to the transcendent and yet eminent divinity or ultimate reality, the 'unicity' of Allah. Allah is uniform, and unites exisiting multiplicities or seeming dualities in both the corporeal and the metaphysical realm' (2006, 28).

> 'Say: [God] is God, the One and Only; God, the Eternal, Absolute; [God] begets not, Nor is [God] begotten; And there is none like unto [God].' (Q112) This unicity of God must be applied to the relationship between his being and his speech and, argues Asma Barlas, it must be the hermeneutical site from which the community then reads the Qur'an (2002, 13).

Drawing together the arguments of various Muslima scholars, Ayesha Hidayatullah proposes that the *Qur'an* is about reminding human beings of their 'origins in God's unity' (2014, loc. 2463). Lamptey applies this principle of *tawhid* by positing it as a 'central theological concept within Islamic thought' that

> as a counter construct, not only affirms the unity of all humanity but also delegitimizes certain possibilities for human beings (2018, 158).

She says that because God is unique no human, neither male nor female, can claim anything that wholly and uniquely belongs to God.

Feminist Muslima scholars and theologians interpret *tawhid* as a foundational principle of reform and contend it should be the basis of reclaiming theological thought concerning the nature and equality of women. According to Hidayatullah, placing males in authority over women is a violation of the *tawhidic* principle because men then put themselves in the place of God (2014, loc. 2495); that is, they take to themselves something that belongs to God alone. The conclusion is that women are created equal before God, and that this should translate into the practices of faith in the everyday of life.

God is incomparable, and also unrepresentable. Muslima scholars like Barlas categorically defend Islam from any 'father' imagery or view of God.

Invent not similitude for God: for God knows, and ye know not (Q16:74);
and,
God has said: 'Take not (For worship) two gods: for [God] is just One God Then fear me (and Me alone)' (Q16:51).

She asserts that anthropomorphising God through the use of gendered language and imagery negatively defines women and subjects them to the violences and abuses of patriarchy (2002, 93-94). Furthering her argument, Barlas says that in neither literal nor symbolic ways can God be described in relationship as father, and that this makes it impossible for Islam to then construct women under patriarchal norms (2002, 98). She points to the *Qur'an*:

(Both) the Jews and Christians say: "we are sons of God, and His beloved." Say: "why then doth [God] punish you for your sins? Nay, ye are but men, - of the men [God] hath created" (Q 5:20).

This rejection of Islam as a 'theological patriarchy' situates women as fully orbed equals in submission to God, able to navigate their identity and being within this framework of equality under God.

This further expands into affirming the role of women as equal viceregents of God on earth. 'And when the Lord said to the angels,

"I am placing a vicegerent upon the earth," they said, "wilt those place therein one who will work corruption therein, and shed blood, while we hymn Thy praise and call thee Holy?" He said, "Truly I know what you know not" (Q 2:30).

Various interpretations of this verse conclude that women are not second-class vicegerents of God (Lamrabet, 2018, 42), and to place them under men so as to exclude them from this God-ordained responsibility is to deny the thrust of the *Qur'an,* and its definition of the nature of God, that human vicegerency is granted to men and women equally. Lamrabet believes that the *Qur'an* considers both men and women to be

Custodians of an eternal promise, the promise to life on earth and perpetuate the divine creation in all its splendor and beauty (2018, 31).

Rereading the *Qur'an* without 'gender dualisms and binaries', and rejecting anthropomorphic definitions of God, opens the opportunity to 'theorise human subjectivity in terms that respect the complete equality and humanity of women and men' (Barlas, 2002, 108).

Exploring the nature of God as a framework for understanding theologies of women challenges the cultural accruements that have become enshrined in orthodox Islamic theologies. Barbara Stowasser believes that within Islam, theological and legal paradigms enshrined cultural norms of the day regarding women and gender, and that this excluded women and the way they were read in the *Qur'an* (1994, 7). Muslima scholars are referencing fundamental theologies on the nature of God to overcome the crusts of culture that have been used to define them within Islam.

Questioning women's deficiency and *fitna*

According to Adis Duderija three criteria have traditionally been used to conceptualise a religiously ideal Muslim woman:

> ... the nature of the female (and by implication male) sexuality; ... [the] role and function of women in broader society/public sphere, especially the purpose and function of seclusion and veiling for women; and ... spousal rights and obligations, especially the role of the wife in marriage (2011, 6).

He says that

> [t]he category of the female gender is constructed primarily in sexual terms. Women are identified with the "irreligious" realm of sexual passion, as repositories of all "lower" aspects of human nature, the very anti-study of [the] "illuminated" sphere of male (religious) knowledge, which is the source of religious authority (Duderija, 2011, 101).

Women are constructed as the source of social and moral chaos, anti-divine and therefore subject to restrictions.

A range of verses from the *Qur'an*, along with many *Hadith*, are used to justify this conceptualisation of women: for example Q24: 2, 14, 28, 30-31; Q33:59; Q33:32-33; Q33:53; Q4:34; Q2:228. Q4:34 reads:

> '*Men are in charge of women by [right of] what Allah has given one*

Barlas, 2002, 183), recent scholars acknowledge that Islam must own its own interpretative frameworks and not absolve itself of responsibility for this conceptualisation of women as deficient and the source of *fitna* (see the work of Lamptey, 2018).

The Prophet Muhammad as Exemplar

In her innovative work to reclaim a fresh theologising of women in the *Qur'an* and *Hadith*, Jerusha Tanner Lamptey attempts something that has been given little attention elsewhere, the Prophet Muhammad's maleness. Prophet Muhammad is held as an example for all Muslims, an example they are exhorted to emulate or imitate. However, a number of questions are being asked concerning the example of the Prophet Muhammad: in what ways is the example of Prophet Muhammad contextual and how does the time and place of his example translate to today's world?; how are women excluded from fully emulating Prophet Muhammad and what does this do for the religious life and experience?; and how does encouraging women to follow the example of Prophet Muhammad's wives marginalise them from the highest example for emulation, the Prophet himself? Lamptey identifies that gender plays a role in the theological discourses around Prophet Muhammad (2018, 123).

Referencing the work of Annemarie Schimmel, Lamptey acknowledges the beauty of Prophet Muhammad's example whilst referencing tensions that arise when the distinctions between the divine and human appear to be blurred (2018, 123-125). At the same time, there are underlying assumptions that need to be problematised by Muslima scholars who seek to interpret those verses of the *Qur'an* that hold the Prophet as worthy of emulation. What should be done with the 'invocation of a historically human male as a universal exemplar?' (Lamptey, 2018, 121). There has been little work done by feminist Muslima scholars on the differing aspects of the Prophet's example and it appears that it would be a challenging topic to address because of the esteem given to the person and role of Prophet Muhammad in Islam. Jerusha Tanner Lamptey is one Muslima scholar who recognises the need for Islamic feminists and Muslima theologians to address concerns with 'the maleness of Prophet Muhammad and the implications of this maleness for emulation of his moral example' (2018, 122). The implications on a theology of women in Islam need to be addressed by those calling for fresh interpretations of the *Qur'an* and *Sunnah*.

While acknowledging that the *Qur'an* says believers should 'obey' the prophet, Asma Barlas rejects ideas of the infallibility of the Prophet, addressing the issue of exemplar by rejecting the possibility of depicting the prophets as either symbolic fathers or symbols of the Divine (2002, 129). How to obey and follow Prophet Muhammad, in accordance with the injunction of the *Qur'an*, becomes an issue. Barlas' approach is twofold. She draws on the arguments of another scholar, Barbara Metcalf, in asserting that the principle of the equality of women and men is informed by the fact that both women and men are called to follow the example of the Prophet. She also argues that Prophet Muhammad does not carry, what she calls, 'hyper-masculinist' traits, concluding therefore that all Muslims have a model to emulate in him (2002, 122).

Not all women scholars agree with Barlas' approach. Kecia Ali is among those who explore the Prophet as exemplar through the lens of context, where his example is seen as representative of the time (Lamptey, 2018, 127). She says that with the changes in time and context it is appropriate for Muslims to ask questions about the example of Prophet Muhammad. Ali continues this argument saying that Muslims must go beyond subsuming all the issues around the example of the Prophet under the rubric of what she calls 'westoxication' (2004, 274). Ali calls into question the absoluteness of the Prophet's example, noting that there are a number of areas of exception, such as the number of wives he can have, where he is exempt from the usual rules. This discussion is pertinent because it confronts the tensions regarding definitions of women in the *Ahadith* in particular, and therefore frames theologies of women. Questions about the role of the Prophet as exemplar are raised because of the misogynistic texts that define women negatively and with limitations. A number of women seem to believe that the *sunnah* of the Prophet should be rejected as a source of example and therefore as the framework for the theological and legal framing of women (Barlas, 2002; Wadud, 1999a). Both Wadud and Barlas seem to add caveats to their rejection, though Ali argues that Wadud concludes her book, *Qur'an and Women*, with an appeal to the *sunnah* of Prophet Muhammad (Ali, 2004, 286).

The topic of exemplar is also approached more circuitously by engaging discussions on the role of the Prophet's wives as exemplars for the community. Or, are they only exemplars for women? Barbara Stowasser (1994) has done extensive work on the examples of women in the *Qur'an*, noting her conviction that female symbols have been important in the construction of Islamic self-identity (Stowasser, 1994, 9). Barlas argues that the wives of Prophet Muhammad were exceptional too, and that while their example was for all, the standard required of them is not required from all Muslims. This allows her to build an argument that, for example, *hijab* and seclusion have limited application because they were specific to that particular context (2002, 124). However, as Lamptey notes, laws have been codified and acceptable social behaviour for women determined around the example of the wives of the Prophet.

While inclusion of the Prophet's wives as examples may appear to open new doors of engagement for women, it also

> vividly reveals the presence of gendered and sexed assumptions in emulation and veneration of Prophet Muhammad. If Prophet Muhammad's *Sunna* [sic] alone does not accommodate female experience, concerns, and obligations, then that *Sunna* [sic] is gendered and sexed (Lamptey, 2018, 129).

Where there are limitations for women in pursuing Prophet Muhammad as exemplar, the construction of theologies of women are constrained within those limitations. Muslima scholars and theologians are confronted with the challenging legacy constructed by historical interpretations of his *sunnah* and the charged emotional environment that surrounds questioning his role as exemplar. Their work is pressing against historical interpretive narratives that have excluded women through an androcentric focus on the exemplary role of Prophet Muhammad.

Community in the practices of leadership and ritual

Creating the public/private divide that institutes social and role boundaries, where the private is the primary arena of women, along with a failure to recognise women's work in that arena as contributing to society and the community, has resulted in women being marginalised from participation as equal members of the community. As theology is made visible in permitted practices, as Muslim women of faith act to reclaim space from which they have previously felt excluded, the tensions of changing theologies are made visible.

Amina Wadud is most widely known in the West for her

23

actions that cut across the previous limitations on women's participation in the most definitive public space in Islam, the mosque. Her widely publicised leadership of prayers in New York in 2005, followed her address at the Claremont Main Road Mosque in Cape Town in 1994. In this address she spoke from her experience as a mother, drawing analogies with what she calls the 'engaged surrender' that defines a Muslim's life in Islam. She concluded her talk saying:

> ... the task of a Muslim is to continually engage in surrender ... Should we even forget that we must consciously be engaged in surrender, surely Allah never forgets ... He ... always accepts our effort to engage ourselves in surrender to Him.

She says of that *khutbah* that the 'words flowed from the centre of my innermost yearning for meaning as a woman in Islam' (2006, 158-162).

Wadud believes that the inclusive participation of women in the leadership of mixed-gender congregational prayers is a matter of theology, where women are not defined theologically differently from men (Lamptey, 2018, 190). She situates her actions within her beliefs and practices with respect to *da'wa*, the belief that all Muslims are called to renewal personally and to call non-Muslims to embrace Islam. Wadud acknowledges that the personal is political and that actions such as hers aim to challenge hegemonic constructions of women under Islam. Women have been theologised about, but through their emergence and activities in spaces from which they have previously been precluded they are seeking to be part of theologising. Wadud, and other scholars like her, have as their starting point a theology of equality regarding all humankind and they pursue this through their leadership and the way they participate in ritual practices.

Women are rooting their activism in their reinterpreted theological principles. Wadud says her actions were founded on her understanding of *tawhid* (discussed in an earlier section), and its fullest expression in 'reciprocal relations between women and men in all aspects of society: Familial, political, and spiritual functions, roles and contexts' (2006, 168). Muslima feminists argue against gender-based restrictions on the basis of what Lamptey has called

24

'theological anthropologies'. In addition to the *tawhidic* principle that roots Wadud's theologising, *khalifa*, *taqwa* and the removal of a man-made division between the moral and social spheres frame Muslima theologising about women (2018, 191). Practice embodies theology.

Lamptey addresses an important, but neglected, aspect of women-led prayers and the importance and role of communal prayers. She identifies the functions of communal prayers as gathering; unifying and shaping the community; foundational in the formation and expression of community identity; the locale of disseminating knowledge, information and perspectives; the site of discourse production where the moral, social and spiritual development of the community is fostered (2018, 193-194). The issue then is not just about permitting women access to public space, it is about the nature of the community and how that community forms and lives out its theologies.

The issue, however, is more than women leading prayers. Muslima scholars are questioning 'androcentric ritual norms', the 'androcentric normativity' of communal ritual practices (Lamptey, 2018, 190, 194). The theological premises of ritual practices demonstrate the inherent biases and assumptions that have developed from masculinised theologies of women. Women's deficiency and *fitna* (discussed in the previous section), as constructed theologies, become the basis on which masculinised rituals are normative. At the most basic outworking, women are problematic to the moral and social well-being of men, and a threat to the purity and sacredness of the mosque.

Muslima scholars, theologians and practitioners have theologised differently and so can claim space and rituals without the burden of moral and social danger based on sexuality and purity that traditional theologies have encumbered them with. Celene Ayat Lizzio concludes that the exclusion of women, based on the natural functions of a woman's body,

> quickly becomes tautological with claims being made that women, as a gender category, are lesser in religion compared to men because they regularly do not participate in devotional rituals (2013, 174).

Theologies that deem women ritually deficient are at the centre of reformation being pursued by Muslima theologians and practitioners as they push back against the marginalisation they experience in their faith.

> Women-led prayer is … a "human enactment of moral agency, an expression of gender justice, and responsive to the right to participate as equally enfleshed, sexual and spiritual subjects in the production of religious meaning and meaning-making (Lamptey, 2018, 196).

Fresh theologies of women are being constructed through women reclaiming space for participation in the ritual practices of their community. Their pursuit of inclusion articulates theologies of equality, inclusion, space, the other and community. Amina Wadud says:

> … the task is not so much for women to claim the centre space as legitimate for female agency. Instead, the whole of the community must enter into the margins with women to affirm the place where women's lives are experienced (2006, 180).

When women speak

I have attempted to listen to the voices of Muslima scholars, theologians and faith practitioners in order to hear how they are reimagining theologies of women. The majority of those to whom I 'listened' are seeking acceptance as credible interpreters of the religious texts, faith practices and laws that impact women. They situate themselves within the schools of reformers, critically reflecting on their position within Islam while challenging the androcentric and patriarchal norms. They want to situate the religious texts of the *Qur'an* and *Hadith*, as well as the example of Prophet Muhammad, within the historical and social context of their revelation. Drawing on what they consider to be the dynamic origins of Islam they are reimagining theologies of women to address the context-specific challenges they face in faith-practice and justice as they negotiate their everyday.

As a Christian woman who has given attention to listening to these voices, I have identified a number of questions to which I have not yet heard answers, or to which I have only heard partial answers with respect to theologies of women.

Firstly, what theologies of women could or would be

26

constructed when they are not set against 'the other', in this case men? The starting point of many of the conversations I have 'listened' in on is opposition to the negative portrayals, theologies, and laws regarding women. The voices of the activist seeking to address social injustices often seems to have catalysed the work of theologising in fresh ways about women. While I don't conclude this is necessarily negative, I am wondering if there are other places to start theologies of women, what they might be and what the outcomes would be.

Secondly, how can women's voices influence theologies of humankind, and not remain marginalised? It is unclear how the development of theologies of women are influencing and/or changing orthodox theologies, which means that women will always remain at the edge. Some Muslima theologians and scholars allude to this challenge, inviting the community to women's space in order to embrace women's being and place holistically within Islam. The question of change in religious spaces is fraught, and it appears that women in Islam are constrained by the continual marginalisation of their voices.

Thirdly, what would reformed or reimagined theologies on women look like? Muslima theologians, academics and activists have different lenses that they use to address this question. They circle around feminist discourses, troubled by the western, colonial, political nature of these imaginations but appear to struggle to rearticulate theologies that embrace women without the language that so troubles them.

Fourthly, how can the challenges for women be problematised without defaulting to a blame game that often focuses on variant Christian theologies? There are refreshing voices that seem willing to own the problems of interpretation within Islam, but little work has been done so far to address what has commonly been a default position in defending the beauty of Islam.

Christian women face similar questions as they consider theologies of women and practices of faith. These questions in no way conclude that Muslima theologians, scholars, faith practitioners and activists are addressing problems isolated to Islam. Women across faith divides are challenged by the gendered nature of social, religious, and political constructs. There are issues that are contextually specific, and there are issues in our basic theologies of God, humankind and the relationship of these. However, there are areas of overlap where we could learn from the way each other is dealing with the challenges as we seek theologies of women that reflect the basic issues of identity, being and justice.

There is, I believe, an opportunity for us to listen to each other, learn together and seek to live faithfully as women who love God.

Bibliography

Ali, K. 2004. "A Beautiful example: The Prophet Muhammad as a Model for Muslim Husbands." *Islamic Studies* 43, no. 2: 273-291.

Amath, N. n.d. *Women: Pillars of Islamic Civilisation* (unpublished paper shared with the author).

Aslan, E., Marcia Hermansen, and Elif Medeni, eds. 2013. *Muslima Theology: The Voices of Muslim Women Theologians*. Frankfurt: Peter Lang.

Barlas, A. 2002. *Believing Women in Islam: Unreading Patriarchal Interpretations of the Qur'an*. Karachi: Sama Editorial and Publishing Services.

Duderija, A. 2011. *Constructing a Religiously Ideal "Believer" and "Woman" in Islam: Neo-traditional Salafi and Progressive Muslims' Method of Interpretation*. New York: Palgrave Macmillan.

Hidayatullah, A. A. 2014. *Feminist Edges of the Qur'an*. New York: Oxford University Press.

Lamptey, J. T. 2018. *Divine Words, Female Voices: Muslima Explorations in Comparative Feminist Theology*. New York: Oxford University Press.

Lamrabet, A. 2018. *Women and Men in the Qur'an*. New York: Palgrave Macmillan.

Lizzio, C. A. 2013. "Gendering Ritual: A Muslima's Reading of the Laws of Purity and Ritual Preclusion." In *Muslima Theology: The Voices of Muslim Women Theologians*, edited by E. Aslan, Marcia Hermansen, and Elif Medeni. Frankfurt: Peter Lang.

Stowasser, B. F. 1994. *Women in the Qur'an., Traditions and Interpretation*. New York: Oxford University Press.

Tatari, M. 2013. "Gender Justice and Gender Jihad: Possibilities and Limits of Qur'anic Interpretation for Women's Liberation." In *Muslima Theology: The Voices of Muslim Women Theologians*, edited by E. Aslan, Marcia Hermansen, and Elif Medeni. Frankfurt: Peter Lang.

Tuksal, H. S. 2013. "Misogynistic Reports in the Hadith Literature." In *Muslima Theology: The Voices of Muslim Women Theologians*, edited by E. Aslan, Marcia Hermansen, and Elif Medeni. Frankfurt: Peter Lang.

Wadud, A. 1999a. *Qur'an and Woman: Rereading the Sacred Texts from a Woman's perspective*. New York: Oxford University Press.

Wadud, A. 1999b. *Qur'an and Woman: Rereading the Sacred Text from a Woman's Perspective*. new York and Oxford: Oxford University Press.

Wadud, A. 2006. *Inside the Gender Jihad*. Oxford: Oneworld Publications.

THE WOMEN IN THE QUR'AN:

Who They Are and the Insights They Provide

Carol Walker[1]

This paper identifies which women feature in the Qur'an and considers what roles they serve in the message of the text. It is largely based on doctoral work I completed some years ago which took a comparative approach, examining whether principles of rhetorical analysis now being used in Biblical Studies are appropriate to the Qur'anic text. Sample texts from both corpuses featured women characters, not least because the more recent reading of biblical texts in the light of rhetorical analysis has exposed how long-assumed interpretations have been based on preconceptions and have given a helpful basis for drawing defendable fresh conclusions for some of those texts. The methodology involves reading small units of text in their wider context (i.e. in their literary, that is 'discourse' context, as well as that of the prevailing milieu).

Mindful that this article is for those engaged in thoughtful and academic reflection on Islam, I begin by giving a summary of the women identified in some way in the Qur'an. I then give an overview of the interests of works that major on looking at women in the Qur'an before taking a particular text as a basis for exploring ways in which individual women contribute to the message of the Qur'an. I then conclude by considering how the emergent insights relate to some assumptions and questions which Christians have when they read the Qur'an.

The women who are identified in the Qur'an

---

[1] Carol M Walker is an Associate Lecturer in Old Testament and Islamic Studies at All Nations Christian College, UK, with over twenty years' experience of Bible teaching in Pakistan and the Middle East. Her PhD explored interpretative methodology for comparing Bible and Qur'an.

There are something like twenty to twenty-five women identified in the Qur'an. Numerical precision is difficult[2] as we don't know how many Egyptian women cut themselves on seeing Yusuf (Q12:30-31), nor, from the Qur'an, how many daughters Lot had (Q11:81). Whilst the accepted tradition, rather than any specific reference in the text, suggests that Q24:11-26 refers to Aisha and Q14:37 to Hagar, the Shi'ite understanding in particular would want us to include Fatima within the reference in Q33:33 as they understand it to be referring to the *Ahl ul-Bayt* (the family comprised of Muhammad, his daughter Fatima and her husband Ali, plus their sons Hasan and Husayn). Only one woman, Mary, is named in the Qur'an. Most others are identified in terms of their relationship to a male character (e.g. as wife of, sister of, or as mothers of). The presence of some women is evidenced through the Arabic verbal nouns being in the feminine form (see the titles of Q58 and Q60). I will later refer to the helpful investigation into their significance which was conducted by Georgina Jardim (2014) at much the same time as I was engaged in the rhetorical analysis.

In summary, sequenced according to the epochs recognised by the Qur'an, the women mentioned within it are:
- the wife of Adam in Q2:35, Q7:18-25, Q20:115-121;
- the wife of Noah in Q66:10;
- the wife of Abraham in Q11:69-73, Q51:24-30;
  - possible allusion to the unnamed Hagar in Q14:37
  - the wife of Lot in Q11:81, Q15:58-60, Q26:171, (Q27:57), Q29:32-33, (Q37:135), Q66:10;
  - the daughters of Lot in Q11:78, Q15:71;
- Women in the story of Joseph:
  - the wife of the Governor of Egypt (known as Potiphar in the Bible) in Q12:21-3;
  - other Egyptian women 'who cut their hands' in Q12:30-31;
- women related to Moses:
  - his mother in Q20:38-40 and Q28:7-13;
  - his sister in Q20:40 and Q28:11;
  - the woman he married Q28:22-28;
  - the wife of Pharaoh in Q28:9-13, Q66:11;

---

[2] It is difficult in the Bible too, because of there being groups of women, whose names could refer to either a man or a woman, and individuals who may be called by different names in different places.

- the queen of Sheba in Q27:20-44;
- women related to 'Isa (Jesus):
  - a woman of Imran (the mother of Mary mother of Jesus) in Q3:35-36;
  - Mary the mother of Jesus in Q3:35-63, Q4:156, Q5:19, 78, 116, Q19:16-34, Q21:91, Q23:50, Q66:12;
- Women from the lifetime of Muhammad:
  - the Mothers of the Believers (the wives of the Prophet Muhammad) Q33:6, 53;
    - direct address to the wives of Muhammad Q33:28-34;
    - a possible revelation in response to a query by the unnamed Umm Salma, wife of Muhammad, Q33:35;
    - a revelation concerning Muhammad's marriage to unnamed Zaynab, Q33:36-40;
    - likely allusions to an event involving 'Ā'isha, wife of Muhammad, Q24:11-26;
    - the rebuking of two unnamed wives, Q66:3-5;
  - 'the woman who pleads' in Q58:1;
  - 'the women to be evaluated' in Q60:10;
  - the wife of Abu Lahab in Q111:4-5.

This list enables us to see that the wife of Adam, the wife of Abraham and the mother of Moses each feature briefly in more than one *sura*, whilst the wife of Lot is second only to Mary in the number of different *suras* in which they feature. We also see that the main *sura* concerned in some way with the wives of Muhammad is Q33, and with careful attention, notice that Q66 has the most diverse range of women characters. Figure 1 provides an alternative way of setting out the detail.

The figure details each reference to a woman in canonical order, setting out the sequence in which each female character would be encountered when the Qur'an is being read from beginning to end. It also gives some immediate sense of the extent to which an individual *sura* may be taken up with the stories of women by indicating how many verses there are in the *sura* and the range of verses in which the particular women feature. This highlights the concentration, and a-typical diversity, of women characters in Q66 even clearer). The right hand column provides information for yet another approach to sequencing, in that it gives an approximate

Figure I– Women characters in the Suras of the Qur'an

Sura no.	total verses	Women Characters	Period of Revelation
2	286	Wife of Adam (v.35)	Medinan
3	200	'A woman of Imran' (vv. 35-36) and her daughter Mary (vv.35-63)	Medinan
4	176	Mary (v.156)	Medinan
5	123	Mary (vv.17&78)	Medinan
7	206	Wife of Adam (vv.18-25)	Late Meccan
11	123	Wife of Abraham (vv.69-73), daughters (v.78) and wife of Lot (v.81),	Late Meccan
12	111	Potiphar's wife (vv.21-35) and Egyptian women who cut their hands (vv.30-31)	Late Meccan
(14)	52	(Hagar (v.37))	Late Meccan
15	99	Wife (vv.58-60) and daughters of Lot (v.71)	Middle Meccan
19	98	Mary (Title and vv.16-34)	Late Meccan
20	135	Mother and sister of Moses (vv. 38-40), wife of Adam (vv.115-121)	Middle Meccan
(24)	64	(A'isha (vv.11-26))	Medinan
26	227	Old woman (= wife of Lot (v.171))	Middle Meccan
27	93	Queen of Sheba (vv.20-44), wife of Lot (v.57)	Late Meccan
28	88	Mother and sister of Moses (vv.7-13), wife of Pharaoh (vv.9-13), the woman Moses married (vv.22-28)	Late Meccan
29	69	Wife of Lot (vv.32-33)	Late Meccan
33	73	Mothers of the Believers (vv.6,28-40,53, etc)	Medinan
37	182	Old woman (= wife of Lot (v.135))	Middle Meccan
51	60	Wife of Abraham (vv.24-30)	Middle Meccan
58	22	'The woman who pleads' (Title and v.1)	Medinan
(60)	13	'The women to be evaluated' (Title and v. 10)	Medinan
66	12	2 wives of Muhammad (vv.3-5), wives of Lot and of Noah (v.10), wife of Pharaoh (v.11), Mary (v.12)	Medinan
111	5	Wife of Abu Lahab (vv.4-5)	Early Meccan

34

indication of when, within Muhammad's prophetic activity, each particular reference to a woman character occurred. This final piece of information is based on the lists in Watt and Bell, *Introduction to the Qur'an* (1970 [rep. 2005, 205-213]), modified in light of careful contemporary analysis as summarized by Nicolai Sinai (2017, 111-137). The emergent chronology broadly accords with classical Islamic chronology. It brings out the unsurprising fact that the wives of Muhammad do not feature in any *Suras* prior to the relocation to Medina. Interestingly, it also indicates that the first woman referred to through revelation was a member of the community in which Muhammad originally lived: Q111 is, chronologically, an early *sura*. The *sura* expresses a curse in response to the hostility of a married couple, Abu Lahab and his wife, whom tradition identifies as his uncle and spouse. Both of them are deemed worthy of ire. As closer consideration of the other women characters will show, Abu Lahab's wife is not particularly representative.

Each approach to sequencing brings its own insights. I draw on these in closer textual analysis after first giving an overview of work that others have done on the women in the Qur'an.

Writings on the women in the Qur'an

In pre-modern times, women associated with the qur'anic text were mostly known about through traditions and the commentaries (*tafsīr*). Even when living in the Middle East around the turn of the millennium, I was surprised to discover that local people were unaware that Mary is the only woman named in the Qur'an and that it neither mentions Khadija (Muhammad's first wife) nor provides the name of Adam's wife (*Hawwa* in Arabic, Eve in English). In circles I have moved in more recently, it would seem that knowledge of these details is increasing nevertheless; one simple way of discovering people's familiarity with the qur'anic text, and the importance of Hadith, is to ask Muslim friends about these women characters.

Stowasser's (1994) *Women in the Qur'an: Traditions and Interpretation,* was the first in-depth survey of Islamic literature dealing with women characters. In the introduction, Stowasser observes the plethora of religious books, booklets and pamphlets providing instruction 'on "women's issues in Islam"' available in the Middle East in contrast to the paucity of any systematic exploration of the Qur'an's female characters. The *sunna* has been the main source for the presentation of the wives of Muhammad as models to be emulated, whilst detail about the individual women associated with the Judeo-Christian scriptures became part of the *tafsīr* material by way of *'isra'iliyat'* (i.e. clarifications gathered from Jewish and Christian sources in the early centuries of Islam). More contemporary Muslim women scholars who are re-reading their texts concur with Stowasser's conclusion that the result of recourse to *'isra'iliyat'* is that 'Bible related traditions, including their symbolic images of the female's defective nature, were seamlessly integrated into an Islamic framework' through the medieval period and up to recent times (1994, 23; cf. Hassan (1985), Wadud (1999, 25), Barlas (2002, 9)). Importantly, though qur'anic detail about each woman character is supplemented by traditions from within the early milieu, the character at the heart of these observations is, of course, *Hawwa*/Eve. Wadud and Barlas make reference to texts referring to Eve whilst expanding on the importance of other key passages and terms which contribute to understanding of the status and role of women in the teaching of the Qur'an. Meanwhile, Hassan's continues to be recognised as the seminal work on Eve (Hidayatullah, 2014, 90). Indeed, she is still engaged in related discussions through writing and teaching (see bibliography in Hidayatullah, 2014, 245-246).

Hassan, born in Pakistan and defining herself as a Sayyid,[3] has long been based in the USA. She explains that the catalyst for her observations came in 1979 through preparing for a '"trialogue" of Jewish, Christian and Muslim scholars who were exploring women-related issues in the three "Abrahamic" faith traditions'. An additional catalyst was a subsequent visit to Pakistan in 1983, when she encountered a Muslim society that insisted on an Islam that conflicted with that which she understood from systematic study of the Qur'an (Hassan in Kvam et al., 1999, 464-465). She came to the conclusion that three assumptions underpin the androcentrism of the three faith traditions. These are:

1. God's primary creation is man, not woman, since woman is believed to have been created from man's rib, hence is derivative and secondary ontologically;
2. That woman, not man, was the primary agent of what is customarily described as the "Fall"... hence all "daughters of

---

[3] A descendent of the Prophet Muhammad.

Eve" are to be regarded with hatred, suspicion, and contempt;

3.   That woman was created not only *from* man but also *for* man, which makes her existence merely instrumental and not of fundamental importance (e.g. Hassan in Kvam et al., 1999, 466).

In her fuller work(s) she demonstrates that the Qur'an gives rise to none of these assumptions: there is no reporting of Adam's wife speaking in the Qur'an, though words in dual forms indicate that she partnered with her spouse in eating the fruit and in being expelled from the garden.

Hassan's summation of the assumptions that come from Judeo-Christian tradition are fair, though her statement that these 'originate' in Genesis 2 and 3 would, arguably, have been better expressed—and been fairer to the observations of women and men who are engaged in fresh systematic study of the Bible—if she said the traditions 'grew out of' particular readings of those texts. Reviewing Hassan's work as well as related work by others, Jardim (2014, 40) more helpfully says, 'the Qur'anic account is elaborated in classical Islamic commentary in accordance with contemporary medieval descriptions of the biblical female character 'Eve'.' As Jardim goes on to summarise, 'Most of the traditions brought together by Tabari (d. 923CE/301CE) blame the woman for human error' (2014, 41). Meanwhile, amongst examples Hassan provides is the following hadith related from Ibn 'Abbas and Ibn Mas'ud (1999, 470):

> When God sent Iblis out of the Garden and placed Adam in it, he dwelt in it alone and had no one to socialize with. God sent sleep on him and then He took a rib from his left side and placed flesh in its place and created Hawwa' from it. When he awoke he found a woman seated near his head. He asked her, 'Who are you?' She answered, 'Woman.' He said, 'Why were you created?' She said, 'That you might find rest in me.' The angels said, 'What is her name?' and he said. 'Hawwa.' They said, 'Why was she called Hawwa?' He said, 'Because she was created from a living thing.'

Hassan notes that this hadith is in conflict with the naming of Eve in the Bible. The reasons for this are lost in the mist of time, for al-

Tabari's report of a tradition from Ibn Ishaq, that God 'cast slumber on Adam – according to what has reached us from the people of the Torah...' (Kvam, 1999, 187), could be an accurate attribution. Precisely how the echoes and negativities emerged is not clear, though it would seem that they became established in the Abbasid period (cf. Ahmed, 1992, 79), when Baghdad became the *de facto* capital of the Islamic world and centre of prodigious intellectual activity. It is to be remembered that Jews and Nestorian Christians made significant contributions to that intellectual activity, and indeed that the first example of a new genre of Jewish writings, *The Alphabet of Ben Sira* (not to be confused with the much earlier Ecclesiasticus, which is also known as 'Ben Sira'), with a degree of witty irony, tells of the sequential creation of first Lillith[4] and then Eve. Given the possibility that ideas about Lillith arise from Mesopotamian roots, and that it was the Baghdad Caliphate which was the conduit through which Aristotle's teachings reached the wider world (Yassif, 1997, 154-155), it is eminently possible that the reframing of attitudes to women that spread into each of the major monotheistic faiths drew on a mix of Greek and Mesopotamian tradition: Aristotle had a famously low view of women (Phipps, 1976, 265).

Whilst the brief references to the wife of Adam provide little material from which to deduce any theology of gender (let alone her personality or ongoing faith), from even less qur'anic material Hagar emerges as 'an empowering figure' in the writings of the first tranche of contemporary women scholars. Hidayatullah (2014, 55) draws attention to the ways 'exegetes' Hassan (2006), al-Hibri (2003), and Wadud (2006, 120ff) all find her to 'embody an exemplary "active female role within Islam"'.[5] Fascinatingly it is the Genesis text and parallels in tradition which provide grist for the empowerment. Consequently, in the search for models from their scripture, Hagar joins Mary as one of the most highly esteemed of women characters shared with the biblical text. However, where Hagar is accorded status through her active role, Mary is more known for her piety. Indeed, Barazangi (2004, 39-42) is at pains to argue that it is wrong to accord Mary the status of an archetype of the Muslim woman. She

---

[4] Ed. According to one of the apocryphal books of the Bible Lillith was Adam's first wife.

[5] Taking her phrase from Hibba Abugideiri, "Hagar: A Historical Model for 'Gender Jihad,'" in *Daughters of Abraham: Feminist Thought in Judaism, Christianity and Islam*, ed. Yvonne Yazbek Haddad and John L. Esposito (Gainsville: University of Florida Press, 2001), 84.

describes Mary as 'the silent pious, the pure, the virgin ...', and gives a detailed defence of her view that, by taking Mary as the preferred 'static' model, an ideal which 'is against the core principle of Islam' has been promoted. Barazangi takes exception to the way in which the predominant characterisation of her as submissive undermines the qur'anic call to believers, male and female, to gain inspiration from the autonomous *uswah hasana* (beautiful example) of each and all prophets. Her key texts are Q33:21, which particularly refers to Muhammad, and Q60:4-6, which especially mentions Abraham but in the context of instructions to test and welcome women emigrants who have taken independent decisions to join the Muslim community. Like those seeking to de-patriarchalise what is to be learnt through Adam's wife, and who seek to find empowerment through Hagar, Barazangi too has sought to demonstrate that the guidance of the Qur'an is liberative for Muslim women.

Jardim (2014), a Christian scholar of the Qur'an, also draws attention to the women to be tested in Q60, especially the way language used within the *sura* reflects the reception context. Her main text, though, is Q58 which takes as its name the (female) disputant (*al-Mujadilah*): the noun being in its feminine form. Her research is complementary to Barazangi's thesis in that she demonstrates how language within the Qur'an endorses the agency of women, and suggests that their questioning is an approved part of the production of qur'anic revelation. The context suggested by these two *Suras* is one in which women are independently choosing to embrace Islam, and where they are approved as they dispute principles of practice within the community. Jardim notes that the *Suras* sit close to the middle of the Qur'an. She floats the possibility that this accords them the status of being paradigmatic. I note that they are Medinan *Suras*, like Q66 to which we now turn, and that specific consideration of the faith and status of women comes more to the fore in that later period.

Women characters in light of text analysis

In that it is not possible to engage in a full analysis of every text featuring a female character in one article, Q66 (*al-Tahrim* / 'Prohibition' or 'Forbidden') is a particularly useful starting point. As noted earlier, it is unique in the range and number of women characters which feature within it. It is also short and, as we will see, has features within it which lend themselves to intra-textual consideration, alongside other parts of the Qur'an, and to reviewing questions of reception context and diachronic development of content. As the last of its twelve verses refers to Mary, it enables us to revisit the question of whether she is presented as an archetype too. And this and other elements lead us to consider how helpful related hadith are for illuminating the interests of the *sura*.

The title of the *sura* reflects its opening verse which urges the Prophet not to forbid to himself something which has not been divinely forbidden. Linguistic detail, including number and gender, in the verses that follow, indicate that the forbidding in view is bound up with Muhammad's relationship with his wives. Tradition provides alternative background scenarios (*asbab al-nuzul*) to do with abstaining from eating honey or withholding sex (Stowasser, 1994, 95-97, provides a good overview of the various traditions). These lively stories have tended to influence what detail is considered when the *sura* is read. Choosing rather to follow principles of rhetorical analysis, taking account of leading words, themes and discourse structure, shifts the focus on to different detail. As it happens this *sura* has a range of features which suggest that it is a ring structure: it makes a major point at the centre, whilst bringing the opening and concluding portions into illuminating conversation with one another:

A O Prophet – 2 women warned   vv 1-5
    B O Believers – 'Hereafter': avoid the Fire   v 6
        C O Unbelievers – Fair recompense Today   v 7
    B' O Believers – 'Hereafter': attain the Garden   v 8
A' O Prophet – 2 x 2 women bad and good examples   vv 9-12

The two women (*azwaj*) referred to at the beginning are unnamed wives of Muhammad. They are threatened with divorce for breaking a confidence which Muhammad had shared with one of them. The concluding portion then presents two women (*imra'a*) who are wives of former prophets (the wife of Noah and the wife of Lot) as examples of unbelievers who do not attain Paradise despite being spouses of 'righteous servants'. This is followed by two examples of women with independent faith: the wife (*imra'a*) of Pharaoh and Mary, daughter of 'Imran. The *sura*, which is generally deemed to be one of the last chronologically, clearly endorses the autonomous faith of women. Indeed, that may be one reason for the unusual description of Mary, who here is not directly associated with *'Isa* (Jesus).

The threat of divorce is expanded (v5) by description of the qualities of better wives (*azwaj*) who could replace them. They are 'devoted to God, true believers, devout, turn to Him in repentance and worship Him, given to fasting, whether previously married or virgins' (Abdel Haleem trans.). That Pharaoh's wife and Mary fulfil these qualities may be why there are traditions which identify them as amongst the heavenly consorts of the Prophet (Stowasser, 1994, 80).

It is interesting, though, to note that terminology seems to be used carefully in the *sura*. There are two main words used to denote a wife in the Qur'an: *zawja* and *imra'a*. Both occur in Q66. Whilst the use of both could be for aesthetic balance, closer consideration yields other possible insights.

The word *zawj* (fem. *zawja*, pl. *azwaj*, and *zawjat*) has a wide range of meaning, indicating a single part of a complementary pair. This might be coupled extremes (Q38:57-58, of boiling and ice cold), pairing in plant and animal life (e.g. palm trees are dioecious, coming as separate male and female trees), husband and wife (e.g. the wife of Adam is always described as his *zawja*, Q2:35, Q7:19, Q20:117), but is also used of the companions of Paradise (Q2:25, Q3:15, Q4:57 and Q43:70). The verse key to discussion of the egalitarian nature of qur'anic depiction of the creation of woman, Q4:1, addresses humankind (*insan*), saying that 'your Lord... created you from a single *nafs*, and from it created its *zawja*, and from the pair spread abroad a multitude of men (*rijallan*) and women (*nisa*)'. For the purpose of exploring interests in Q66, we simply note that in Q4:1 the *zawja* is the partner in producing future generations. This would also seem to be the major role of Adam's wife. She is the partner to be enjoyed in the bliss of the Garden where, in the chronologically later two references (Q2:35 and Q7:19), Adam is encouraged to dwell (*uskun*) with his wife: a phrase echoed in a parallel passage (Q7:189) that brings the instruction to wider humanity to y*askuna ilayha* / 'Dwell in mutual comfort with your female spouse' (cf. Muhammed Azad trans.) and which also shares phrasing with Q4:1 about humanity origination from a single *nafs*. The women being rebuked in Q66 are two of Muhammad's consorts (*azwaj*). Notably, even though in Medinan *Suras* the companions of Paradise are only called *azawj* (Q2:25, Q3:15, Q4:57), rather than *kawā'iba atrābān* / 'round breasted mates' (Q78:33 – Wild, 2010:627), *al-ḥūr al- ʿīn* / 'wide-eyed maidens' (Q44:54, Q52:20, Q56:22), *qāṣirāt aṭ-ṭarf* / 'maidens restraining their glances' (Q37:48, Q38:52, Q55:56), Q66 makes clear that being the earthly *zawja* of a man of faith does not guarantee partnership with him in Paradise.

The women through whom the Consorts are to learn are not identified as *azwaj* (or *zawjat*). Like all female characters in the Qur'an, other than the wives of Muhammad and of Adam, those within Q66 who are married are called *'imra'a*, whilst Mary is identified in terms of a forebear. The term *'imra'a* (pl. *nisa*) has more the sense of a female who has passed through puberty than necessarily that of sexual partner. It is probably used with that sensitivity when Mary is described as 'chosen above all women (*nisa*)' in Q3:42. In Q66 the wives of Noah, Lot and Pharaoh are all referred to as *'imra'a*. It is notable that the wife of Noah is not mentioned anywhere else in the Qur'an, nor as an active character in the Bible. What is said about her here is unique. In contrast, the reference to Lot's wife is the last of the seven occasions where she is mentioned in the Qur'an. Even so, it is noteworthy that in the previous occurrences she is mainly referred to in a formulaic kind of way, identifying her with those who turn back (*al-ghabirin*):

Q26:171	*ajūzan* (old woman) *fi al-ghabirin*	(Early Meccan)
Q37:135	*ajūzan* (old woman) *fi al-ghabirin*	(Early Meccan)
Q27:57	*imra'a Lūt... Min al-ghabirin*	(Mid. Meccan)
Q15:60	*imra'a Lūt... Min al-ghabirin*	(Mid. Meccan)
Q11:81	'your wife... will happen what happens to the people'	(Mid. Meccan)
Q29:32	*imra'a Lūt... Min al-ghabirin*	(Mid. Meccan)
Q66:10	*imra'a Lūt...* False to their husbands	(Medinan)

Only here, in Q66, is Lot's wife described as being false to her husband: the *sura* exhibits a degree of freshness in the way in which it deals with already familiar stories. As in the case of the term *zawja*, diachronic evaluation of reference to the wife of Lot hints at development of a theme over the years of qur'anic revelation. Meanwhile, the reference to the wife of Pharaoh mirrors that in Q28:9, where it is Pharaoh's wife who protects the infant Moses, but also develops the implications.

At first glance the choice of *imra'at* might seem random. However each, along with Mary, is linked to a different epoch within qur'anically recognised monotheism: the times of Noah, of Abraham, of Moses and of Jesus. Even as each period provides a lesson for the Consorts the effect of the whole is to create parallels between the experience of Muhammad and those of earlier prophets. Read in light of principles of rhetorical analysis it would also seem that detail in the reference to Mary contributes both to the lesson and to exoneration of the Prophet.

The distinctive nature of the final verse which features Mary, along with the preceding prayer by Pharaoh's wife that indicates fulfilment of the eschatological hope set out in the central portion of the *sura*, suggests that we have here a double closure such as is commonly found in ring structures (cf., Douglas, 2007:126). Consistent with this, it would also seem that the final verse is centred:

> *And Mary the daughter of 'Imrān*
> *She guarded her 'chastity',*
> > *so We breathed into her (fīhi) from Our spirit.*
> *She accepted the truth (ṣaddaqat) of her Lord's words and Scriptures:*
> *She was one of (min) the devout (qānitīn).*

The opening designation of Mary, as daughter of 'Imrān, resonates with detail in Q3 which gives account of Mary's birth to the wife of 'Imrān in the textual context of a prior identification of chosen figures who are clearly representatives of earlier monotheistic epochs: Adam, Noah, the family of Abraham, the family of 'Imrān (Q3:33). The closing reference to Mary as being one of the devout would also seem to be associating her with key figures within (Judaism) monotheism (see also Q33:7). Work on contemporary milieu by Neuwirth (2005 and 2010) and Marx (2010) provides suggestive evidence that the references to 'Imrān's family, and the description of Mary as 'sister of Aaron' in *Surat* Maryam (Q19:28), intentionally associate Mary genealogically with the Aaronid line in ways that echo iconography and hymns of the contemporary Syriac church. Textual analysis alone cannot corroborate this proposal which has implications for identifying the interests of Q66. This *sura* opens with reference to the self-imposed restraint by the Prophet, who is then inspired by Allāh, and closes with deferential reference to Mary, in terms of her sexual restraint paralleled to her faithful response to

God's word (the language of *kalimāt rabbihā wa kuttubihi* probably refers to fresh revelation as well as previous scriptures). On this reading, Mary is not so much an archetype for Muslim women as a template for the behaviour and characteristics of the Prophet himself.

Indeed, whilst Q66 indicates that women are consigned to Hell or admitted to the Gardens of Paradise on the basis of their own response to Allah, it also indicates that men of faith are not tainted by the misdemeanours of their wives, and so do not need to become celibate ascetics in order to attain religious perfection. In this context the Prophet is told not to forbid to himself what Allah does not forbid: to be celibate would be to erect human rules which go against *fitr* and the permissions of Allah. The *sura* presents a high view of Mary. It also presents her in a fresh way, without obvious association with her son, and in the process opposes the exaltation of perpetual virginity which was prevalent within Christianity of the time.

Concluding observations

Q66 is a late Medinan *sura*. Tradition, and in particular the *asbab al-nuzul*, draws attention to Muhammad's lively, polygamous household at that time, but masks some other aspects of the milieu towards which the detail in the *sura* hints. Nevertheless, it is important to observe that the *sura* provides evidence which endorses content of the *Sira* (the traditional biography of Muhammad).

The *Sira* informs us that Muhammad had an Egyptian concubine, Marya the Copt, who was the only woman to bear him a son. It is possible that reference to the wife of Pharaoh provides allusive support for her presence within the Prophet's household (Stowasser, 1994, 100, 112-113). The *sura* (Q66) certainly seems to address concerns of those whose religious sensibilities have been influenced by the contemporary expressions of Christianity.

The briefly considered diachronic intra-textual observations made in the review of Q66 suggest that insights on a range of themes and topics developed as time passed and the community grew. For example, initial references to the wife of Adam and the wife of Lot are little more than labels. Later references have more substance. We saw that in Q66, which is the last *sura* to make reference to women (other than focus on Mary in Q5), existing stories of women are reframed to make fresh points. The *sura* also seems to provide something of a conclusion to communal uncertainties about who the companions in Paradise are to be: Q43:70 might have been understood to hint that Paradise could be gained by being married to a believer. However, legislative detail in Q2 and Q4 made it clear that there is a difference between the original and future bliss of Paradise and earthly realities, which may well have left nagging doubts. Alongside the slightly earlier Medinan *Suras* Q58 and Q60, which both endorse the agency of believing women, Q66 brings the clarification that women attain Paradise through their own autonomous faith. It does so by referring to women from past periods of monotheism and by censuring the women of Muhammad's world who are not following their example.

References to Mary are deferential. They are different in detail to biblical material, which some Christians assume is due to misunderstandings. From the detail in Q66 it would seem that difference is due more to polemical interest than limited information, and whilst giving clues to issues within the original reception context. The references are geared to endorsing the prophetic role of Muhammad rather than to illuminating the message of Jesus the Messiah.

Bibliography

Ahmed, Leila. 1992. *Women and Gender in Islam: Historical Roots of a Modern Debate*. New Haven, CT: Yale University Press.

Al-Hibri, Azizah Y. 2003. "Hagar on My Mind." In *Philosophy, Feminism, and Faith*, edited by Ruth E. Groenhout and Marya Bower, 198-210. Bloomington, IN: Indiana University Press.

Barazangi, Nimat Hafez. 2004. *Women's Identity and the Qur'an: A New Reading*. Gainesville: University Press of Florida.

Barlas, Asma. 2002. *"Believing Women" in Islam: Unreading Patriarchal Interpretations of the Qur'an*. Austin, TX: University of Texas Press.

Douglas, Mary. 2007. *Thinking in Circles: an Essay on Ring Composition*. New Haven, CT: Yale University Press.

Hassan, Riffat. 1985. "Made from Adam's Rib: The Woman's Creation Question." *Al-Mushir: Theological Journal of the Christian Study Centre* (Autumn): 124-156.

------- 2006. "Islamic Hagar and Her Family." In *Hagar, Sarah, and Their Children: Jewish, Christian, and Muslim Perspectives*, edited by Phyllis Trible and Letty Russell, 149-167. Louisville, KY: Westminster John Knox Press.

Hidayatullah, Aysha A. 2014. *Feminist Edges of the Qur'an.* Oxford, UK: Oxford University Press.

Jardim, Georgina L. 2016. *Recovering the Female Voice in Islamic Scripture: Women and Silence.* Oxford, UK: Routledge.

Kvam, Kristen E., Linda S. Schearing, and Valerie H. Ziegler, eds. 1999. *Eve and Adam: Jewish, Christian, and Muslim Readings on Genesis and Gender.* Bloomington, IN: Indiana University Press.

Marx, Michael. 2010. "Glimpses of a Mariology in the Qur'an: From Hagiography to Theology via Religious-Political Debate." In *Qur'an in Context: Historical and Literary Investigations into the Qur'ānic Milieu*, edited by A. Neuwirth, N. Sinai, and M. Marx, 533-563. Leiden: Brill.

Neuwirth, Angelika. 2005. "Mary and Jesus – Counterbalancing the Biblical Patriarchs: A re-reading of *sūrat Maryam* in *sūrat Al 'Imrān* (Q3:1-62)." *Parole de l'Orient* 30: 231-260.

------- 2010. "The House of Abraham and the House of Amram." In *Qur'an in Context: Historical and Literary Investigations into the Qur'ānic Milieu*, edited by A. Neuwirth, N. Sinai, and M. Marx, 499-531. Leiden: Brill.

Phipps, William E. 1976. "Adam's Rib: Bone of Contention." *Theology Today* 33, no. 3: 263-273.

Sinai, Nicolai. 2017. *The Qur'an: A Historical-Critical Introduction.* Edinburgh: Edinburgh University Press.

Stowasser, Barbara F. 1994. *Women in the Qur'an, Traditions and Interpretation.* Oxford, UK: Oxford University Press.

Wadud, Amina. 1999. *Qur'an and Woman: Rereading the Sacred Text from a Woman's Perspective.* Oxford, UK: Oxford University Press.

------- 2006. *Inside the Gender Jihad: Women's Reform in Islam.* Oxford, UK: Oneworld.

Watt, M., and R. Bell. 1970 (repr. 2005). *Introduction to the Qur'an.* Edinburgh: Edinburgh University Press.

Wild, Stefan. 2010. "Virgins of Paradise and the Luxenburg Hypothesis." In *Qur'an in Context: Historical and Literary*

Investigations into the Qur'ānic Milieu, edited by A. Neuwirth, N. Sinai, and M. Marx, 625-647. Leiden: Brill.

Yassif, Eli. 1997. "The Hebrew Narrative Anthology in the Middle Ages." Translated by Jacqueline S. Teitelbaum. *Prooftexts* (May): 153-175.

MOTHERS of the FAITHFUL:

How Muhammad's wives have shaped Islamic culture

Tara MacArthur[1]

Introduction

'Aïsha, favourite wife of the prophet Muhammad, observed, "Allah's Messenger forbade celibacy."[2] Her remark was surprising, for Muhammad had nineteen wives. These "Mothers of the Faithful" shaped aspects of Islam both actively, through their virtues and mistakes, and passively, through their life-circumstances. Our purpose is to map how some of their contributions, as detailed in the *hadith* and *sira* literature, impact on Muslim women to this day as is reflected in many a fatwa.[3] We shall focus on the lesser-known wives as well as casting new light on some familiar stories.

Khadija: first among the faithful

Deservedly famous is Muhammad's first wife, Khadija, described as "determined, noble and intelligent"[4] and "wise and forbearing".[5] He married her when he was a poor goatherd[6] and she was "a merchant of dignity and wealth".[7] We note that Khadija's

---

[1] Tara MacArthur is a pseudonym. Tara has extensively researched into Islam and is the author of *Unsheathed*, a biography of Muhammad, and of *Unveiled*, a group biography of his wives.

[2] Ahmad an-Nasa'i, *Sunan an-Nasa'i*, 4:26:3215.

[3] Ed. For more information on fatwas see Chap 6 in this volume *Women and Fatwas.*

[4] Muhammad ibn Ishaq, *The Life of Muhammad*, trans. Alfred Guillaume (Oxford: Oxford University Press, 1955), 82.

[5] Muhammad ibn Saad, *Ibn Sa'd's Kitab al-Tabaqat al-Kabir*, trans. S. Moinul Haq (Delhi: Kitab Bhavan, 1967), 1:147.

[6] Ibn Saad, *Tabaqat*, 140-141.

[7] Ibn Ishaq, *Muhammad*, 82.

accomplishments in business owed nothing to Islam, as the restrictions of veiling were only imposed after her death.[8]

Khadija was Muhammad's only wife as long as she lived,[9] and he "never opposed her."[10] She "helped him in his work" (although details are infuriatingly sparse) and consoled him when he was discouraged.[11] He was so distraught by her death "that people feared for him."[12] He told 'Aïsha: "Allah never gave me a better wife than Khadija. She believed in me when others disbelieved; she called me truthful when others called me a liar; she financed me when others gave me nothing; and she alone bore me a son. Allah himself nurtured love for her in my heart!"[13, 14, 15]

Despite Khadija's importance in launching Islam,[16, 17] she had limited impact on the lives of Muslim women, for the paradigm for Islamic marriage shifted after her death. Within three weeks, her grief-stricken widower proposed to two women on the same day,[18, 19, 20] thus endorsing polygyny. Muhammad required his subsequent wives to obey him because "men are superior to women;"[21] if any human had been permitted to prostrate to another, he would have ordered wives to prostrate to their husbands.[22] He believed women to be less intelligent than men, which he said was proved by Allah's ruling that the testimony of two women was equal to that of one

[8] Bukhari, *Mufrad*, 43:1051.

[9] Muslim 31:5975.

[10] Ibn Ishaq, *Muhammad*, 313.

[11] Ibn Ishaq, *Muhammad*, 191.

[12] Muhammad ibn Saad. *The Women of Madina*, trans. Aisha Bewley (London: Ta-Ha Publishers, 1995), 44.

[13] Ahmad ibn Hanbal, *Musnad* (Cairo: Qurtuba Organisation, 1890), 6:24908. This conversation occurred in 628, two years before Muhammad's Egyptian concubine Mariya bore his last son Ibrahim. All of his sons died in infancy.

[14] Muhammd ibn Ismail ibn Kathir, *The Life of the Prophet Muhammad*, trans. Trevor Le Gassick (Reading, UK: Garnet Publishing, 1998), 2:90.

[15] Muslim 31:5972.

[16] Muhammad al-Bukhari, *Sahih al-Bukhari*, 1:1:3.

[17] Ibn Ishaq 106-107, 111-112; Bukhari 1:1:3; Muslim 1:301.

[18] Muhammad ibn Jarir al-Tabari. *Volume 9: The Last Years of the Prophet*, trans. Ismail K. Poonawala (Albany, NY: State University of New York Press, 1990), 129-130.

[19] Muhammad ibn Jarir al-Tabari. *Volume 39: Biographies of the Companions and Their Successors*, trans. Ella Landau-Tasseron (Albany, NY: State University of New York Press, 1998), 170.

[20] Ibn Saad, *Women*, 39, 152.

[21] Quran 4:34.

[22] Abu Dawud 11:2135.

man.[23] He promised the wives who accepted this new paradigm: "Any woman who dies having pleased her husband will enter Paradise."[24]

Saowda: a veiled bargain

Muhammad's second wife was Saowda, an early convert to Islam.[25] He married her when his fortunes were at their lowest ebb[26] and his choice of brides was limited. Saowda was a tanner[27] whose work could supplement his income, and her cheerful quips amused him.[28] 'Aïsha recalled: "No woman was ever more loving to me than Saowda. I wished I could be exactly like that devoted woman."[29]

As Muhammad became more powerful in Medina, he did not have much to do with Saowda,[30] who was "a fat, huge lady;"[31] slow-moving and weak.[32] When he had four wives, he proclaimed that four was the maximum number that any Muslim should have.[33] In due course, he wanted to marry a fifth woman,[34] so he decided to divorce Saowda.[35]

Saowda, fearing abandonment, intercepted Muhammad at her doorstep and asked, "Are you angry with me?" When he admitted that she had not done anything wrong, she pleaded: "Will you take me back? I am too old to desire men; I only want to be raised up as your wife at the Resurrection. So do not divorce me, but give my day on your roster to 'Aïsha."

---

[23] Quran 2:282; Bukhari 1:6:301.
[24] Ibn Maja 3:9:1854 (*hasan*). Ed Note: Hadith are categorised according to the quality of the reports. A *sahih* Hadith is said to be sound; *hasan* fair, *da'if* weak (cf. Bernie Power, *Engaging Islamic Traditions* [Pasadena, CA: William Carey Library), 2016], 23.
[25] Ibn Ishaq, *Muhammad*, 148.
[26] See Ibn Ishaq, *Muhammad*, 191-194 for some of these circumstances.
[27] Bukhari 8:78:677; Nasa'i 5:41:4245.
[28] Ibn Saad, *Women*, 41.
[29] Ibn Saad, *Women*, 40; Muslim 8:3451.
[30] Ibn Saad, *Women*, 40, 123.
[31] Bukhari 6:60:318.
[32] Ibn Saad, *Women*, 145; Bukhari 2:26:740.
[33] Quran 4:3. This ayah can be dated to early 625.
[34] Bukhari 7:62:134. See Ibn Saad, *Women*, 40 for confirmation that the couple in question are Muhammad and Saowda. The "other lady" would have been Zaynab bint Jahsh.
[35] Ibn Saad, *Women*, 40. Abu Dawud 11:2130 (*hasan sahih*).

Muhammad accepted this compromise. Saowda remained legally married to him, but he never spent another night in her house.[36, 37] A revelation from Allah confirmed that it was permissible for a wife to bargain away some of her rights in exchange for not being divorced.[38] Such bargains remain an option for an unloved Muslim wife, as shown in this recent *fatwa*: "The reader wants to divorce his first wife in order to marry another. His first wife, however, has offered to relinquish some of her rights in order to stay married... This offer is a gift which you may accept. There is nothing wrong with this."[39]

At the same time, Umar was urging Muhammad to veil his wives. When Muhammad appeared too busy to take immediate action, Umar lurked at nightfall near a field that Muhammad's wives used as a toilet. He discerned Saowda by her height and shouted, "Saowda, I recognise you!" Embarrassed, Saowda complained to Muhammad. He did not admonish Umar for harassing his wives; rather, he heeded the warning of how vulnerable they were to harassment. Therefore "Allah revealed the verse of veiling."[40] Umar talked afterwards of how "Allah agreed with me," because the revelation came exactly as he had requested it.[41]

After that Saowda had to be veiled up to the eyes whenever she left her house.[42] But Umar was still not satisfied. He returned to spying on the toilets. The veiled Saowda was still taller than everyone else, and Umar once again shouted at her. "You can't hide, Saowda! Think of a way not to be recognised when you go out!" Saowda ran back to the mosque and found Muhammad eating supper in 'Aïsha's house. Without replacing his meat-bone on his plate, he immediately

---

[36] Abu Isa Muhammad at-Tirmidhi, *Jamii at-Tirmidhi*, 5:44:3040.

[37] Ibn Saad, *Women*, 40, 99, 123; Bukhari 3:47:766; 3:48:853; 7:62:5; Muslim 8:3451, 3452, 3455; Abu Dawud 11:2130 (*hasan sahih*); Ibn Kathir, *Tafsir Ibn Kathir* on Q4:128.

[38] Quran 4:128 (Shakir); Bukhari 7:62:134; Ibn Saad, *Women*, 40; Ibn Kathir, *Tafsir* on Q:128.

[39] Dara Al-Ifta Al-Missriyyah, "Is it permissible to keep my first wife who waived her conjugal rights and marry a second one?" (n.d.), https://www.dar-alifta.org/Foreign/ViewFatwa.aspx?ID=8249&text=divorce, accessed December 30, 2019.

[40] Ibn Saad, *Women*, 127-129; Bukhari 1:4:148; 1:8:395; 8:74:257. See below for more about the exact circumstances of the order of veiling.

[41] Bukhari 1:8:395.

[42] Quran 33:59; 24:31. See also Ibn Saad, *Women*, 129; and Ibn Kathir, *Tafsir* on Q33:59.

produced the revelation that Allah gave his wives permission to go to the toilet.[43]

Though Muhammad was more reasonable than Umar, Saowda was from that day secluded. She was not to leave her house without permission and she was not to conduct social relationships with men outside her family.[44] For a woman who was ignored by her own husband, that left few options.

The segregation of men and women remains a defining distinctive of the Muslim lifestyle as is reflected in these fatawa: "It is an unavoidable duty. Such a separation keeps temptation away and prevents the evils caused by the two sexes mingling. So, it is better to avoid co-education even at the basic stage of education so that children are not brought up to become accustomed to a bad form of social life."[45] This is achieved by confining women to their homes as far as practicable. "In principle a woman should stay at home and not go out… if there is a need for a woman to go out and it is safe for her to do so, then there is no harm on her, Allah willing, provided the religious requirements are met, like seeking the permission of the husband, wearing Hijab, avoiding mixing with men, and the like."[46]

'Aïsha: the child-bride

Abu Bakr was Muhammad's closest friend. His daughter Aïsha was legally married to Muhammad a few days after Saowda; but the consummation occurred three years later,[47] when 'Aïsha was nine and a quarter years old.[48]

'Aïsha never offered any explanation for why her elders decided on this premature defloration. It was not a misguided response to an early menarche; on the contrary, 'Aïsha was still a

[43] Ibn Saad, *Women*, 127-128; Bukhari 6:60:318; Muslim 26:5395, 5396.

[44] Quran 33:32-33, 53; Ibn Saad, *Women*, 128-130.

[45] Islamweb.net, "Fatwa #84367: Girl attending school in first years" (2002), https://www.islamweb.net/en/fatwa/84367, accessed December 30, 2019.

[46] Islamweb.net, "Fatwa #92001: Her husband is too busy to go out with her" (2006), https://www.islamweb.net/en/fatwa/92001, accessed December 30, 2019.

[47] Bukhari 7:62:65; Tabari, *Companions*, 171.

[48] Ibn Saad, *Women*, 54-55; Bukhari 7:62:65; Muslim 8:3311, 3312. A careful comparison of the dates shows that 'Aïsha must have been born in January or February 614 (cf. Ibn Ishaq, *Muhammad*, 689 for Muhammad's death-date).

jariya[49] ("prepubescent girl") playing with her dolls[50] some five years later. The surrounding political situation is a better clue. Muhammad, still new in Medina, depended on the support of the Najjar clan.[51] Their chief died in April 623, and they invited the prophet to become their new chief.[52] Muhammad took the dead man's womenfolk to live in the mosque as members of his own family[53] and he sealed the bargain by proposing marriage to one of them.[54] It was at precisely this point that Abu Bakr waylaid Muhammad and asked, "What prevents you from consummating your marriage with my daughter?"[55] Perhaps he was wondering if the Najjar clan would usurp his place in Muhammad's counsels. Finalising the prophet's marriage to 'Aïsha would have been one way to consolidate her father's importance in the Muslim hierarchy.

'Aïsha set a precedent of normalising child-marriage in Islam. This is assumed in the regulations for a prepubescent widow (her mourning takes the same form as an adult widow's[56]) and a prepubescent divorcée (her three-month transition period is calculated by observing the moon[57]). A father can marry off his small daughter without consulting her, although some scholars allow her the right to declare an annulment when she reaches puberty.[58] After puberty a girl must consent to her marriage; but a maiden's consent is inferred from her silence.[59] Even today, child marriage occurs in many cultures;[60] but it is no accident that child-brides are

---

[49] Bukhari 7:62:118; Muslim 37:6673.

[50] Abu Dawud 42:4914. See also Ibn Hajar's note to Bukhari 8:73:151, pointing out that dolls were forbidden after menarche because they were too much like idols.

[51] Ibn Ishaq, *Muhammad*, 59, 198, 201, 228, 230.

[52] Ibn Ishaq, *Muhammad*, 235.

[53] Muhammad ibn Saad, *The Companions of Badr*, trans. Aisha Bewley (London: Ta-Ha Publishers, 2013), 475.

[54] Ibn Saad, *Women*, 288. The marriage did not take place because the Najjar girl was unwilling to participate in polygyny.

[55] Ibn Saad, *Women*, 45. Tabari, *Companions*, 172-173.

[56] Malik 29:108.

[57] Quran 65:4. This refers strictly to a consummated marriage; there is no waiting-period for a woman who is divorced before consummation (Quran 33:49).

[58] Tirmidhi 2:11:1109.

[59] Bukhari 7:62:68.

[60] See, for example, Stephanie Sinclair, "Too Young to Wed," *Stephanie Sinclair Studio*, https://stephaniesinclair.com/too-young-to-wed.

disproportionately Muslim, or that all thirteen nations that still lack a legal minimum age for marriage are Islamic.[61]

Muhammad admitted that it was not possible for a man to love all his wives equally,[62] and 'Aïsha remained his favourite.[63] When asked, "Which person do you love best?" he replied, "'Aïsha!"[64] She was "superior to all other women as a meat stew is superior to all other food."[65] Although he set up a roster so that he spent a night with each wife in turn,[66] this turned out to be a mere approximation. He spent more time with 'Aïsha than with any of his other wives[67] and he shared gifts of luxury food only with her.[68]

Despite her favoured position, 'Aïsha was jealous of her co-wives. She was even distressed by Muhammad's chatter about the long-dead Khadija.[69] She soon had the women divided into two factions: those who accepted her precedence (Saowda, Hafsa and Safiya) and those who did not (all the others, including Muhammad's daughter Fatima).[70] If even the Mothers of the Faithful resented their co-wives, how could higher standards be expected of other women? Once 'Aïsha suspected Muhammad of going to visit another wife on her night. By the time he returned, she was so agitated ("How could I not be jealous of a husband like you?") that he said her devil had overcome her.[71] Another night she followed him out of the house to track his movements. He was so angry over her distrust that he thumped her chest, "which hurt."[72]

This blow was an anomaly, however, for 'Aïsha claimed elsewhere that Muhammad "never" slapped a woman or a servant.[73]

---

[61] "Age of Consent Laws by Country," (2020), https://www.ageofconsent.net/world. The age of consent is eleven in Nigeria, twelve in Angola and the Philippines, and thirteen in Japan and in four other Muslim countries. It is at least fourteen in all other jurisdictions.
[62] Quran 4:129; Abu Dawud 11:2129; Tirmidhi 2:11:1140.
[63] Ibn Saad, *Women*, 46; Bukhari 3:47:755; Muslim 8:3312; 31:5984.
[64] Bukhari 5:57:14.
[65] Bukhari 7:65:330.
[66] Bukhari 3:47:766; Tirmidhi 2:11:1140.
[67] Ibn Saad, Women, 123-124, 126; Abu Dawud 11:2129.
[68] Bukhari 3:47:755.
69 Ibn Hanbal, *Musnad*, 24908. Bukhari 5:58:165, 166; Muslim 31:5972, 5976.
[70] Bukhari 3:47:755.
[71] Muslim 39:6759.
[72] Muslim 4:2127; Nasa'i 3:21:2039.
[73] Ibn Saad, *Tabaqat*, 1:431; Ibn Saad, *Women,* 143. See also Muslim 30:5756.

He cautioned that the best men did not beat their wives[74] and he advised a divorcée with three suitors to reject the habitual wife-beater.[75] Sometimes he protected 'Aïsha from Abu Bakr,[76] who beat his married daughter several times[77] (as well as subjecting her to constant verbal rebuke[78]). Muhammad's last word was that beating should not be "severe" and only for some reason: "Treat women well, for they are domestic animals with you."[79]

Yet although Muhammad found wife-beating distasteful, he was not committed to eliminating it altogether. At one stage he commanded, "Do not beat Allah's handmaidens," but when Umar complained that this encouraged disobedient wives, Muhammad reversed his policy.[80] If wives remained rebellious after verbal rebuke or being sent to their rooms, "beat them."[81] A whip should be placed prominently in the home.[82] Wives who complained about beatings were likely to go to Hell.[83] A man should not be asked why he had beaten his wife.[84] Abu Bakr and Umar each boasted a similar exploit: "I smacked my wife so hard that I knocked her to the floor!" and Muhammad laughed as if it were a joke.[85]

Muhammad's reservations proved too weak to deter 'Aïsha from following her father's example. Decades later, when she had custody of her dead brother's children,[86,87] she was asked what to do about a disobedient child. She replied, "I would beat him until he submitted."[88]

---

[74] Abu Dawud 11:2141. The word "they" is masculine.

[75] Muslim 9:3526.

[76] Ibn Saad, *Women*, 56; Abu Dawud 41:4981 (*da'if*).

[77] Bukhari 1:7:330; Muslim 9:3506.

[78] Muslim 8:3450.

[79] Tabari, *Last Years*, 113.

[80] Abu Dawud 11:2141.

[81] Quran 4:34.

[82] Bukhari, *Mufrad*, 50:1229.

[83] Bukhari 7:62:125.

[84] Ibn Maja 3:9:1986 (*hasan*). See also Abu Dawud 11:2142 (*da'if*).

[85] Ibn Saad, *Women*, 131; Muslim 9:3506.

[86] Muhammad ibn Saad, *Ibn Sa'd's Kitab al-Tabaqat al-Kabir*, trans. S. Moinul Haq (Delhi: Kitab Bhavan, 1972), 2:481-482.

[87] Muhammad ibn Saad, *The Men of Madina*, trans. Aisha Bewley (London: Ta-Ha Publishers, 2000), 2:122.

[88] Bukhari, *Mufrad*, 7:142.

Some present-day Muslims seem embarrassed that the *sharia* permits wife-beating and downplay it. Beating is "permitted on a very limited scale. Therefore, it is very rare for a husband to beat his wife."[89] "The beating should be very light using a *miswaak*[90]… it should not fall on the face."[91] However, few scholars raise an absolute case against wife-beating, for "Beating is among the requirements of being a protector and maintainer of the wife."[92]

There is palpably less embarrassment about child-beating. "The educator is requested to resort to corporal punishment while teaching Qur'an and good ethics, when the child swears, lies, steals or does any bad things that are forbidden for an adult. He can also punish the child if he flees from the school."[93]

Hafsa: the power of words

Hafsa, daughter of Umar, is remembered as the custodian of the first written Qur'an.[94] She was literate[95] in a culture where this skill was so rare that one of her "books" was an inscribed shoulder-bone. It contained the biblical story of Joseph, which Hafsa read out loud to Muhammad. His reaction to the story was one of displeasure: "If Joseph were here today, you would be wrong to follow him instead of me!"[96]

Hafsa, "in every way her father's daughter,"[97] was never afraid to speak her mind. Muhammad asked if there were a spell against her

---

[89] Islamweb.net, "Fatwa #84120: Explanation of Surah an-Nisa':[4:34]" (2002), https://www.islamweb.net/en/fatwa/84120/explanation-of-surah-an-nisa434, accessed December 30, 2019.

[90] *Miswaak* is often translated "toothbrush", which is the intended message here; but a *miswaak* branch could also be used as a clothes-hanger (see Ibn Saad, *Women*, 305).

[91] Islamweb.net, "Fatwa #85402: How to deal with an ill-conduct wife" (Author, 2008), https://www.islamweb.net/emainpage/printarticle.php?id=142504&lang=E&id=142504&lang=E, accessed December 30, 2019.

[92] Islamweb.net, "Fatwa #84120: Explanation of Surah an-Nisa':[4:34]," (2002), https://www.islamweb.net/en/fatwa/84120, accessed December 30, 2019.

[93] Islamweb.net, "Fatwa #85764: What is the Islamic opinion about physical punishment for children?" (2003), https://www.islamweb.net/emainpage/PrintFatwa.php?lang=E&Id=85764, accessed December 30, 2019.

[94] Bukhari 9:89:301.

[95] Abu Dawud 28:3878.

[96] Abdalrazzaq ibn Hammam al-Sanaani, *Al-Musannaf* (Beirut: Publisher, 1972), 6:10165; Abdalrazzaq ibn Hammam al-Sanaani, *Al-Musannaf* (Beirut: Publisher, 1972), 11:20061.

[97] Malik 18:18:50.

blistering tongue,[98] which sometimes put him out of humour for a whole day. At other times, she ignored him for hours.[99] She set a bad example to her own mother, who had never contradicted Umar until she heard Hafsa contradicting Muhammad.[100]

Hafsa screamed at Muhammad when she found him in her house in her bed with his concubine Mariya. He retaliated with the legally-binding words: "I divorce thee!"[101] A Muslim man who utters these words is legally divorced, even if he speaks in anger or as a joke.[102] When Umar found Hafsa weeping over it, he called her a "loser" and castigated her for inviting such ruin upon herself.[103]

A month later, Muhammad announced that Gabriel had commanded him to take Hafsa back. Allah guaranteed her place in Paradise because she fasted so often and kept the night prayers.[104] This was an extraordinary assurance in the light of Muhammad's uncertainty about his own eternal destiny.[105] According to Islamic theology, a good work cancelled a sin.[106] Hafsa's careful rituals and ascetic habits had kept her balance permanently in credit.

Muhammad's wives were not troubled by a mother-in-law as Muhammad's mother had died when he was six.[107] Nevertheless, the dominance of the mother-in-law so typically found in Muslim families can be directly traced to Muhammad's teaching that a man's parents should be more important to him than his wife.[108] Hafsa's brother Abdullah learned this to his cost. Their father Umar took a dislike to Abdullah's wife and instructed the young man to divorce

---

[98] Abu Dawud 28:3878.

[99] Bukhari 5:43:648; 6:60:435; 7:62:119; 7:72:734; Muslim 9:3506, 3511.

[100] Bukhari 6:60:435; 7:62:119; 7:72:734; Muslim 9:3506, 3511.

[101] Ibn Saad, *Women*, 58-59, 134-140; Bukhari 3:43:648; 6:60:435; 7:62:119; 7:72:734; Muslim 9:3508; Abu Dawud 12:2276.

[102] Islamweb.net, "Fatwa #355444: "Divorcing second wife under pressure from parents and first wife" (2017), https://www.islamweb.net/emainpage/PrintFatwa.php?lang=E&Id=355444, accessed December 30, 2019.

[103] Bukhari 3:43:648.

[104] Ibn Saad, *Women*, 58-60.

[105] Bukhari 8:75:398.

[106] Bukhari, *Mufrad* 50:1216; Tirmidhi 4:1:1987 (*hasan*). See also Bukhari 8:76:498.

[107] Ibn Ishaq, *Muhammad*, 73.

[108] Tirmidhi 4:25:1897 (*hasan*).

her. When Abdullah delayed, Muhammad settled the question in Umar's favour, and the obedient son lost his beloved.[109]

Although a Muslim wife has an absolute right to food and accommodation, in all matters beyond these essentials she must defer to her parents-in-law. So a man who genuinely cannot afford to pay the medical expenses of both his wife and his mother must prioritise his mother.[110] Another *fatwa* settles a dispute about a family outing with: "You should avoid making your mother angry, even if this leads to angering your wife, because the right of the mother is a priority."[111]

Zaynab: "Mother of the Beggars"

Not much is known about Zaynab, who died only eight months after marrying Muhammad.[112, 113] She acquired the by-name "Mother of the Beggars" while she was still a polytheist and still a teenager.[114, 115] Generosity was a traditional Arabian virtue, and this moral imperative of almsgiving was continued under Islam.[116] We only wish we had details of exactly how Zaynab's special acts of charity exceeded both pagan and Islamic norms.

Yet, to give credit where it is due, Zaynab's example still inspires Muslim women to steward their resources in charitable endeavours. Indeed, Muslims still frequently ask questions concerning charitable acts: whether vegetables are a suitable donation (yes);[117] whether alms may be directed to non-Muslims (yes,

---

[109] Abu Dawud 42:5119. See also Tirmidhi 4:25:1900 (hasan) and Ibn Maja 3:10:2089 (*hasan*).

[110] Islamweb.net, "Fatwa #99471: Discrepancy between the right of mother and the right of wife" (2007), https://www.islamweb.net/en/fatwa/99471/discrepancy-between-the-right-of-mother-and-the-right-of-wife, accessed December 30, 2019.

[111] Islamweb.net, "Fatwa #173227: Wife objects to husband to bring his mother along" (2012). https://www.islamweb.net/en/fatwa/173227, accessed December 30, 2019.

[112] Muhammad ibn Jarir al-Tabari, *Volume 7: The Foundation of the Community*, trans. M. V. McDonald (Albany, NY: State University of New York Press, 1987), 150.

[113] Ibn Saad, *Women*, 82; Tabari, *Companions*, 164.

[114] Abdulmalik ibn Hisham, "Notes to Ibn Ishaq's *Sirat Rasul Allah*," in *The Life of Muhammad*, ed. Muhammad ibn Ishaq, trans. Alfred Guillaume (Oxford: Oxford University Press, 1955), 794#918.

[115] Tabari, *Companions*, 163-164.

[116] Bukhari 2:24:478.

[117] Islamweb.net, "Fatwa #85476: "Giving vegetables as sadqa" (2003), https://www.islamweb.net/emainpage/PrintFatwa.php?lang=E&Id=85476&lang=E&Id=85476, accessed December 30, 2019.

but helping poor Muslims is better);[118] whether a wife may give alms without her husband's permission (yes, if the money is her own;[119] she may give away small quantities of his property, for which Allah will reward them both[120]); and the problem of helping charlatans who only pretend to be poor (Allah will reward the donor's intention regardless).[121]

Hind, Umm Salama

It is well known that Hind refused Muhammad twice before accepting his third proposal. He enticed her by promising to take care of her children.[122] Let us track how effectively he kept that promise.

He gave her a milch-camel named *al-Aris*, and Hind's household lived off the dairy. Unfortunately, *al-Aris* proved a poor milker. Sometimes Muhammad gave Hind the surplus milk from his camel *Burda*; but if he was hosting guests, they might drink *Burda*'s whole yield. Then Muhammad would lament, "May Allah make thirsty whoever kept my family thirsty tonight!"[123] The reality was that he habitually kept his whole family at subsistence level. 'Aïsha said that they "never ate their fill of wheat-bread with meat for three days in a row."[124]

Hind was a working mother. She tanned leather[125] and apparently processed wool and palm-fibres too.[126] The family owned

---

[118] Islamweb.net, "Fatwa #399793: Giving Charity to Orphanage With Religious Indoctrination other than Islam" (2019), https://www.islamweb.net/en/fatwa/399793/giving-charity-to-orpahanage-with-religious-indoctrination-other-than-islam, accessed December 30, 2019.

[119] Islamweb.net, "Fatwa #364171: "Wife giving charity without husband's knowledge" (2017), https://www.islamweb.net/en/fatwa/364171/wife-giving-charity-without-husbands-knowledge, accessed December 30, 2019.

[120] Islamweb.net, "Fatwa #21063: The woman's reward if she fairly gives in charity from the house of her husband" (2015), https://www.islamweb.net/en/fatwa/21063/the-womans-reward-if-she-fairly-gives-in-charity-from-the-house-of-her-husband, accessed December 30, 2019.

[121] Islamweb.net, "Fatwa #85294: "The ruling concerning begging" (2002), https://www.islamweb.net/emainpage/PrintFatwa.php?lang=E&Id=85294&lang=E&Id=85294, accessed December 30, 2019.

[122] Ibn Saad, *Women*, 64-66.

[123] Ibn Saad, *Tabaqat*, 1:586-588.

[124] Bukhari 8:78:678.

[125] Muhammad ibn Ismail in Kathir, *The Life of the Prophet Muhammad*, trans. Trevor Le Gassick (Reading, UK: Garnet Publishing, 2000), 3:123-124.

[126] Ibn Saad, *Tabaqat*, 1:583.

half a date-orchard,[127] and Muhammad confirmed that guardians were entitled to eat from the children's share.[128] That Hind relied principally on her own enterprises to feed her family is suggested by her question: "Will Allah reward me if I support my children? Even if he doesn't, I am not going to abandon them, for they are mine!" Muhammad assured her that Allah would indeed reward her for all of it.[129]

Hind's eldest daughter and younger son grew up to be notable narrators of hadith;[130] but their narrations do not reveal many personal memories of their famous stepfather. The girl remembered that Muhammad had disliked her original name, Barra, and renamed her "Zaynab".[131] The boy, Umar, recalled that Muhammad taught him how to eat politely, using his right hand and not grabbing at the food.[132] It is also said that one of the boys interrupted Muhammad's prayer by passing in front of him but moved back when Muhammad waved him away. When Zaynab also passed in front of him, she ignored his gesture and kept walking. Muhammad remarked, "Females are more stubborn!"[133] Both Zaynab and Umar convey the decided impression that they were not close to their stepfather.

Hind's older son, Salama, never transmitted a single hadith.[134] We do not know why he had so little to say about Islam. Our one cryptic clue is a biographical note that he was "crazy and lazy".[135]

Two stories about Hind's youngest child, Durra, strike a more chilling note. When Muhammad first married Hind, he would enter her house and find her too busy to receive him because she was nursing Durra. After some days, Hind's foster-brother instructed: "Stop injuring Allah's Messenger with this ugly foulness!" He carried the baby out of the house and handed her to a wet-nurse in the

---

[127] Muhammad ibn Umar al-Waqidi, *The Life of Muhammad*, trans. Rizwi Faizer, Amal Ismail, and AbdulKader Tayob (London: Routledge, 2011), 186.
[128] Nasa'i 5:44:4455.
[129] Bukhari 2:24:546; Muslim 5:2190.
[130] Ibn Saad, *Women*, 298; Tabari, *Companions*, 113.
[131] Muslim 25:5336.
[132] Bukhari 7:65:288.
[133] Ibn Maja 1:5:948. Granted, this hadith is ranked *da'īf* (weak), but it sounds too trivial to be deliberately fabricated.
[134] Tabari, *Companions*, 113.
[135] Ahmad ibn Yahya al-Baladhuri, *Ansab al-Ashraf* (Jerusalem: Jerusalem University Press, 1936), 1283; translation by a friend of the author.

suburbs. Only then did Hind find the time to perform her duty to her bridegroom.[136]

Durra returned to Hind's house after being weaned. Her sister Zaynab's one significant memory of Muhammad concerns Durra. A rumour circulated the mosque that Muhammad had plans to marry this child. Another wife, Ramla, confronted Muhammad about it directly. Fortunately, he confirmed that "my stepdaughter, brought up under my guardianship" was forbidden to him, "so do not offer me your daughters and sisters."[137] Nevertheless, we must ask how the rumour arose. It is quite likely that it was Hind who sent Ramla to Muhammad, and that she did so because she found the rumour credible – both she and others had noticed something suspicious in Muhammad's interactions with her child. Muhammad lived until Durra was six, the same age that 'Aïsha had been when he married her.

The default *sharia* ruling is that financial responsibility for fatherless children falls on their paternal blood-relations, typically their uncles. A stepfather has no moral duty to provide for his wife's children; if he chooses to do so, this is a supererogatory act of generosity.[138] It is not expected that a Muslim stepfather will aspire to a higher standard than his prophet, for Muslims have Muhammad's own word that "I treat my wives better than any of you."[139]

Zaynab: a convenient revelation
There is a danger of remembering the second Zaynab solely for the scandal surrounding her marriages. First Muhammad forced her to marry his adopted son Zayd.[140], [141] A year or so later, he accidentally glimpsed her half-dressed. Inflamed by admiration, he

---

[136] Ibn Saad, *Women*, 63-66.
[137] Nasa'i 4:26:3286. See Muslim 8:3413 for Ramla's account of the same incident.
[138] Dar al-Ifta al-Missriyyah, "Caring for the financial needs of a widow's children," Author, https://www.dar-alifta.org/Foreign/ViewFatwa.aspx?ID=8329&LangID=2, accessed December 30, 2019.
[139] Tirmidhi 6:46:3895.
[140] Jalal al-Deen al-Mahalli and Jalal al-Deen al-Suyuti, *Tafsir al-Jalalayn* on Q33:36-38.
[141] Quran 33:36. Ibn Saad, *Women*, 72; Tabari, *Companions*, 9-10, 180; Jalal al-Deen al-Mahalli and Jalal al-Deen al-Suyuti, *Tafsir al-Jalalayn* on Q33:36-38.

kept exclaiming, "Praise be to Allah, who turns hearts around!" Zayd took the hint and divorced Zaynab.[142, 143]

Muhammad then produced a string of new revelations. Adopted sons did not count as real sons, and in fact adoption did not exist in Islam, so Zaynab was not his daughter-in-law.[144] After deciding not to divorce Saowda,[145] Muhammad revealed that the limit of four wives did not apply to prophets, who might take as many wives as they liked.[146] Finally, Allah required Muhammad to marry Zaynab.[147]

Muhammad hosted an elaborate wedding-banquet, where seventy guests dined on roast lamb and date pudding.[148] A prominent warrior tactlessly boasted that when Muhammad died, he would marry 'Aïsha. Three of the guests sat around talking long after everyone else had gone home; Muhammad had to walk out of and return to Zaynab's house twice before they took the hint to leave him alone with her. Muhammad immediately announced a new revelation.[149] Guests must leave the prophet's house as soon as dinner was finished; his future widows were never to remarry; and, above all, his wives must veil their faces, segregate themselves from other men and not leave their houses without some approved reason.[150]

Hence the immediate sequel to Muhammad's marriage to Zaynab was the veil. Nobody could gaze at Muhammad's wives in the way that he had gazed at Zayd's wife. The veiling of other Muslim women soon followed, for Allah did not accept the prayers of an unveiled woman,[151] although a woman who was not married to

---

[142] Muhammad ibn Jarir al-Tabari, *Volume 8: The Victory of* Islam (translated by Michael Fishbein; Albany: State University of New York Press, 1997) 2-4. Tabari, 39: *Companions*, 180-181.

[143] Bukhari 9:93:516. Tabari, 39: *Companions*, 180-181.

[144] Quran 33:4-5, 40. Bukhari 6:60:305. Tabari, *9: Last Years*, 134. Ibn Kathir, *Tafsir* on Q33:5.

[145] See above.

[146] Quran 33:50. Ibn Saad, *Women*, 143.

[147] Quran 33:38. Ibn Hisham, *Notes*, 793 #918. Bukhari 9:93:516. Muslim 1:338. Nasa'i 4:26:3253. Tabari, *8: Victory*, 3-4. Tabari, 39: *Companions*, 180-181.

[148] Ibn Saad, *Women*, 74, 76. Bukhari 7:62:84, 97, 100. Muslim 8:3328, 3331.

[149] Ibn Saad, *Women*, 76-77, 142. Bukhari 6:60:315, 316, 317; 7:62:84, 92, 95; 7:65:375; 8:74:255, 256, 288; 9:93:517. Bukhari, *Mufrad* 43:1051. Muslim 8:3333, 3334, 3336.

[150] Quran 33:53. See also Quran 33:32-33 and Ibn Kathir's *Tafsir* on this.

[151] Abu Dawud 2:641.

Muhammad was allowed to reveal her hands and face.[152] Men must treat veiled women with respect;[153] but slave-women did not veil.[154]

Veiling remains a distinctive of the devout Muslim woman. "Wearing Hijab is a form of worship... It is Divine Order and Godly legislation that people have no right to change or neglect."[155] This subject arouses strong emotion in many Muslims. Discarding the hijab "is a deathblow and a form of alienation and loss of the Muslim personality and even 'dissolution' into non-Muslim habits and customs. They, i.e. non-Muslims, suffer the worst forms of pain and moral dissolution in their societies; it is the natural result of nakedness and displaying charms," therefore, "inviting/urging others to be naked constitutes a form of bestiality and life in caves and forests."[156]

A further consequence of Muhammad's marriage to Zaynab is that adoption does not exist in Islam. Muslims are encouraged to foster orphans,[157] but in practice they are reluctant to care for children who are not blood-relatives. This is because of the practical difficulties that will arise after puberty when male and female members of one small house will need to be veiled from each other.[158]

An even more serious issue arises from this chronicle of convenient revelation. Was there anyone left in Medina who still believed that Muhammad was a true prophet who genuinely spoke for God? Doubtless there were many who followed him gladly as the political leader of choice. But others must have been thinking what 'Aïsha voiced: "Your Lord seems so quick to grant your desires!"[159]

---

[152] Abu Dawud 33:4092.

[153] Quran 33:58-59; Ibn Kathir, *Tafsir* on Q33:59.

[154] Bukhari 7:62:22; Ibn Saad, *Women*, 129, 317.

[155] Islamweb.net, "Fatwa #84304: Wife wants her husband and his family to let his sister wear Hijab" (2002), https://www.islamweb.net/emainpage/PrintFatwa.php?lang=E&Id=84304, accessed December 30, 2019.

[156] Islamweb.net, "Fatwa #84304." accessed December 30, 2019.

[157] Islamweb.net, "Fatwa #82371: Adoption in Islam" (Author, 2001), https://www.islamweb.net/en/fatwa/82371/ cited 30 Dec 2019

[158] Islamweb.net, "Fatwa #84422: Islamic rules for adoption" (2002), https://www.islamweb.net/en/fatwa/84422/islamic-rules-for-adoption, accessed December 30, 2019.

[159] Bukhari 6:60:311.

Zaynab maintained a high status in Muhammad's household.[160] 'Aïsha said that Zaynab and Hind were his favourite wives after herself.[161] Hind said that Muhammad liked Zaynab but that he was often vexed with her,[162] perhaps because she lost her temper easily but was also quick to calm down.[163] More than once, Zaynab was so displeased with a gift from Muhammad that she sent it back.[164] Perhaps it was down to artistic temperament, for she was a skilled craftswoman who tanned leather, dyed cloth and sewed textiles.[165] She gave away all her profits in alms.[166]

Zaynab was openly competitive among her co-wives.[167] She used to boast to them: "You were all married by your families, but I was married by Allah in the seven heavens."[168] She often exchanged angry words with 'Aïsha,[169] and once she refused to lend her spare camel to Safiya.[170, 171] Yet when she was asked if she knew anything incriminating against 'Aïsha, she honestly declared: "I know only good."[172]

Rayhana: the slave-bride

Rayhana was Muhammad's first slave-wife. After ordering the decapitation of the Qurayza men and enslavement of the women,[173] Muhammad selected the "beautiful and graceful" Rayhana for himself.[174] He offered to manumit and marry her if she would convert to Islam; but she answered, "I hate Islam, and I would rather remain a slave than marry you."[175]

---

[160] Bukhari 5:59:462; Muslim 31:5984; Ibn Saad, *Women*, 123.

[161] Ibn Saad, *Women*, 81.

[162] Ibn Saad, *Women*, 74.

[163] Muslim 31:5984.

[164] Ibn Saad, *Women*, 138.

[165] Ibn Saad, *Women*, 74, 77-79; Muslim 8:3240, 3241. Abu Dawud 32:4060 (*da'if*).

[166] Ibn Saad, *Women*, 74, 78-79; Tabari, *Companions*, 182.

[167] Bukhari 3:33:249; 3:48:829; 6:60:274; Muslim 37:6673.

[168] Bukhari 9:93:516; Tabari, *Companions*, 182.

[169] Bukhari 3:47:755; Muslim 8:3450.

[170] Ibn Saad, *Women*, 90.

[171] See also Muhammad ibn Ismail ibn Kathir, *The Life of the Prophet Muhammad*, trans. Trevor Le Gassick (Reading, UK: Garnet Publishing, 2000), 4:435.

[172] Bukhari 3:48:829; 5:59:462; 6:60:274; Muslim 37:6673. See also Bukhari 6:60:281.

[173] Bukhari 4:52:280; 5:58:148; 5:59:362; 8:74:278; Muslim 19:4368.

[174] Ibn Ishaq, *Muhammad*, 466; Waqidi, *Muhammad*, 255; Ibn Saad, *Women*, 92-94. Tabari, *Companions*, 164-165. In fact Rayhana was not Qurayza-born; she was a member of the Nadir tribe whose Qurazi husband had been killed in the massacre.

[175] Ibn Ishaq, *Muhammad*, 466; Tabari, *Victory*, 39.

Muhammad countered that he would keep her in slavery if that was what she really wanted, but that she had no choice about whether she slept with him, for her body was his legal right as her owner.[176] Then Rayhana received advice from a Jew who had escaped the massacre by converting to Islam at the last minute.[177] Whatever he said to her in private, the result was that Rayhana agreed to accept Islam and marry Muhammad.[178] So he set her free, paid her a dower and ordered her to be veiled.[179]

Although Muhammad gave Rayhana everything she asked, she remained proud and aloof. In a matter of weeks, he divorced her;[180] and she returned to her family.[181] Since Muhammad had exiled the Nadir tribe,[182] she must have rejoined them in Khaybar. The following summer, Muhammad invaded Khaybar, laid siege to its fortresses and captured numerous women.[183] It is not stated that Rayhana was among them, but this is the most parsimonious explanation for how she once again fell into Muhammad's power.

This time Muhammad did not marry Rayhana. He kept her as a slave-concubine.[184] When he shared out gifts among his wives, he sometimes included Rayhana and sometimes left her out.[185] Muhammad manumitted all his slaves on his death-bed,[186] but this was too late to benefit Rayhana. She had died a few weeks earlier, still a slave in his possession.[187]

While Muhammad outlawed self-selling and kidnap-slavery, he encouraged the enslaving of civilian war-captives.[188] Given the vast extent of the Islamic conquests, the net effect was a great increase

---

[176] Waqidi, *Muhammad*, 256.
[177] Ibn Ishaq, *Muhammad*, 463; Waqidi, *Muhammad*, 247.
[178] Ibn Ishaq, *Muhammad*, 466; Waqidi, *Muhammad*, 255.
[179] Waqidi, *Muhammad*, 256; Ibn Saad, *Women*, 92-93; Tabari, *Companions*, 165.
[180] Ibn Saad, *Women*, 93.
[181] Ibn Kathir, *Muhammad*, 4, 416, 426, 434-435.
[182] Ibn Ishaq, *Muhammad*, 437-438.
[183] Ibn Ishaq, *Muhammad*, 510-511; Waqidi, *Muhammad*, 329, 332; Bukhari 1:8:367.
[184] Ibn Ishaq, *Muhammad*, 466; Tabari, *Last Years*, 141.
[185] Ibn Kathir, *Muhammad*, 4, 435.
[186] Ibn Saad, *Tabaqat*, 2:394-395; Bukhari 4:51:2.
[187] Ibn Ishaq, *Muhammad*, 466. Tabari, *Companions*, 165.
[188] Islamweb.net, "Fatwa #84431: Slavery in Islam" (2002), https://www.islamweb.net/emainpage/PrintFatwa.php?lang=E&Id=84431, accessed December 30, 2019.

in the quantity of world slavery.[189] The official position for today is that Islamic slavery no longer exists.[190] However, Islam has not yet conquered the world; there is no Islamic reason why the wars could not resume, resulting in more slavery in the future. It may not be an accident that Muslim countries were the last in the world to abolish slavery;[191, 192] it is difficult for a Muslim to denounce as wrong something that Muhammad permitted.

Tukana: the slave-concubine

Tukana was from the Qurayza tribe, and Muhammad captured her at the same time as Rayhana.[193] Muhammad's wives worried that Tukana was beautiful enough to supplant all of them should Muhammad notice her, so they colluded to keep her out of his sight.[194]

Eventually Muhammad did notice Tukana and she became his concubine.[195] However, she appears to have been a low-ranking handmaid who was not granted an official turn on his roster.[196] A man should not go to a free wife on another wife's day but he could visit a concubine at any time (and there was no need to perform the ritual washing if he moved straight from one concubine to another).[197] Hence when 'Aïsha awoke in the night to find Muhammad missing from her bed, her first thought was that he must have gone to one of the concubines.[198]

It is not known whether Muhammad continued to call Tukana to his bed for the rest of his life or whether he lost interest and

---

[189] Samuel Green, "Islam and Slavery," *Answering Islam* (2007), https://www.answering-islam.org/Green/slavery.htm, accessed December 30, 2019.
[190] Islamweb.net, "Fatwa #386479: Buying Women in Modern Times as Slaves" (2018), https://www.islamweb.net/en/fatwa/386479/buying-women-in-modern-times-as-slaves, accessed December 30, 2019.
[191] Free the Slaves, "Slavery in History" (n.d.), https://www.freetheslaves.net/about-slavery/slavery-in-history, accessed December 30, 2019.
[192] Tim Lambert, "A Short History of Slavery," *A World History Encyclopedia* (2019), http://www.localhistories.org/slavery.html, accessed December 30, 2019.
[193] Muhammad Baqir al-Majlisi, *A Detailed Biography of Prophet Muhammad (S)*, trans. H. S. H. Rizvi (Qum: Ansariyan Publications, 2010), 1180.
[194] Ibn Kathir, *Muhammad*, 4:435.
[195] Ibn Kathir, *Muhammad*, 4:435.
[196] Majlisi, *Muhammad*, 1180.
[197] Malik 2:90.
[198] Nasa'i 2:12:1125. However, 'Aïsha then discovered him prostrating on her floor.

discarded her. However, her fortunes took a turn for the better after he died. Not only did she become free,[199] but she is said to have married Muhammad's uncle Abbas.[200]

Juwayriya: another slave-bride

Juwayriya was also a war-captive. Her original name was Barra; it was Muhammad who called her Juwayriya,[201] which translates as "lassie" or perhaps "slavey".

Muhammad raided Juwayriya's tribe while they were watering their cattle at Muraysi Wells.[202] Her husband was killed in the battle, and Juwayriya was taken prisoner.[203] The Muslims wanted to rape their captives;[204] but since a pregnant slave was worth less on the slave-market,[205] they asked Muhammad if it was a good idea to practise coitus interruptus. He replied that, "If Allah wills a child to be conceived, it will be, whether you try to reduce your odds or not."[206] He did not forbid the rapes.[207]

This precedent illuminates why terrorist groups like Boko Haram[208] and ISIS[209] kidnap and rape women in conquered territories. It is the traditional behaviour of victorious armies everywhere, but Islam is the only major religion that actively endorses such behaviour.

'Aïsha took an instant dislike to Juwayriya because she was "a sweet, beautiful woman who captivated anyone who looked at

---

[199] Bukhari 4:51:2.

[200] Majlisi, *Muhammad*, 1180.

[201] Muslim 25:5334.

[202] Bukhari 3:46:717; Muslim 19:4292.

[203] Ibn Saad, *Women*, 83.

[204] Malik 29:32:95; Bukhari 3:46:718; 5:59:459; 9:93:506; Muslim 8:3371.

[205] Waqidi (Faizer) 202.

[206] Malik 29:32:95; Bukhari 3:46:717, 718; 5:59:459; 9:93:506; Muslim 8:3371; Abu Dawud 2:2167.

[207] Waqidi (Faizer) 201.

[208] Premium Times, "How Boko Haram militants rape, abuse girls, women – Report," https://www.premiumtimesng.com/news/headlines/170218-how-boko-haram-militants-rape-abuse-girls-women-report.html, published October 27, 2014.

[209] Yuka Tachibana, Ben Adams, and Kelly Cobiella, "Yazidi Women Tell of Rape and Enslavement at Hands of ISIS," *ABC News*, https://www.nbcnews.com/storyline/isis-uncovered/yazidi-women-tell-rape-enslavement-hands-isis-n462091, published November 29, 2015.

her;"[210] and predictably enough, Muhammad selected her for himself.[211] Later her father and two brothers arrived in Medina to redeem her. Muhammad took their payment; but Juwayriya, perhaps seeing that her relatives were surrounded by armed Muslims, said that she would stay with Muhammad.[212]

Nevertheless, the few traditions about Juwayriya's married life suggest that she tried to avoid Muhammad's company. Once she scheduled a fast (which meant abstaining from sex as well as food) on her rostered day with him. He asked: "Did you fast yesterday? Do you plan to fast tomorrow?" No. "Then break your fast."[213] Another day Muhammad left her house as she was prostrating for dawn prayers. He returned toward noon to find her still in the same position. He taught her that a brief sentence that he said was worth more than a whole morning's prayer.[214] In other words, prayer was no excuse for avoiding one's husband.[215]

Safiya: strategy for survival

Safiya was yet another war-captive: Muhammad gave her this name because the *safi* was his chosen portion from the battle-plunder.[216]

She was the daughter of Muhammad's Jewish nemesis, Huyayy, chief of the Nadir.[217] Huyayy and his son were decapitated alongside the Qurayza tribe.[218, 219] The following year the Muslims captured Safiya at the siege of Khaybar.[220] After Khaybar surrendered, Safiya's husband, Kinana, was interrogated about some jewellery that Muhammad believed should have been included in his conqueror's spoil. Kinana would not confess where he had hidden it,

---

[210] Tabari, *Victory*, 57. See also Ibn Saad, *Women*, 83. Tabari, *Companions*, 183.

[211] Ibn Ishaq, *Muhammad*, 493.

[212] Ibn Hisham, *Notes*, 793#918. Ibn Saad, *Women*, 8:84.

[213] Bukhari 3:31:207.

[214] Muslim 35:6575. "Glory be to Allah, who deserves praise according to the size of his creation, to the pleasure of his self, to the weight of his throne and to the ink of his words."

[215] See also Bukhari, *Mufrad*, 30:279:639, where a similar conversation with 'Aïsha makes the point more directly.

[216] Abu Dawud 19:2988.

[217] Ibn Ishaq, *Muhammad*, 511, 514-515.

[218] Ahmad ibn Yahya al-Baladhuri, *The Origins of the Islamic State: Part 1*, trans. Philip Khuri Hitti (New York: Longmans, Green and Co., 1916), 41.

[219] Ibn Ishaq, *Muhammad*, 464.

[220] Ibn Ishaq, *Muhammad*, 511, 514-515; Waqidi, *Muhammad*, 329; Bukhari 1:8:367; 2:14:68; 3:34:431; 5:59:512, 513; Muslim 8:3325, 3328.

so Muhammad ordered him to be tortured with a firebrand. Kinana still refused to speak, so after being tortured until he could not speak, he was beheaded.[221] We note that Islam forbids burning as a means of execution[222] (technically, it was not the fire that killed Kinana); but the example of Kinana may explain why ISIS insurgents felt justified in burning alive a captured Jordanian pilot.[223]

Only minutes after Safiya first saw Kinana's severed head,[224] Muhammad proposed to her. She replied: "I have always desired Islam and I already believed in you before you called me. I have no father or brother and no desire for their religion. I prefer Allah and his messenger to my own people's way."[225] As she later described it: "The Prophet was so polite that all my hatred melted away. He apologised profusely for destroying my people by explaining that it had all been the fault of my father, whose conspiracies had forced the Muslims to march to Khaybar to defend themselves. By the time I stood up again, I loved him more than anyone in the world."[226, 227]

Safiya's words cannot be taken literally. If her hatred did not "melt" until after she heard Muhammad's apology, then she certainly did not "desire" him before he called her over. Although she managed to convince Muhammad of her sincerity,[228] her florid speeches are better understood as sarcasm.

At first Muhammad's other wives resented Safiya's beauty and Jewish origin.[229] They laughed when she fell off a stumbling camel.[230] Hind snapped at Muhammad for "talking to her on my day."[231] 'Aïsha denigrated her for being too short.[232] Hafsa simply called her

---

[221] Ibn Ishaq, *Muhammad*, 515. Waqidi, *Muhammad*, 330-331. Baladhuri, *Islamic State 1*, 42-47. Abu Dawud 19:3000 *(hasan)*.

[222] Bukhari 9:84:57.

[223] BBC News, "Jordan pilot hostage Moaz al-Kasasbeh 'burned alive'" (Author, 3 February 2015), https://www.bbc.com/news/world-middle-east-31121160

[224] Ibn Ishaq, *Muhammad*, 514-515. Waqidi, *Muhammad*, 331.

[225] Waqidi, *Muhammad*, 332, 348. Ibn Saad, *Women*, 86, 88. See also Tabari, *9: Last Years*, 135.

[226] Abu Bakr Ahmad ibn Hussayn al-Bayhaqi, *Dalaïl al-Nubuwwa Volume 4* (Cairo: Dar al-Hadith, 2007) #1575.

[227] See also Baladhuri, *Islamic State 1*, 45.

[228] Waqidi, *Muhammad*, 349. Ibn Saad, *Tabaqat 2*, 390. Ibn Saad, *Women*, 87, 91.

[229] Waqidi, *Muhammad*, 332, 349. Ibn Saad, *Women*, 90.

[230] Muslim 8:3329.

[231] Ibn Saad, *Women*, 67.

[232] Abu Dawud 42:4857.

"Jewess".[233] When Safiya cooked for Muhammad's dinner-guests, 'Aïsha smashed the dish.[234] Sometimes Muhammad stood up for Safiya;[235] but when 'Aïsha denigrated Safiya's father, and Safiya retaliated with words about Abu Bakr, Muhammad dropped the pretence that he was Safiya's champion. "Safiya, do not insult Abu Bakr!"[236]

Within months, however, 'Aïsha befriended Safiya.[237] She never explained why, but she most likely discovered that Safiya had no desire to be her romantic rival.

On the family's journey to Mecca, Safiya was impeded by a slow camel and she began to cry. Muhammad stopped beside her and wiped away her tears; but the more he urged her not to cry over it, the more uncontrollably she wept. Muhammad lost patience and rebuked her, then halted the caravan. Safiya became afraid. She wanted to avoid Muhammad, but it was her rostered night with him. She approached 'Aïsha and begged, "Can you restore me to Allah's Messenger's favour? I'll give up my night to you." 'Aïsha put on a saffron veil and entered Muhammad's tent. When he began to tell her that tonight was not her turn, she replied, "This is Allah's gift, which he bestows on whomever he pleases!" She presented Safiya's apologies and soothed over Muhammad's annoyance.[238]

We question, of course, whether Safiya was really weeping over a camel. It seems that she negotiated her way through the Muslim community by hiding and dissembling. Nevertheless, one of her speeches rings true. She said: "I hated the prophet more than anyone in the world because he had killed my husband, my father and my brother."[239]

Ramla, Umm Habiba

Ramla was from the aristocratic Umayya family.[240] Her father, Abu Sufyan, was the leader of the opposition in Mecca,[241] but Ramla

---

[233] Waqidi, *Muhammad*, 332. Tirmidhi 6:46:3894.
[234] Bukhari 7:62:152; Abu Dawud 23:3560, 3561 (*da'if*); Nasa'i 4:36:3409 (*hasan*).
[235] Waqidi, *Muhammad*, 332.
[236] Ibn Saad, *Women*, 56.
[237] Bukhari 3:47:755; Muslim 31:5984; Abu Dawud 42:4880 (*da'if*).
[238] Ibn Hanbal, *Musnad*, 6#26908, #24684. Ibn Maja 3:9:1973. 'Aïsha was quoting Quran 62:4.
[239] Baladhuri, *Islamic State*, 44-45; Ibn Kathir, *Muhammad*, 3:271.
[240] Ibn Saad, *Women*, 68. Tabari, *Companions*, 177.
[241] Ibn Ishaq, *Muhammad*, 168, 187, 203, 274, 277, 323, 540, etc.

was an early convert to Islam.[242] Her first husband died[243] at about the time when Abu Sufyan forced Muhammad into the humiliating armistice of Hudaybiya.[244] Soon afterwards, Muhammad sent Ramla a proposal of marriage, which she joyfully accepted.[245] Hence his motive seems to have been primarily political: he could snub Abu Sufyan by showing him where his daughter's loyalties lay.

Two years later, Abu Sufyan visited Medina in a desperate attempt to renew the armistice. Ramla had not seen her father for thirteen years, but when he entered her house, she snatched up her rug and folded it away. "My dear," exclaimed Abu Sufyan, "is the rug too good for me, or am I too good for the rug?" She clarified: "It's the Prophet's rug, and you are a dirty pagan. I don't want you sitting on it." Abu Sufyan could only lament, "O daughter, your misfortunes have rotted your mind!"[246]

Ramla had not broken any rule of Islam, for while a man must prioritise his parents over his spouses, the opposite is true for a woman. This *fatwa* was issued to a woman whose father and husband had given her conflicting instructions: "Your obedience to your husband takes priority over your obedience to your father; the fact that your husband mistreated your father is not a sound reason for not traveling to join him."[247]

Ramla was meticulous in her observation of Islamic rituals. She knew to ablute after drinking barley-water,[248] not to travel with a bell,[249] to avoid gatherings at night[250] and not to mourn a dead relative for longer than three days.[251] She never neglected her extra prayers, for Muhammad told her that Allah built a house in Paradise for every

---

[242] Ibn Ishaq, *Muhammad*, 146; Abu Dawud 11:2081; Tabari, *Last Years*, 133; Tabari, *Companions*, 177.

[243] Ibn Ishaq, *Muhammad*, 527-528; Abu Dawud 11:2102; 11:2102; Tabari, *Companions*, 177-178.

[244] Ibn Ishaq, *Muhammad*, 499, 504-505.

[245] Ibn Saad, *Women*, 69-70; Tabari, *Victory*, 109-110; Tabari, *Last Years*, 133-134. Tabari, *Companions*, 178-180.

[246] Ibn Ishaq, *Muhammad*, 543; Waqidi, *Muhammad*, 390-391.

[247] Islamweb.net, "Fatwa #119697: Her parents forbid her from traveling to join her husband" (2009), https://www.islamweb.net/en/fatwa/119697, accessed December 30, 2019.

[248] Abu Dawud 1:195.

[249] Abu Dawud 15:2548.

[250] Ibn Saad, *Women*, 71.

[251] Bukhari 2:23:371; Muslim 9:3539.

Muslim who prayed twelve extra prayer-units every day… if Allah willed.[252] He also advised her that it was no good to pray for blessing on earth, as her lifespan and wealth were already predestined: "It would be better to pray to avoid Hellfire."[253] It is therefore not clear whether Ramla was praying out of confidence that she would earn Paradise or fear that she might not.

She was as devoted to the messenger as to the message. She referred to Muhammad as "my beloved Abu Qasim,"[254] a public declaration of her love not made by any of his other wives. She perfumed her house and her person with ambergris and musk, which he approved.[255] After the conquest of Mecca, Ramla was an important link between Muhammad and the old Quraysh nobility. Her brother Muaawiyah served in the prophet's scriptorium,[256] while their father was appointed a governor in Yemen.[257] But none of this earned her a particularly high status in Muhammad's household or his heart.

Maymuna: ritually undefiled

Maymuna was Ramla's cousin;[258] and, like Ramla, she was obsessed with ritual correctness. Cleanliness was her running theme: the order in which Muhammad washed his body-parts;[259] how to manage menstruation;[260] what to do about a dead mouse found in the butter.[261] Carrion meat was forbidden but the same animal's hide was permitted.[262] Eating lizard was permitted, but since Muhammad disliked it, Maymuna did not touch it either.[263]

Despite her care, Maymuna's house became defiled. One day Muhammad told her that angels were avoiding it because she had images and there was a puppy under her bench. Maymuna had to

---

[252] Muslim 4:1579, 1581; Nasa'i 20:1814.
[253] Muslim 6:6440.
[254] Nasa'i 2:20:1814.
[255] Ibn Saad, *Women*, 69; Tabari, *Victory*, 110; Tabari, *Companions*, 179.
[256] Muslim 31:6095. Muwaawiyah was destined to become the fifth Caliph of Islam.
[257] Muhammad ibn Jarir al-Tabari. *Volume 10: The Conquest of Arabia*, trans. Fred M. Donner (Albany, NY: State University of New York Press, 1993), 158.
[258] Ahmad ibn Hajar al-Asqalani, *Al-Isaba fi Tamyiz al-Sahaba* (Riyadh: Dar 'Aalim al-Kutub, 2013), 3#4050. Ramla's paternal grandmother was Maymuna's paternal aunt.
[259] Bukhari 1:5:259.
[260] Bukhari 1:6:300
[261] Bukhari 7:67:446.
[262] Bukhari 2:24:569
[263] Muslim 21:4796.

behead her sculpture "so that it looks like a tree" and to tear down some curtains that were decorated with animals. Muhammad threw out the puppy and ordered the slaying of every dog in Medina.[264]

Maymuna's concern with ceremonial purity is widespread in the Muslim world. One observer noted: "Their daily lives and religious rituals seem to revolve around... their ceremonial purity... because eating pork is the worst possible state of defilement, and more attention is given to ceremonial purity than moral purity, the pork eater (George Bush) is worse off than a murderer (Saddam Hussein)." Therefore: "Perhaps the greatest need felt by these Muslim people is not for assurance of salvation from sin but for deliverance from the tyranny of being in a near constant state of defilement. Every element of their daily lives is ordered by this insecurity."[265]

Little is told of Maymuna beyond her passion for reciting, obeying and enforcing "the rules". When she was not busy with ritual prayers or household chores, she liked to sit and clean her teeth.[266]

Mariya: the Copt
Mariya was an Egyptian slave, born to a Coptic father and a Greek mother. She was in the service of the Governor of Alexandria until he sent her to Medina as a diplomatic gift for Muhammad.[267] In Arabia she agreed to convert to Islam.[268] She may have assumed that Islam was a branch of Christianity, for she could not have understood much Arabic, and the Muslims spoke of Jesus.

Mariya was beautiful with curly hair,[269] and Muhammad took her as a concubine.[270] His official wives, led by 'Aïsha and Hafsa, protested furiously. Muhammad at first appeased them by promising

---

[264] Muslim 24:5248; Abu Dawud 33:4146. 'Aïsha also had to tear down some animal-patterned curtains (Bukhari 3:43:659; 8:73:130).

[265] Bruce Thomas, "The Gospel for Shame Cultures," *Evangelism and Missions Information Service* (July, 1994), https://missionexus.org/the-gospel-for-shame-cultures, accessed December 30, 2019.

[266] Ibn Saad, *Women*, 98.

[267] Ibn Ishaq, *Muhammad*, 653; Ibn Hisham, *Notes*, 711#129; Ibn Saad, *Women*, 148; Tabari, *Victory*, 100; Tabari, *Last Years*, 147; Tabari, *Companions*, 193-194.

[268] Ibn Saad, *Women*, 149; Tabari, *Victory*, 131; Tabari, *Companions*, 194.

[269] Ibn Saad, *Tabaqat*, 1:151; Ibn Saad, *Women*, 149. Tabari, *Victory*, 131; *Companions*, 194.

[270] Ibn Saad, *Women*, 136, 149; Tabari, *Last Years*, 141.

to give Mariya up, but later he thought better of letting his women dictate to him and said that Allah had absolved him of his promise.[271] When his wives remained angry, he swore not to speak to them for a month, and he spent that month alone with Mariya in his neighbour's attic.[272] He then made his wives a generous offer: they could choose to divorce him, in which case he would pay them handsomely; or they could agree to be obedient wives who were destined for Paradise. They all chose to remain.[273]

To the distress of the official wives, Mariya was pregnant. 'Aïsha, the most jealous of them all, confesses that they "alarmed" Mariya, although she does not specify what they did to her. Mariya was so uspet that Muhammad moved her out of the mosque to a house in the suburbs.[274] Rumours followed her to her new residence. It was whispered that Muhammad was infertile and Mariya's pregnancy must have been the result of an infidelity. Suspicion fell on her cousin Maabur, who often visited her with supplies of water and firewood, and Muhammad sent his son-in-law Ali to kill his rival. The two cousins were reprieved when Ali reported back that the gossip was wrong: he had seen that Maabur was a eunuch.[275]

If Mariya had been convicted of infidelity, she would have been flogged;[276] but a married freewoman convicted of adultery was stoned to death.[277] Adultery is still punished by lapidation in some

---

[271] Quran 66:1-3; Ibn Saad, *Tabaqat*, 1:152. Ibn Saad, *Women*, 124-125, 135-138, 149; Bukhari 3:43:648; 6:60:434; 7:62:119; 7:63:192; 8:78:682; 9:86:102; Muslim 9:3496; Nasa'i 4:36:3410, 3411. In some of these traditions, Muhammad's promise is to stop eating mimosa honey, which gives him bad breath. In fact there is no real conflict over which version is correct, for "tasting honey" was a commonplace Arabic metaphor for sexual intercourse (cf. Abu Dawud 12:2302). The "honey" narrative is therefore an allegorical recasting of Mariya's story.

[272] Ibn Saad, *Women*, 135-137, 149; Bukhari 3:31:134; 3:43:648; 7:62:119, 130; 7:72:734; Muslim 6:2387; 9:3509.

[273] Bukhari 3:43:648; Muslim 9:3507.

[274] Ibn Saad (Haq) 1:152; Ibn Saad, *Women*, 149.

[275] Ibn Saad, *Women*, 150; Tabari, *Last Years*, 147.

[276] Muslim 17:4219.

[277] Bukhari 4:56:829

Islamic jurisdictions, though not universally.[278, 279]

When Mariya gave birth to a son, Ibrahim,[280] it seemed that her status in the household was secured. Yet although Mariya veiled herself like a wife, Muhammad never married her legally.[281] Nor is there any evidence that his infatuation with her continued; rather, he seems to have transferred his affections to their son.[282] Ibrahim died within two years.[283] Muhammad forbade Mariya to wail over her child's death,[284] but his own eyes leaked.[285] Then he preached a gloomy sermon on the evils of adultery,[286] as if his old suspicions had never quite been laid to rest.

Mulayka, Asma and Fatima: seeking refuge with Allah

In 630 Muhammad divorced three brides in quick succession. The first was Mulayka, whose father had been killed while resisting the conquest of Mecca. Her family presumably offered her to Muhammad to appease him. Within weeks, 'Aïsha challenged the newcomer: "You should be ashamed of marrying the man who killed your father!" Mulayka took the point. On her next rostered turn with Muhammad, she announced: "I seek refuge in Allah from thee!" These solemn words were a pre-Islamic divorce formula, and Muhammad gave Mulayka what she wanted. Her family begged that she was "too young to know her mind," but Muhammad would not take her back. Mulayka never returned to Mecca; she mysteriously died before the divorce was final.[287]

---

[278] 'Abdul-'Azeez Bin Baz, "There are no Conditions Attached to One Who Stones the Adulterer," *FatwaIslam.com*,
http://www.fatwaislam.com/fis/index.cfm?scn=fd&ID=421, accessed December 30, 2019.

[279] See also Emma Batha and Ye Li, "Stoning – where is it legal?" *Thomas Reuters Foundation News*, http://news.trust.org//item/20130927160132-qt52c, published September 29, 2013.

[280] Ibn Saad (Haq) 1:152; Ibn Saad, *Women*, 149; Tabari, *Last Years*, 39; *Companions*, 194.

[281] Ibn Saad, *Women*, 149. Tabari, *Last Years*, 141, 147; *Companions*, 194.

[282] Ibn Saad (Haq) 1:152-155.

[283] Muslim 30:5734; Abu Dawud 20:3181 (*hasan*). The exact date of Ibrahim's death is disputed.

[284] Ibn Saad, *Women*, 151.

[285] Bukhari 2:23:390; Muslim 30:5733.

[286] Bukhari 2:18:154.

[287] Ibn Saad, *Women*, 106; Tabari, *Victory*, 187; *Companions*, 165.

A nobleman from the south converted to Islam and sealed the alliance by giving Muhammad his daughter Asma, "the most beautiful widow in Arabia."[288] 'Aïsha and Hafsa visited the bride, flattered her on her regal deportment, and offered to comb her hair. They advised her that the prophet would be driven wild with passion if Asma played the prude in the nuptial chamber.[289] She naïvely took their advice and spoke the rehearsed words. "Does a princess give herself to the rabble? I seek refuge in Allah from thee!" Muhammad told her: "You have sought refuge in the Almighty, so return to your family!"[290] Asma was distraught when Muhammad gave her a gift of two linen gowns and sent her back to the desert.[291]

Fatima's father, a middle-weight in the Muslim army,[292] probably handed over his daughter to advance his career. She later claimed that he had never asked for her consent.[293] Fatima did not adapt well to the lifestyle of veiling. She used to lift her curtain to peep at the men in the mosque courtyard. 'Aïsha caught her in the act and reported to Muhammad,[294] and Muhammad warned Fatima about appropriate conduct for a Mother of the Faithful. At his anger, Fatima became hysterical. She had seen how Mulayka and Asma had released themselves from him, and she recited that she sought refuge in Allah from him.[295] After the divorce, Fatima supported herself by collecting camel-dung and drying it to sell as fuel. Sometimes she visited Muhammad's wives, announcing herself as, "It's the wretch, the miserable woman!"[296]

Although Muhammad agreed that 'Aïsha and Hafsa had been "immensely devious" to trick Asma, he maintained that this divorce formula was inviolable.[297] Nevertheless, it seems that he reconsidered

---

[288] Ibn Saad, *Women*, 101-102; Tabari, *Companions*, 188.

[289] Ibn Saad, *Women*, 102-104; Tabari, *Companions*, 189-191.

[290] Ibn Hisham, *Notes*, 794#918; Ibn Saad, *Women*, 102-104; Bukhari 7:63:181, 182; 7:69:541; Ibn Maja 3:10:2050; Tabari, *Last Years*, 137; *Companions*, 188-191. Ibn Hisham has confused the names "Asma" and "Amra," and the tradition recorded in Tabari, *Last Years*, repeats this mistake.

[291] Ibn Saad, *Women*, 104; Bukhari 7:63:182; 7:69:541; Tabari, *Companions*, 190-191.

[292] Ibn Ishaq, *Muhammad*, 590-591; Waqidi, *Muhammad*, 170, 477, 481.

[293] Tabari, *Last Years*, 136.

[294] Ibn Saad, *Women*, 101; Tabari, *Companions*, 187-188.

[295] Ibn Saad, *Women*, 100-101; Tabari, *Last Years*, 39. Tabari, *Companions*, 186-188.

[296] Ibn Saad, *Women*, 100-101; Tabari, Companions, 187. We are not told why Fatima did not revert to being her father's responsibility; but it would appear that he did not want her.

[297] Ibn Saad, *Women*, 103.

after Fatima used the same formula to call his bluff. It was not used again, and this form of divorce does not appear in the hadith as a legal option.

A Muslim woman now has two routes out of a bad marriage, but neither is "inviolable". She can tell her husband that she wants to "ransom" herself, and he either refuses or sets the price that he will accept before allowing her to leave.[298] Or she can plead to a sharia court that she needs a separation, and the permission and its price are determined by the judge.[299, 300] Muhammad warned that a woman who attempted either route without a "strong reason" would "never smell Paradise";[301] a broken arm qualified[302] but a bruised face did not.[303]

The burden of proof still lies on the woman, as this typical *fatwa* shows: "If what you mentioned is true that your husband beat you, and he has no sound reason for doing so... then he is wrong. However, you also was [*sic*] wrong by going out of the marital home without the consent of your husband... We advise you to be patient with your husband especially that he wishes to reconcile with you..."[304]

Amra: the Lepress

Another short-lived bride was Amra. Muhammad saw on the wedding night that she had white patches on her skin. "Your people have deceived me!" he exclaimed. "Take your clothes and go home."[305]

---

[298] Quran 2:229.

[299] Bukhari 7:63:197, 198.

[300] Dar al-Ifta, "Rights upon a woman who sought divorce in return for reimbursement of her dowry" (n.d.),
https://www.dar-alifta.org/Foreign/ViewFatwa.aspx?ID=454&text=divorce

[301] Abu Dawud 12:2218. See also Malik 29:32; Tirmidhi 2:13:1186.

[302] Nasa'i 4:27:3527 (hasan); Abu Dawud 12:2220. The woman who was granted a divorce because her husband had broken her arm was the same woman who had refused Muhammad's marriage-proposal in 623.

[303] Bukhari 7:72:715. The two husbands of this woman were Qurayza survivors.

[304] Islamweb.net, "Fatwa #130103: She feels unable to return to her husband who beat her" (2009); "Fatwa #130103: She feels unable to return to her husband who beat her" (2009); "Fatwa #130103: She feels unable to return to her husband who beat her" (2009),
https://www.islamweb.net/emainpage/PrintFatwa.php?lang=E&Id=130103&lang=E&I
d=130103, accessed December 30, 2019.

[305] Ibn Saad, *Women*, 101. Tabari, 39: *Companions*, 186-188. Ibn Kathir, Muhammad 4, 416, 427. Amra and Fatima were from the same tribe, Kilab, with the result that some

Muhammad ruled that a guardian who neglected to warn a prospective bridegroom about a girl's leprosy or insanity was liable for damages, although the bride would keep her dower.[306] He took it for granted that the outcome would be divorce, for he never touched lepers.[307] "One should flee from the leper as one flees from a lion."[308]

Nafisa

Nafisa was Muhammad's last slave-concubine. She originally belonged to his wife Zaynab. Following a quarrel, Muhammad refused to speak to Zaynab for over two months. When he was ready to reconcile, she gave him Nafisa as a gift. A few days later, Muhammad was stricken by his final illness.[309, 310]

Nobody knows what happened to Nafisa afterwards. Her intimacy with the most important man in the world did not render her of sufficient importance to have her biography recorded.

Conclusion

To the Western world, Muslim attitudes to women, and Muslim women's attitudes to life, can seem strange, archaic and resistant to progress. Women are constrained and segregated in social relationships, leading to disadvantage in marriage and divorce, reduced economic opportunities and threats to physical safety. Muslim children are also inadequately protected from violence and poverty, and female children are at risk of premature marriage. Slavery, including concubinage, is not a major feature of Islam today, but it has been in the past and could be again in the future. Only the mothers of adult sons enjoy relative security and independence. In such a culture, women are perhaps even more vulnerable than men to the psychological stress caused by the demands of Islam's rules, rituals and the fear of damnation.

---

historians have treated them as one person. However, there is no real problem in distinguishing them, as their names, clans and biographies are quite different.

[306] Malik 28:3:9. It is not known whether he made this rule as a specific response to his experience with Amra.

[307] Muslim 26:5541.

[308] Bukhari 7:71:608.

[309] Ibn Hanbal, Musnad 6, #26908. Abu Dawud 3:4588; 41:4585 (daïf). Ibn Saad, *Women*, 90. See also Ibn Kathir, *Muhammad 4*, 435.

[310] Shams al-Deen Muhammad ibn Ahmad al-Dhahabi al-Dimashqi, *Siyar a'lam al-Nubala* (Beirut: Mu'assassat al-Risalah, 2014) #117.

These attitudes are not arbitrary. Many of them can be traced directly to the experiences of Muhammad and his wives, as presented in the hadith and sirat literature. If Muhammad is a prophet who cannot be wrong, it is understandable that the Muslim community would perceive no need to change its attitudes, except to align them ever more closely to the life and teachings of Muhammad. Any hope for change must lie in undermining the authority of Muhammad by questioning his claim to be a prophet!

Bibliography

Qur'an, The. Qur'an Gateway: A world of Qur'anic research at your fingertips. https://info.qurangateway.org/
The Hadith of the Prophet Muhammad at your fingertips, https://sunnah.com/ (This compendium includes Malik, Bukhari, Muslim, parts of Abu Dawud, Nasa'i al-Asghar, Tirmidhi and ibn Maja.)

al-Asqalani, Ahmad ibn Hajar. *Al-Isaba fi Tamyiz al-Sahaba*. Riyadh: Dar 'Aalim al-Kutub, 2013.

al-Baladhuri, Ahmad ibn Yahya. *Ansab al-Ashraf*. Jerusalem: Jerusalem University Press, 1936.

al-Baladhuri, Ahmad ibn Yahya. *The Origins of the Islamic State: Part 1*. Translated by Philip Khuri Hitti. New York: Longmans, Green and Co., 1916.

al-Bayhaqi, Ahmad ibn al-Hussayn. *Dala'il al-Nubuwwa wama'rifat Ahwal Sahib al-Sharia*. Cairo: Dar al-Hadith, 2007.

Hisham, Abdulmalik ibn. "Notes to Ibn Ishaq's Sirat Rasul Allah." In *Muhammad ibn Ishaq: The Life of Muhammad*, translated by Alfred Guillaume. Oxford: Oxford University Press, 1955.

Hanbal, Ahmad ibn Muhammad ibn. *al-Shaybani: Musnad Ahmad ibn Hanbal*. Cairo: Qurtuba Organisation, 1890.

Ishaq, Muhammad ibn. *The Life of Muhammad*. Translated by Alfred Guillaume. Oxford: Oxford University Press, 1955.

Kathir, Muhammad ibn Ismail ibn. *The Life of the Prophet Muhammad*. Vol. 2. Translated by Trevor Le Gassick. Reading, UK: Garnet Publishing, 1998.

_____. *The Life of the Prophet Muhammad*. Vol. 3. Translated by Trevor Le Gassick. Reading, UK: Garnet Publishing, 2000.

_____. *The Life of the Prophet Muhammad*. Vol 4. Translated by Trevor Le Gassick. Reading, UK: Garnet Publishing, 2000.

_____. *Quran Tafsir*. http://qtafsir.com/

al-Mahalli, Jalal al-Deen, and Jalal al-Deen al-Suyuti. *Tafsir al-Jalalayn.* https://www.altafsir.com/al-jalalayn.asp

al-Majlisi, Muhammad Baqir. *A Detailed Biography of Prophet Muhammad (S).* Translated by H. S. H. Rizvi. Qum: Ansariyan Publications, 2010.

Saad, Muhammad ibn. *Ibn Sa'd's Kitab al-Tabaqat al-Kabir.* Vol 1. Translated by S. Moinul Haq. Delhi: Kitab Bhavan, 1967.

_____. *Ibn Sa'd's Kitab al-Tabaqat al-Kabir.* Vol 2. Translated by S. Moinul Haq. Delhi: Kitab Bhavan, 1972.

_____. *The Companions of Badr.* Translated by Aisha Bewley. London: Ta-Ha Publishers, 2013.

_____. *The Men of Madina.* Vol. 2. Translated by Aisha Bewley. London: Ta-Ha Publishers, 2000.

_____. *The Women of Madina.* Translated by Aisha Bewley. London: Ta-Ha Publishers, 1995.

al-Sanaani, Abdalrazzaq ibn Hammam. *Al-Musannaf* (Beirut: 1972).

al-Tabari, M. ibn J. *Volume 7: The Foundation of the Community.* Translated by M. V. McDonald. Albany, NY: State University of New York Press, 1987.

_____. *Volume 8: The Victory of Islam.* Translated by Michael Fishbein. Albany, NY: State University of New York Press, 1997.

_____. *Volume 9: The Last Years of the Prophet.* Translated by Ismail K. Poonawala. Albany, NY: State University of New York Press, 1990.

_____. *Volume 10: The Conquest of Arabia.* Translated by Fred M. Donner. Albany, NY: State University of New York Press, 1993.

_____. *Volume 17: The First Civil War.* Translated by G. R. Hawting. Albany, NY: State University of New York Press, 1996.

_____. *Volume 39: Biographies of the Companions and Their Successors.* Translated by Ella Landau-Tasseron. Albany, NY: State University of New York Press, 1998.

al-Waqidi, Muhammad ibn Umar. *The Life of Muhammad.* Translated by Rizwi Faizer, Amal Ismail, and Abdul Kader Tayob. London: Routledge, 2011.

PART II

WOMEN IN ISLAM

LIVING AS MUSLIM WOMEN

WOMEN PRACTITIONERS OF ISLAM

Moyra Dale[1]

Introduction

In considering women as practitioners of Islam, there are two factors that affect our reading of their place in history and current practice.

1. When a religion has been defined primarily by male scholars and through male exemplars, the shape of women's place will inevitably be contested. One of the ways in which place and honour are traditionally challenged has been through verbal jousting matches in the Middle East and beyond.[2] Linda Boxberger cites such an exchange in medieval Yemen:

A female religious scholar of fifteenth-century Hadramawt, Yemen, al-Shaykha Sultana bint 'Ali al-Zubaydy was well-known for her piety, knowledge, and teachings. One of her male counterparts, expressing the conventional opinion that religious scholarship and teaching were the domain of men, challenged her in verse: "But can a female camel compete with a male camel?" She completed the couplet, responding: "A female camel can carry the same load as a male, and

---

[1] Moyra Dale (Ph.D, D.Th) spent over two decades in the Middle East including work in education and ethnographic research. She now writes and teaches on Islam and Cultural Anthropology.

[2] S. A. Sowayan, "'Tonight My Gun Is Loaded': Poetic Duelling in Arabia," *Oral Tradition* 4, no. 1-2 (1989): 23. For a discussion of the context of these exchanges in the gospels, see also B. J. Malina, *The New Testament World: Insights from Cultural Anthropology*, 3rd ed. (Louisville: Westminster John Knox Press, 2001), 33-36; Fedwa Malti-Douglas, *Woman's Body, Woman's Word: Gender and Discourse in Arabo-Islamic Writing* (Princeton: Princeton University Press, 1991), chapter 2 gives further examples of male-female exchanges.

produce offspring and milk as well.[3]

2. How women practice Islam will be influenced by their place and responsibilities in wider society. So their practices of Islam must be considered within their whole life context. People don't perform religious practices in isolation: piety finds its place within the daily routines, responsibilities and opportunities of all of life and living. Generally, in communities around the world, men fit in family around their commitments in study, work and religious duties. Women are more likely to fit in study, work and pious practices around the needs of their families.

What does it mean to be a woman practitioner of Islam? This article examines different places of women's religious practice. We begin with asking about their role as scholars, writers and activists in the history of Islam and now. Then we look at the official pious practices required of all Muslims, and what enables or restricts women's participation in them. In particular we explore the ways in which women pray. The article concludes by noticing what practices may be evoked by women's responsibilities in family and society.

Scholars

Virginia Woolf's reflection on what might have happened if Shakespeare had a gifted sister invites us to look at the traditional expectations, roles and possibilities for women. If a young man shows aptitude or learning he is more likely to have the opportunity to go to school or learn under a scholar. A young woman needs to be prepared for her domestic and family duties. Considerations of cost commonly deter the option of schooling; or, more importantly, the risk that travel beyond the household realm would bring to a woman's reputation and thus her family's good name.

Given the restricted options that women have faced, it is all the more remarkable that so many are recognized in Muslim history among the significant transmitters of *hadith*. Some had an advantage: proximity to Muhammad, founder of the faith. Hence there is an

---

[3] Boxberger 1998, 'From Two States to One: Women's Lives in the Transformation of Yemen'. In *Women in Muslim* Societies: *Diversity Within Unity*. Boulder & London: Lynne Rienner Publishers, 1998. 119–33

extensive body of *hadith* that are ascribed to Aisha, his favourite wife. Alwani ascribes one thousand two hundred and ten hadith narrations of Muhammad to Aisha, of which "one hundred and seventy four found their way into Al-Bukhari's and al-Muslim's collections of *hadith*."[4] Among Muhammad's other wives, Umm Salamah is often cited as a transmitter of *hadith*.[5] Hafsa's role as keeper of the transcribed Qur'an suggests that she was probably literate: Aslan suggests that Hafsa could read and write, and Umm Salamah and Aisha could read but not write.[6] The advantage of proximity was not limited to spouses: some of the women among Muhammad's companions were also described as narrators of *hadith*, including Naseebah and Umm Sulaym.[7]

The participation of women religious scholars didn't stop at the time of Muhammad. Early examples include Al-Khansa' and 'Umara bint Abdel-Rahman in the first century of Islam, together with 'Aishah 'Abd-al-Hadi and Nafissah (great-granddaughter of Muhammad); and Rabia'a al-Adawiyya towards the end of that century.[8] Umm al-Darda' was a famous female *muhaddithah* and jurist in Syria in the early years, whose students included 'Abd al-Malik ibn Marwan, the sixth Ummayad Caliph. Women were part of a revival in *hadith* scholarship in Syria in the seventh century A.D., learning and teaching *hadith* in some of the main mosques in Damascus, in gardens and private houses.[9] Nadwi in his book on women scholars notes examples also of women involved in *fiqh*,

---

[4] Zainab Alwani, "Muslim Women as Religious Scholars: A Historical Survey," in *Muslima Theology* (New York: Peter Lang, 2013), 57.

[5] Lara Deeb, "Religious Practices: Preaching and Women Preachers: Arab States (Excepting North Africa and the Gulf)," in *Encyclopedia of Women and Islamic Cultures* (Leiden: Brill, 2007), 5:335; Mohammad Akram Nadwi, *Al-Muhaddithat: The Women Scholars of Islam* (Oxford: Interface Publications, 2007), 248; Ruth Roded, ed., *Women in Islam and the Middle East: A Reader*, 2nd ed. (New York: I. B. Tauris, 2008), 49.

[6] Joseph T. Zeidan, *Arab Women Novelists: The Formative Years and Beyond* (Albany, NY: State University of New York Press, 1995), 12; Ednan Aslan, "Early Community Politics and the Marginalisation of Women in Islamic Intellectual History," in *Muslima Theology*, 39.

[7] Muhammad 'Ali Qutb, *Women Around the Messenger* (Riyadh: International Islamic Publishing House, 2007), 189, 212.

[8] Aziza Abdel-Halim, *Did You Know? Refuting Rigid Interpretations Concerning the Position of Women in Islam and Muslims' Interactions with Non-Muslims* (Sydney: Muslim Women's National Network of Australia, 2008), 19.

[9] Nadwi, *Al-Muhaddithat*, 266-267.

including *tafsir* and giving *fatwas*, insisting "women scholars acquired and exercised the same authority as men scholars."[10]

Nadwi and other contemporary writers are able to draw on detailed historical records of women within Islam. Al-Khatib al-Baghdadi (392-463A.H./C10th A.D.) in his *Ta'rikh Baghdad* included 29 women in his list of 7831 scholars over a 300-year period. Mernissi lists the names of no less than ten religious histories written from the ninth to the fourteenth centuries which mention prominent women in Islam.[11] Lindsay also refers to Ibn Asakir's description of how women in the 12th century were able to study, earn *ijazahs* and qualify as scholars and teachers (particularly in families of scholars), and notes that Ibn Asakir himself had studied under eighty different female teachers.[12] Roded comments on al-Sakhawi (d. 902/1497) following al-Asqalani in devoting the final section of his biographical dictionary to female scholars, including over one thousand, among whom "38% of these women studied, received licenses (*ijazahs*) to transmit their learning and/or taught others."[13] Alwani mentions significant women legal jurists from the 9th to 13th centuries, together with the names of Fatima Ibrahim Mahmud Ibn Jawhar (d.c 1300) and Zaynab bint al-Shar 'ri (d.1218) who taught hadith to notable hadith scholars.[14] Leila Ahmed also records a number of other women scholars from the fifteenth to eighteenth centuries A.D.[15]

Given the restrictions faced by women, how did this impressive list of women find opportunities to learn, let alone to contribute to the religious rulings and teaching of their times? Female religious scholars were often relatives of male clerics from the *'ulama* (scholar) class, who had been taught by their father or perhaps their brother: a few in wealthier families had access to private tutors.[16]

---

[10] Ibid., xviii, chapter 10; also Roded, *Women in Islam and the Middle East*, 96.

[11] Fatima Mernissi, *Women's Rebellion and Islamic Memory* (London: Zed Books, 1996), 82-100.

[12] James E. Lindsay, *Daily Life in the Medieval Islamic World* (Wesport, CT: Greenwood Press, 2005), 196-198.

[13] Roded, *Women in Islam and the Middle East*, 132.

[14] Alwani, "Muslim Women as Religious Scholars," 52, 54.

[15] Leila Ahmed, *Women and Gender in Islam* (New Haven, CT: Yale University Press, 1992), 113-114.

[16] Ibid.; Nadwi, *Al-Muhaddithat*, xii; E. W. Lane, *Manners and Customs in the Modern Egyptians*, 3rd ed. (London: Everyman's Library, 1966), 64; Debbie J. Gerner, "Roles in Transition: The Evolving Position of Women in Arab-Islamic Countries," in *Muslim*

Records show that in the 18th-19th centuries a few girls, mostly of middle class families, attended the small local Qur'anic schools (*kuttab*) present throughout the Muslim world.[17] Given that female literacy was generally low, and even privileged women with private tutors describe being discouraged in their desire to learn more of the Qur'an because they were women, the strong numerical presence of these Muslim women scholars is even more remarkable.[18]

Towards the end of the 1800s and early 1900s, Muslim women were becoming more actively involved in nationalist and social movements.[19] This movement coincided with the growth of women's press, where women were actively writing and publishing, some under their own name, some under pseudonyms.[20] Significant publications included *Sultana's Dream*, a feminist utopian story written in English by Rokeya Sahkawat Hossain (1880-1932), which was published in 1905 in Bengal: and *Unveiling and Veiling: Lectures and Views on the Liberation of the Women and Social renewal in the Arab*

Women (Beckenham, UK: CroomHelm Ltd., 1984), 77; Beth Baron, "The Rise of a New Literary Culture: The Women's Press of Egypt, 1882-1919" (PhD diss., University of California, 1988); Mervat Hatem, "A'isha Taymur's Tears and the Critique of the Modernist and Feminist Discourses on Nineteenth Century Egypt," in *Remaking Women: Feminism and Modernity in the Middle East* (Cairo: The American University in Cairo Press, 1998), 74.

[17] Ivor Wilks, "The Transmission of Islamic Learning in the Western Sudan," in *Literacy in Traditional Societies* (Cambridge: Cambridge University Press, 1968), 165; D. F. Eickelman, "The Art of Memory: Islamic Education and Its Social Reproduction," *Comparative Studies in Society and History* 20, no. 4 (1978): 493; Daniel A. Wagner, *Literacy, Culture and Development: Becoming Literate in Morocco* (New York: Cambridge University Press, 1993), 44.

[18] Shaarawi, H., 1998. Harem Years: The Memoirs of an Egyptian Feminist (1879-1924). (Cairo, The American University in Cairo Press, 1998), 40; Mernissi, *Women's Rebellion and Islamic Memory*, 102-103.

[19] https://whenwomenspeak.net/blog/feminism-muslimahs-and-christians-where-do-they-meet/

[20] Beth Baron, *The Women's Awakening in Egypt: Culture, Society, and the Press* (New Haven, CT: Yale University Press, 1994. Women's use of pseudonyms when writing is not restricted to the Muslim world. Virginia Woolf asks how many of the poets who signed their work only 'Anon' were women. Examples of famous women writers who chose to publish under other (male or ambiguous) names include the three Bronte sisters, George Eliot (Mary Ann Evans), Louisa Alcott, Harper (Nelle Harper) Lee, and J.K. Rowling. In 2015, Catherine Nichols sent out a novel manuscript under her own name, and then under a male pseudonym (George), with 50 queries under each name. She reported receiving two requests under her own name while 'George' received seventeen requests, concluding wryly that "He is eight and a half times better than me at writing the same book." https://jezebel.com/homme-de-plume-what-i-learned-sending-my-novel-out-und-1720637627

World (*Al-Sufur wal hijab*) published in 1928 by Nazir Zayn al-Din (1908-1976), a young Druze woman in Lebanon, who used the Qur'an to support her arguments. In Egypt Aisha Abd al-Rahman (1913-1988), professor of Arabic literature at the Women's College at a Cairo university, wrote a Qur'anic exegesis under the name 'Bint al-Shati.'[21] More recently the two last decades in particular have seen a plethora of books and articles written by women on the Qur'an and *Hadith*, beginning with Amina Wadud's *Qur'an and Women: Rereading the Sacred Text from a Woman's Perspective.*[22]

Gatherings and Movements among Muslim Women

Muslim women scholars and activists are part of Islamic history, and their presence is growing today. This coincides with a significant increase in women memorizing the Qur'an: around the Muslim world women and girls can be encountered clustering around the entrances to mosques, whether major suburban centres or in the small back streets of towns, to attend classes in the Qur'an.

Religious gatherings for Muslim women are not a new phenomenon. They can be seen in many different expressions around the world, including Sufi gatherings in homes as well as religious centres, vowing rituals at shrines and tombs, women's mosques among the Hui people in central China, women's *pesantren* in Indonesia, Shi'ite women's mourning ceremonies, Ismaili ritual meal trays, regional pilgrimages in India, and Bori cult rituals in central Africa.[23]

---

[21] Maria Jaschok and Jingjun Shui, *The History of Women's Mosques in Chinese Islam* (Richmond, UK: Curzon Press, 2000); Marcia Hermansen, "Introduction: The New Voices of Muslim Women Theologians," in *Muslima Theology*, 15; Alwani, "Muslim Women as Religious Scholars," 51.

[22] Amina Wadud, *Qur'an and Woman: Rereading the Sacred Text from a Woman's Perspective* (Oxford: Oxfod University Press, 1999). Some other examples include Nimat Hafez Barzangi, *Women's Identity and the Qur'an: A New Reading* (Gainesville: University Press of Florida, 2004); Aysha A. Hidayatullah, *Feminist Edges of the Qur'an* (New York: Oxford University Press, 2014); Georgina L. Jardim, *Rediscovering the Female Voice in Islamic Scripture: Women and Silence* (London: Routledge, 2014); Asma Lamrabet, *Women in the Qur'an: An Emancipatory Reading*, trans. Myriam Francois-Cerrah (Kube Publishing, 2016); and *Women and Men in the Qur'an*, trans. Muneera Salem-Murdock (New York: Palgrave Macmillan, 2018).

[23] Doumato, E.A., *Getting God's Ear: Women, Islam, and Healing in Saudi Arabia and the Gulf.* (New York: Columbia University Press, 2000), 112ff; Barbara M. Cooper, "Gender and Religion in Hausaland: Variations in Islamic Practice in Niger and Nigeria," in *Women in Muslim Societies: Diversity Within Unity* (London: Lynne Rienner Publishers, 1998), 21-37; van Doorn-Harder, P., *Women Shaping Islam. Reading the*

In the 1800s and early 1900s, early women's movements drew on more liberal foundations, as Huda Shaarawi's (1879-1947) Egyptian Feminist Union, and were linked with international women's movements. There has since been considerable growth in religiously based women's movements. In particular, the numbers of Muslim women involved in *da'wa* movements has been increasing across the Muslim world. Zaynab al-Ghazali (1917-2005), an early *da'iyya* in Egypt, is a prominent example. Initially involved with Huda Shaarawi in the Egyptian Feminist Union, she left the Feminist Union when she was eighteen to found the Muslim Women's Association.[24] The Association published a magazine and offered lessons for women and help to orphans and poor families. Hasan al-Banna, founder of the Muslim Brotherhood, proposed a merger of her association with the Brotherhood. Zaynab declined, but herself worked closely with al-Banna and the Brotherhood, including spending six years in prison under Nasser. While Zaynab argued for women's primary place in domestic space and obligations to husband and family, she also encouraged women to play an active role in public life, providing this did not interfere with their central familial duties. She divorced her first husband, claiming that the marriage held her back from her involvement in *da'wa*.[25] Zaynab wrote extensively and also taught large groups of up to thousands of women.[26]

This growth in Muslim women's pious activism has attracted attention in a number of recent studies, both written and film. Saba

---

Qur'an in Indonesia, (Urbana and Chicago, University of Illinois Press, 2006). Mary Elaine Hegland, "Shi'a Women's Rituals in Northwest Pakistan: The Shortcomings and Significance of Resistance," *Anthropological Quarterly* 76, no. 3 (2003); Rehana Ghadially, "A Hajari (Meal Tray) for Abbas Alam Dar: Women's Household Ritual in a South Asian Muslim Sect," *The Muslim World* 92, no. 2 (2003).

[24] Rokeya Sakhawat Hossain, mentioned above, also founded the Muslim Women's Association in 1916 in Bengal, which sought to promote women's education and employment.

[25] Commentators are divided on whether this contradicted her own teaching on the place of women – Ahmed, *Women and Gender in Islam*, 197-202; Larnia Rustum Shehadeh, *The Idea of Women in Fundamentalist Islam* (Gainesville: University Press of Florida, 2003), 121-140; Saba Mahmood, *Politics of Piety: The Islamic Revival and the Feminist Subject* (Princeton: Princeton University Press, 2005), 67-72; Margot Badran, *Feminism in Islam: Secular and Religious Convergences* (Oxford: One World, 2009).

[26] Baron, "The Rise of a New Literary Culture," and *Woman's Identity and the Qur'an*; Miriam Adeney, *Daughters of Islam: Building Bridges with Muslim Women* (Leicester, UK: Inter Varsity Press, 2002), 41; Shehadeh, *The Idea of Women in Fundamentalist Islam*, 124; Roded, *Women in Islam and the Middle East*, 258-259.

Mahmood's influential study explores the individualization of moral responsibility in the women in the mosque movement in Egypt, with the formation of the pious self through ritual performative behaviour. Other writers consider the relationship between religious and secular/social activities in women's piety movements; investigate women Qur'anic reciters in SE Asia; or discuss particular groups such as the elusive Qubaysiyyat movement in Syria which had already spread internationally before the disruption and population moves in Syria. There is more attention being given to these pious movements among Muslim women in the diaspora, both in the Arab world and also increasingly Europe and North America.[27] Marcia Hermansen comments that:

> When contemporary Muslim women engage in scriptural interpretation and theology they are breaking new ground in a number of areas, not only as females, but also as interpreters of the religious tradition in the context of significant contemporary challenges.

> The emergence of female teachers and preachers… has opened up new spaces for issues of women's rights, religious practice, and dignity to be discussed and challenged.[28]

Social activism and textual interpretation accompany one another, as in the notable work of Sisters in Islam in Malaysia,[29] and also the example of Aziza al-Hibri, who founded 'Karamah: Muslim Women Lawyers for Human Rights' in 1993, and has also published a first

---

[27] Bridget Maher, *Veiled Voices*, DVD, Documentary (Typecast Releasing, 2010); Julia Meltzer and Laura Nix, *The Light in Her Eyes*, DVD, Documentary (Clockshop and Felt Films, 2012); Saba Mahmood, "Feminist Theory, Embodiment, and the Docile Agent," *Cultural Anthropology* 16, no. 2 (2001): 202-237; and "Rehearsed Spontaneity and the Conventionality of Ritual," *American Ethnologist* 28, no. 4 (2001): 827-853; and *Politics of Piety*; Hafez, S., An Islam of Her Own. Reconsidering Religion and Secularism in Women's Islamic Movements. (New York: University Press, New York & London, 2011); Anne Rasmussen, *Women, the Recited Qur'an, and Islamic Music in Indonesia* (Berkeley, CA: University of California Press, 2010); Wanda Krause, *Women in Civil Society: The State, Islamism, and Networks in the UAE* (New York: Palgrave Macmillan, 2008); Masooda Bano and Hilary Kalmbach, eds., *Women, Leadership, and Mosques: Changes in Contemporary Islamic Authority*, vol. 11 (Leiden: Brill, 2012); Rachel Rinaldo, "Women and Piety Movements," in *The New Blackwell Companion to the Sociology of Religion*, Blackwell Companions to Sociology (Chichester, UK: Wiley-Blackwell, 2010).
[28] Hermansen, "Introduction," 13, 23.
[29] https://www.sistersinislam.org.my/

volume of *Islamic Worldview: Islamic Jurisprudence, An American Muslim Perspective,* and is working on the second volume.

These movements have a variety of responses to both Islamic religion and patriarchy. Women living within conservative Muslim societies generally need to exhibit a more conservative position in public voice, behaviour and dress if they are to retain place and influence within their social context. Susan Sered suggests four positions that are taken on women and religion:

> i). 'Patriarchal and proud of it.' Patriarchy is divinely mandated.
> ii). Religious founders were first feminists, but their egalitarian messages were suppressed – we need to recover the original message of gender justice.
> iii). Religion is not female-friendly, we need activism to bring theological and institutional change.
> iv). Religion is irreparably patriarchal and oppressive.[30]

The restrictions around the extent to which some of these views can be openly publicly espoused within many conservative Muslim countries gives a significant place to the growing contribution in research and writing from Muslim women in places like Europe and North America.

Pious practices

The practice of *salah* (mandated liturgical prayer) five times daily, fasting in the month of Ramadan and making the pilgrimage to Mecca if possible, are part of the fundamental pillars of Islam required of all believing Muslims – obligations as part of their daily, yearly and life-time cycles.

Ramadan

For the Muslim community, Ramadan is a time for enjoying the evening break-fast meals with family members or friends, after fasting from food and drink during the daylight hours. The beginning and the end of Ramadan are times when people make a particular effort to be with their relatives. *Eid al-Fitr,* which concludes the fast, and *Eid al-Adhha* (the Feast of the Sacrifice), are times when families gather for a meal together, and visit the members of the extended kin,

---

[30] Cited by Hermansen, "Introduction," 22-23.

usually starting with the eldest. For women, Ramadan is also marked by extra effort in hospitality, involving long hours in cooking for the extended break fasts each night, and also house cleaning, especially before a feast day.

The month of Ramadan for the devout is when they 'bank' up religious observance for the rest of the year. Ramadan is synonymous with reading the Qur'an right through, and so women can be seen reciting the Qur'an in the mosque or in their homes, to complete it during the month. People pray more, and even women who don't go to the mosque much or at all in the rest of the year will attend the evening *tarawih* (recommended evening prayers during Ramadan) after the '*isha*' (evening) prayer. Similarly the pre-dawn (*suhur*) prayers typically attract large crowds of women and men to spend a few hours from about 2am in *salah*, listening to the Qur'an and to supplication led by the sheikh of the mosque; then they return home for the last light meal of the night after which the daily fast from food and water recommences. It is a time of intense emotional and physical engagement with the words of *salah*, supplication and scripture. The *tarawih* prayers culminate in the Night of Vigil (*laylat al-qadar*) when they continue through the night to the early hours before sunrise. As the night wears on, rounds of *raka'at* (cycles of standing, kneeling, prostrating) continue, interspersed with recitations from the Qur'an and teaching from the sheikh. Intercessions are offered, emotions are high, people are weary, space is tightly crowded, and participants gather strength from the congregated community to complete the arduous duties of *tarawih*, finishing in the darkness of the mid-morning hours, an hour or so before sunrise. Ramadan is the most focused time of pious practice for many women, a time for experiencing community solidarity with other women, for being in the mosque, as well as in family homes for breaking fast.

Salah prayer

How do Muslim women engage in prayer? The times of *salah* intersperse the daylight hours, stretching and contracting with the seasons, marking the passage of day with the muezzin call in Muslim countries. Rhythms of creation rather than intervals of the clock define times of *salah*. A *shaykah* described them to me:

> Dawn prayer (*al-fajr*) - begins when the sun begins to rise, about an hour and a half before the sun is risen, when the time of dawn prayer

finishes.

Midday prayer (*al-dhuhr*) – takes place at midday.

Mid-afternoon prayer (*al-'asr*) – is about two and a half hours after midday prayers, when a shadow is about twice the length of the object, and it lasts until sunset.

Sunset prayer (*al-maghrib*) – extends from the going down of the sun, and lasts as long as there is still a red glow or red line in the sky.

Evening prayer (*al-'asha'*) – is when the sun has completely gone.[31]

The devout also practice *qiyam al-layl* (*tahajjud*) – optional prayer in the early hours of the morning.

Within the five prayer times there are gradations of duty and devotion, involving more *raka'* (the set rounds of standing, kneeling and prostration, and the words that go with them). There is the prescribed *fard* prayer, which entails a penalty if it is missed. Then there are the additional recommended *sunna* prayers, which bring more merits. I would see women attending a mosque-teaching programme who would often pray these *sunna* prayers when there was no time pressure on them to finish the *salah* quickly, particularly in the evening and there is the optional *nafilah* prayer, which carries no set reward or penalty beyond that of devotion. Saqib notes that, "Prophet Muhammad (pbuh) encouraged the believers to pray *Nafl* to help make up for any minor omissions or other defects in the obligatory prayer."[32] Whether performed at the mosque, or more commonly for women, in their homes, *salah* remains a corporate act, joining with the wider community in set patterns of prayer, at set times, facing the same direction. Gendered patterns are reproduced at home: if men join the women there in prayer, the women pray behind. Women performing *salah* are required to wear *hijab* and ensure they are covered from the neck to the wrists and ankles – dress that corresponds generally to covering required in front of male non-family members.

Purity and Piety

However, for women, their practice is constrained by the requirements of purity and of family responsibilities and duties. Khattab comments that:

---

[31] Moyra Dale, *Shifting Allegiances: Networks of Kinship and Faith*, ACT Monograph Series (Eugene, OR: Wipf and Stock, 2016), 46.

[32] Muhammad Abdul Karim Saqib, *A Guide to Salat* (Riyadh: Darussalam, 1997), 18-20.

In Islam, religious duties are to be performed by men and women alike... Having said that, there are some differences in the ways in which men and women are to go about performing these acts of worship, which sisters need to be aware of. [33]

The differences include when women and men are in a state of ritual purity and thus allowed to complete religious duties.

Islam describes two categories of impurity (*najasah*). Minor impurity (*hadath*) proscribes the believer from *salah*, circumambulating the Ka'aba, and touching the Qur'an. It is incurred by defecation, urination, secretion from the penis, flatulence, bleeding, sleeping, touching the genitals, laughing, eating camel flesh, and some other debated categories; and the believer becomes ritually pure by performing ablutions, washing head, forearms and feet (*wudu'*). Major impurity (*janabah*) prohibits the believer from fasting, and many authorities hold that it also proscribes entering a mosque and reciting the Qur'an. This is incurred through menstruation, ejaculation, sexual intercourse, childbirth and post-birth bleeding. Purification of *janabah* requires complete washing of the body (*ghusl*).[34]

Gauvain, discussing the egalitarian nature of Sunni Islamic purity, notes that, "According to Sunni Islam, no human being is deemed purer than any other, and none—*with the arguable exception of women*—is isolated or disadvantaged in any way through purity strategies."[35] A glance at the list of major impurities above shows that women are far more implicated than men: we may estimate that for at the very least during a quarter of their lives between about thirteen

---

[33] Huda Khattab, *The Muslim Woman's Handbook*, 2nd ed. (London: Ta-Ha Publishers, 1994), 1.

[34] Yaya Emeric, *What Islam is All About* (Kuala Lumpur: A. S. Noordeen, 2002); Richard Gauvain, "Ritual Rewards: A Consideration of Three Recent Approaches to Sunni Purity Law," *Islamic Law and Society* 12, no. 3 (2005): 333-393; Ze'ev Maghen, "Close Encounters: Some Preliminary Observations on the Transmission of Impurity in Early Sunni Jurisprudence," *Islamic Law and Society* 6, no. 3 (1999): 348-392; Etin Anwar, "Bodily Waste," in *Encyclopedia of Women and Islamic Cultures*, ed. Suad Joseph (Leiden: Brill, 2006), 3:29. Coming into contact with physical impurities (bodily emissions of humans and animals, wine, dead bodies, dogs and pigs all come under the category of *najasah*) causes impurity, and should be kept away from Muslims, clothes, and places of prayer – see Gauvain, "Ritual Rewards," 342.

[35] Gauvain, "Ritual Rewards," 350.

and sixty years of age (menarche to menopause) women are in a state of ritual pollution. If they are involved in sexual relations with their husband and care for young children, they may be impure for the majority of their daily/nightly lives, and thus unable to participate in the pious duties required of all believers.[36] Jaschok and Shui observe that:

> Women... are faced with an in-built contradiction: in order to be a good Muslim, they must be good wives and mothers. The Muslim's duty of increasing her religious knowledge to attain perfect faith, to attend to the daily duties of purification and praying, are in daily life at odds with her inability to reconcile time-consuming domestic duties with the time-consuming task of learning, ablution and prayer.[37]

Buitelaar comments that although "this only means that women are more often impure but certainly not inherently more impure than men, in practice women tend to be more strongly associated with impurity than men."[38]

The subject of ritual purity, with its impact on so much of their daily lives, is a frequent part of women's discussions in religious and also domestic gatherings, included amid recipes and household concerns. Women have to decide when they are in a state of impurity or not, according to the conditions and length of their *hayd* (menstruation), and other considerations, and thus required to perform the requirements of *salah* and fasting, or to makeup the prayers and pious observances that they have missed.[39] One acquaintance recounted how she had taken a pill to avoid menstruating during Ramadan: however it had such a severe impact

---

[36] Al-Faisal links ascribed deficiency with fertility: "Women's deficiency lies in the fact that she becomes pregnant, gives birth and menstruates. This clearly means that motherhood is the cause of her deficiency!... these writers have forgotten to tell us whether we should deduce from all this that the barren woman is more complete than the one that is fertile, and whether women who do not menstruate are more complete than the other women." Toujan al-Faisal, "They Insult Us... and We Elect Them!" in *Faith and Freedom: Women's Human Rights in the Muslim World* (London: Tauris, 1995), 232-233.

[37] Jaschok and Shui, *The History of Women's Mosques in Chinese Islam*, 8.

[38] Marjo Buitelaar, "Space: Hammam – Overview," in *Encyclopedia of Women and Islamic Cultures* (Leiden: Brull, 2007), 4:542; also Roded, *Women in Islam in the Middle East*, 98-101.

[39] Anwar, "Bodily Waste," 27; Abu Ameenah Bilal Philips, *Islamic Rules on Menstruation and Post-Natal Bleeding* (Kuala Lumpur: A. S. Noordeen, 1995).

on her body that she didn't take it again, and returned to missing the fast during her menstrual period, and needing to make up the missed days on her own at another time of the year, the normal practice for Muslim women.

Ahadith collections include detailed sections on issues of impurity, as do collections of *fatwa*; similarly *fiqh* classes incorporate multiple sessions in scrupulous description of what constitutes states of impurity and purity, particularly with regard to degree and colour of menstrual flow and other bodily emissions. Intricate details among the different schools of Islam, determined by medieval male scholars, determine women's practice of daily piety.

Other responsibilities also shape women's involvement in prayer. While men can often interrupt their work to pray, women are required to fit prayer and other pious practices around care for family, domestic duties and domestic space. Saqib assures us that, "wherever a Muslim might be he can offer his *salah* (prayer)." Cragg confirms his words: "everyone's prayer mat is a portable mosque and wherever they choose to spread it they can find their Qiblah and worship God."[40] But Saqib and Cragg write only of men. Women cannot turn public places into prayer sites as men can. I have met women in sheltered places, even in old and ruined mosques, putting their handbag in front as a *sutra* (barrier) and prostrating on the bare and dusty stone floor; but they do not pray in public spaces with the same freedom as men. Requirements of modesty constrain their freedom to turn outside space into spaces of worship – their primary place of *salah*, as well as of their duties, is the home. Even where there are women's spaces in mosques for them to join the community prayer (which entails increased merits) and to learn, those spaces are often occupied by men for the Friday community prayer (Friday prayer in the mosque has a reduced number of *raka'at* which must be performed). The home, as women's place of prayer, entails less merits and more rigorous requirements.

Beyond *salah*

Muslim women's performance of pious duties, including fasting, reciting the Qur'an, and carrying out the required *salah* prayer is constrained by requirements of purity, modesty and domestic

---

[40] Saqib, *A Guide to Salat*, 17; Kenneth Cragg, *The Call of the Minaret*, 2nd ed. (London: Collins, 1985), 99.

duties. However, they are also involved in other forms of prayer that offer them more access.

Dhikr

Many Muslim women in different parts of the world participate in *dhikr* prayer. *Dhikr* is associated with Sufism, and women have been part of Sufi practice in Islam from the time of Rabia of Bosra (717-801), one of the earliest and best-known examples. Silvers suggests that historically women made up nearly a quarter of participants of those on the Sufi path.[41] Helminski describes how:

> There have often been Mevlevi shaykhas (female of shayk) who have guided both women and men. Mevlana (Rumi) himself had many female disciples, and women were also encouraged to participate in sema, the musical whirling ceremony of the Mevlevis (women usually had their own semas, but sometimes performed semas together with men).[42]

Women continue to be involved in Sufi orders today, in Muslim countries and among Muslim women in the western world also. Orders such as the Naqshabandi, Chishti, Bektashi and Mehlevi are among those with numerous adherents across the world, including women leaders as well as participants. North African Sufi groups where women are involved include the Tijanni, Qadiri, Rahmani, Isawi and Nasiri. Women make pilgrimage to the tombs of saints (both female and male saints) seeking blessing or healing and perform *dhikr*s there or in their own homes. Meeting in homes, older women in Muslim regions of the Central Asian Caucuses continue to carry out *dhikr* practices which were proscribed in official male mosque space during the communist era.

The practice of *dhikr* is not restricted only to Sufis. Those who practise *dhikr* point back to Muhammad meditating in a cave, and to Qu'ranic verses; the most quoted verse is *Al-Baqarah* 2:152, "So remember Me, I will remember you" (*fa-adhkuruni 'adhkurkum*).[43]

---

[41] L. Silvers, "Representations: Sufi Women, Early Period, Seventh-Tenth Centuries," in *Encyclopedia of Islam* (Leiden: Brill, 2007), 5:541.

[42] Camille Adams Helminski, *Women of Sufism: A Hidden Treasure* (Boston: Shambhala Publications, 2003), xxiv.

[43] Some verses refer to the coming of Gabriel (*An-Najm* 53:1-18; *At -Takwir* 81:19-25) and Muhammad's night journey (*Al-Kahf* 17:1). Other verses suggest a mystical consciousness of God (*Al-Baqarah* 2:115, 186; *Al-Taubah* 9:123; *Al-'Ankabut* 29:20; *Qaf* 50:16), and especially the famous verse of light (*Al-Nur* 24:35). The word *dhikr*

The use of *wird* (litany) in morning and evening devotional practice is deeply embedded across the Muslim world in Orthodox Islam, including among those with no connection to Sufi orders.[44] Describing *dhikr* in a mosque programme in Aleppo, Shannon comments that "Many participants... understand *dhikr* to be an orthodox Sunni practice, and not something associated primarily with Sufism."[45] Conservative reform streams of Islam such as the *Tablighi Jamaat* draw on disciplines including *dhikr* as a required means of pious formation for their members. The *Tablighi Jamaat* now exists in between 150 and 200 countries, with anything between 12 million and 150 million adherents, both men and women.[46]

Dhikr can be silent but is more commonly verbal. I have seen this include extended songs (*tarnim*) by the woman leading the *dhikr*, sometimes with women joining in the chorus; and also lively chants (*anashid*) accompanied by a drum with more repetition, where a small chorus leads the extended group of women, on days of special remembrance or feasts. While women's voices may be considered *awrah* (shameful) and forbidden in some contexts, in *dhikr* women's talent in singing can be taken up and honoured.

Conditions of purity and covering that are required for Muslim women to perform *salah* are desirable, but not mandated for doing *dhikr* prayer. Thus for Muslim women, more constrained by the restrictions of purity requirements from activities like *salah* and fasting, *dhikr* offers a way to access God and his power for daily life. For some women in mosque programmes, *dhikr* is an essential part of preparation before lectures, allowing them to put aside the preoccupations of home, family, work, in order to focus and take in the teaching. Others say that regular practice of *dhikr*, including asking God for forgiveness, makes people more aware of themselves and their actions, less likely to sin.

---

appears often in the Qur'an (such as *Al-Ma'idah* 5:91; *Al-Jum'ah* 62:9; *Al-A'la* 87:15, and more particularly *Al-Baqarah* 2:200; *Al-'imran* 3:41; *Al-A'araf* 7:205; *Al-Muzzammil* 72:17).

[44] *Al-Ma'thurat* is a *wird* written by Hassan al-Banna, founder of the Muslim Brotherhood.

[45] Constance E. Padwick, *Muslim Devotions: A Study of Prayer-Manuals in Common Use* (Oxford: One World, 1996), xii; Jonathan H. Shannon, "The Aesthetics of Spiritual Practice and the Creation of Moral and Musical Subjectivities in Aleppo, Syria," *Ethnology* 43, no. 4 (2004): 381.

[46] Begun by Muhammad Ilyas al-Kandhlawi in 1927 in India, the Tablighi Jamaat is one of the biggest reform/missionary movements worldwide.

Dhikr is also associated with emotional expression. The preferred leader of group prayer is often the one whose leading and voice is most likely to elicit emotion and tears among those in the group. When I attended the early morning Ramadan prayer in a Middle Eastern mosque, at 2-3am the mosque was tightly packed with 500-700 women in the upper section and many more men below, crying '*Amin*' with rising emotional intensity after each prayer from the *sheikh*. Spontaneous tears are expected as a normal part of prayer, and this is facilitated by the communal experience of worship.

While much is written about *salah* prayer, we need to pay more attention to the place of *dhikr* in the lives of Muslim women. *Dhikr* offers them a rich and also emotionally engaged form of prayer in which they can participate. I suggest that *dhikr* reminds us of the longing of Muslim women to know the God who is with us, not just closer than our jugular vein (Qur'an *Qaf* 50:16), but who is always accessible, who can offer refuge and safety in the precariousness of daily life, whatever our condition or state of purity or impurity.

Du'a

Du'a is universal across the Muslim world, a deep stream of popular piety: but there is surprisingly little on it in writings about Islam. Incorporated into the formal *salah*, but not as bounded by rules of purity and language, *du'a* finds its way also into every part of life. It includes invocations for rewards in the next life, but is perhaps even more important for seeking power and protection for the needs of this life. Hence it has a vital place in the lives and practices of Muslim women, who must find a way to access divine power to fulfill their responsibilities for family harmony and welfare, amid the restrictions of bodily purity that are so weighted against women. Written, recited or spontaneously uttered, *du'a* voices the piety and deep desires of people across the Muslim world.

Du'a is not so often for specific needs but rather related to particular situations. God is not called so much to intervene in daily life as to protect the worshipper through it. There are invocations or *du'a* for every situation, from the mundane to the poignant – walking out of one's home or into a mosque, in or out of the bathroom, putting on new clothes or undressing, when it thunders, or the new moon is sighted, when afraid, when travelling, when you hear a dog bark, before and after eating, at a child's funeral, when you see the first dates of a season. And while the words of *du'a'* can be the informal expression of the worshipper's heart, often they are phrases which are also used in *dhikr*, said with intent. The relatively small amount written in books and articles on Islam about *du'a'* belies the multitude of the cards and small booklets containing prayers of appeal that can be found everywhere in markets, bookshops, mosques and at shrines throughout the Muslim world.[47] Popular prayer books in non-Arabic language will usually include the Arabic form, both written in Arabic script and often also transliterated, for the non-Arabic speakers' use. The set phrases frequently have particular efficacy or protection associated with them:

> Whoever recites this three times in the evening, will be protected from insect stings,

> Whoever recites this with conviction in the evening and dies during that night, shall enter Paradise; and whoever recites it with conviction in the morning and dies during that day, shall enter Paradise.

> Allah will spare whoever says this four times in the morning or in the evening from the fire of Hell.

> Whoever recites this one hundred times a day will have the reward of freeing ten slaves. One hundred Hasanah will be written for him and one hundred misdeeds will be washed away. He will be shielded from Satan until the evening. No one will be able to present anything better than this except for someone who has recited more than this.[48]

A widespread *du'a* is the 'taking refuge' in God (*a'udh birabb/billah*) from danger. This finds Qur'anic authority in *Al-Nahl* Q16:98, "and when you recite the Qur'an seek refuge with God from Satan the accursed." (Also *Al-Falaq* Q113:1 and *Al-Nas* Q114:1, the last two frequently-quoted chapters of the Qur'an.) It occurs frequently in the books of recommended *du'a*. Padwick describes it as the 'cry of frightened humanity'... 'in a demon-haunted world, in a world... where the evil eye is to be feared as well as the attacks of less uncanny human enemies'. [49] 'Taking refuge' is a part of formal *salah* as well as the exclamation of the ordinary person in the street who has a fright. Some of the perils from which the worshipper seeks

---

[47] Padwick's 1961 authoritative study, *Muslim Devotions*, is a notable exception.
[48] Sa'id bin Ali bin Wahf al-Qahtani, *Private Devotions for Morning and Evening from the Qur'an and the Sunnah* (Riyadh: Darussalam, 1996), 50, 52, 53, 59.
[49] Padwick, *Muslim Devotions*, 97.

refuge in God include: 'the evil of the whisperer who withdraws,' 'the evil of today and the days after it, laziness and old age, the punishment of hellfire and the grave,' and similarly, 'the grave and its torture,' 'the evil of my soul and the evil of the devil and his helpers,' and 'the evil of the created world'. Other times to take refuge are at the conclusion of *salah* (as well as its beginning), going into the mosque, in the evening, before going to sleep.[50]

Du'a can take place anywhere, on any occasion, and anyone can do it. Muslim women often ask me to petition for them, or say, "Supplicate for me, and I supplicate for you." However, while *du'a* can happen anywhere, some conditions are believed to make it more effective, more likely to elicit a favourable divine response. These conditions include where the *du'a* is prayed. I have seen women as well as men gathering at shrines from Syria to Sumatra, murmuring prayers from the booklets that are usually in a small pile for the visitor seeking extra efficacy or *baraka* (blessing) from the holy person buried there. The Night of Power near the end of the month of Ramadan is well known as a night when petitions are answered. Mornings (daybreak) and evenings are often quoted as times to recite prayers, often a set number of repetitions (three times in the evening, or ten or a hundred times in the morning and in the evening; or thirty-three times and thirty-four for the culminating invocation). Particular days or months may have their associated invocations and attendant rewards.

While *du'a* can be in any language, use of Arabic is believed to enhance its potency, which is why booklets and cards will often include the Arabic with its translation and sometimes transliteration for non-Arabic-speaking Muslims.[51] Actions may also contribute. Petitioning after drinking water from the spring of Zamzam at Mecca is said to carry extra efficacy. One prayer is to be 'read three times when you lie down, placing your right hand under your right cheek'.[52] *Du'a* is most often said with hands spread out, palms up, or cupped, to receive blessing; and the hands are often wiped over the worshipper's face at the end, as a physical application of blessing. The prayer for rain (*salah al-istisqa* – usually part of public prayer) may

---

[50] Al-Qahtani, *Private Devotions*; Shaykh Khaalid al-Husaynaan, *More than 1,000 Sunan (Sayings and Acts of the Prophet) Every Day and Night*, 2nd ed. (Riyadh: Darussalam, 2006).
[51] About 20% of Muslims speak Arabic as their mother tongue.
[52] Al-Husaynaan, *More than 1,000 Sunan*, 134.

be performed with raised hands and the outer garments of the petitioners turned inside out, following the example of Muhammad, Prophet of Islam.

Du'a can go also beyond formal phrases, repetitions, and conditions of purity and pious practice, to express the inner hopes of the petitioner, whether in Arabic, in another language, or the most inarticulate expressions of heart longing.

Women's responsibilities

While Muslim women are involved in formal study and official pious practices, their role as practitioners of Islam has to be seen in the context of their family responsibilities. An Egyptian woman described to me her responsibilities to bring up her children and marry them off well as her *risalah*, her vocation. This is the same word that is used for the prophetic vocation ascribed to Muhammad himself. Muslim women's practice of Islam does not just lean towards growing in personal merit, or even social reform, but is about enabling them to carry out their responsibilities to maintain health and harmony among family members, ensure children's success in schooling, and appropriate marriages. This is the urgent daily/nightly context for women of what it means to practice Islam. And for many of them, they must work out how to fulfill their responsibilities in situations where education, medical resources and even government can be unreliable or precarious; or in the face of natural or human disasters such as famine, floods, riots and war. When access to official pious practices are limited by requirements of modesty and purity, or by cultural or religious gender constraints, how are they to find access to the power and resources needed to fulfill their vocation, their role and functions in the immediate and extended family?

The concerns around pious practices and family affairs can be best seen in the questions that are asked in talk-back shows of broadcasting *shaykhs* and *shaykahs*, or those that are handed up on anonymous pieces of paper to the *da'iyya* at the end of a mosque lecture. As well as the enquiries around the difficulty of precise definitions concerning purity and pious duties, or about what to say in *salah* and what it means to read the Qur'an. Questions can include how to bring up children and answer their questions, deal with recalcitrant or irreligious husbands, when girls should start wearing *hijab*, how to relate to difficult in-laws, particularly when they were

104

opposed to the woman leaving her home and domestic duties to attend mosque classes. Other questions asked about subjects such as taking contraceptive pills, having sexual relationships with your spouse while still breast-feeding, having *jinn* help with housework, giving bribes, and magic. Women's practice of Islam is deeply entwined with their family obligations and how they can fulfill them.

This is the context of a wider range of customs not always mentioned in books introducing Islam, but part of daily life for Muslim women as well as men throughout the world. Practices such as reciting the Qur'an right through for *barakah* (blessing); reciting particular Qur'anic verses or other invocations two or three, seven or a hundred times, at prescribed times in the day or year; writing the names of the prophets on paper, then submerging the paper in olive oil for anointing an afflicted part of the body or in water for drinking with medicinal intent, were well-used ways of accessing blessing, healing, protection or forgiveness, that women described to me. Other customs included drinking water from Zamzam, or use of amulets and other protective devices against sickness or envy/the evil eye. This was the intent also for the routine motion by women at the end of prayer, to wipe their faces with the palms of their hands, bringing the flow of *barakah* (blessing/power) from the recited words back on to themselves. These practices and other rituals may seem far removed from official delineations of Islam, from the theological schools of law and the debates studied in colleges. While there is not space to develop it here, these traditions must be recognized as an accepted part of Muslim practice which is deeply ingrained in everyday life for Muslims in every continent, and which gain their authority from the example of or connection with Muhammad himself, or the early authoritative companions.[53]

Finally, as part of their vocation Muslim women practice Islam in their role as purveyors of faith to the next generation. While official Islam defines children according to the religion of their father, it is at their mother's knee, in daily observance of her practice as well as listening to her precepts, that children are often deeply formed in their own faith allegiance and observance.[54] Handayani observed in an informal survey of children of mixed Christian and Muslim

---

[53] See Dale, *Shifting Allegiances*, 88-97 for further discussion.
[54] Sardar provides a typically evocative description of learning to read the Qur'an and understand it with his mother. Ziauddin Sardar, *Desperately Seeking Paradise: Journes of a Sceptical Muslim* (London: Granta Books, 2004), 40-44.

parentage that almost three times as many of the children followed the faith of their mother compared to those who took their father's faith.[55]

Conclusion

What does it mean (for a woman) to practice Islam? Muslim women participate in faith practices in a variety of ways. History shows us unexpectedly large numbers of Muslim women scholars and teachers that have been perhaps hidden from popular view. Observers may look to women's involvement in the obvious pillars of faith such as *salah* and fasting. While women face particular constraints in their participation in these required rites, we find them also involved in other forms of prayer and piety. Less obvious are the daily practices of life and faith which derive from women's responsibilities to care for immediate and extended family, and to pass on their faith to the next generation.

This article has explored how Muslim women seek to follow the teachings and requirements of their faith, and to find from God the power to fulfil their daily duties. A deeper appreciation of their desires and duties enables us to understand and love them more in the name of the Messiah who welcomed both women and men as his disciples.

Bibliography

Abdel-Halim, Aziza. *Did You Know? Refuting Rigid Interpretations Concerning the Position of Women in Islam and Muslims' Interactions with Non-Muslims*. Sydney: Muslim Women's National Network of Australia, 2008.

Adeney, Miriam. *Daughters of Islam: Building Bridges with Muslim Women*. Leicester, UK: InterVarsity Press, 2002.

"AEL - 40 - Issue 3 - Eight Important Things to Know about The Experiential Learning Cycle." Accessed February 27, 2019. https://www.acel.org.au/ACEL/ACELWEB/Publications/AEL/2018/3/Lead_Article_1.aspx.

Ahmed, Leila. *Women and Gender in Islam*. New Haven, CT: Yale University Press, 1992.

---

[55] Dwi Handayani, "Veiled: Muslim Women in Modern Mission Strategies, Response 1," in *When Women Speak...* (Oxford: Regnum Books, 2018), 20.

Al-Banna, Imam Shaheed Hasan. *Al-Ma'thurat*. Swansea, UK: Awakening Publications, 2001.

Al-Faisal, Toujan. "They Insult Us… and We Elect Them!!" In *Faith and Freedom: Women's Human Rights in the Muslim World*, 232–237. London: Tauris, 1995.

Al-Husaynaan, Shaykh Khaalid. *More than 1,000 Sunan (Sayings and Acts of the Prophet) Every Day & Night*. 2nd ed. Riyadh: Darussalam, 2006.

'Ali Qutb, Muhammad. *Women Around the Messenger*. Riyadh: International Islamic Publishing House, 2007.

Al-Qahtani, Sa'id bin Ali bin Wahf. *Private Devotions For Morning and Evening From the Qur'an and the Sunnah*. Riyadh: Darussalam, 1996.

Al-Qahtani, Sa'id bin Wahf. *Fortress of the Muslim: Invocations from the Qur'an and Sunnah*. 5th ed. Riyadh: Darussalam, 2006.

Alwani, Zainab. "Muslim Women as Religious Scholars: A Historical Survey." In *Muslima Theology*, 45–58. New York: Peter Lang, 2013.

Anwar, Etin. "Bodily Waste." In *Encyclopedia of Women & Islamic Cultures*, vol. 3., edited by Suad Joseph, 27-33. Leiden: Brill, 2007.

Aslan, Ednan. "Early Community Politics and the Marginalisation of Women in Islamic Intellectual History." In *Muslima Theology*, 35–44. New York: Peter Lang, 2013.

Aslan, Ednan, Marcia K. Hermansen, and Elif Medeni, eds. *Muslima Theology: The Voices of Muslim Women Theologians*. New York: Peter Lang, 2013.

Badran, Margot. *Feminism in Islam: Secular and Religious Convergences*. Oxford: One World, 2009.

Bano, Masooda, and Hilary Kalmbach, eds. *Women, Leadership, and Mosques. Changes in Contemporary Islamic Authority*. Vol. 11. World. Leiden: Brill, 2012.

Barazangi, Nimat Hafez. *Woman's Identity and the Qur'an: A New Reading*. Gainesville: University Press of Florida, 2004.

———. *Woman's Identity and the Qur'an: A New Reading*. Gainesville: University Press of Florida, 2004.

Baron, Beth. *The Women's Awakening in Egypt: Culture, Society, and the Press*. New Haven, CT: Yale University Press, 1994.

Baron, Beth. "The Rise of a New Literary Culture: The Women's Press of Egypt, 1882-1919." PhD, University of California, 1988.

Buitelaar, Marjo. "Space: Hammam – Overview." In *Encyclopedia of Women and Islamic Cultures*, 4:541-43. Leiden: Brill, 2007.

Cooper, Barbara M. "Gender and Religion in Hausaland: Variations in Islamic Practice in Niger and Nigeria." In *Women in Muslim Societies: Diversity Within Unity*, 21–37. London: Lynne Rienner Publishers, 1998.

Cragg, Kenneth. *The Call of the Minaret*. 2nd ed. London: Collins, 1985.

Dale, Moyra. *Shifting Allegiances: Networks of Kinship and of Faith, The Women's Program in a Syrian Mosque*. Australian College of Theology Monograph Series. Eugene, OR: Wipf and Stock, 2016.

Deeb, Lara. "Religious Practices: Preaching and Women Preachers. Arab States (Excepting North Africa and the Gulf." In *Encylopedia of Women and Islamic Cultures*, 5:335–36. Leiden: Brill, 2007.

Doorn-Harder, Pieternella van. *Women Shaping Islam: Reading the Qur'an in Indonesia*. Chicago: University of Illinois Press, 2006.

Doumato, E.A., *Getting God's Ear: Women, Islam, and Healing in Saudi Arabia and the Gulf*. New York: Columbia University Press, 2000.

Eickelman, D. F. "The Art of Memory: Islamic Education and Its Social Reproduction." *Comparative Studies in Society and History* 20, no. 4 (1978): 485-516.

Emerick, Yaya. *What Islam Is All About*. Kuala Lumpur: A. S. Noordeen, 2002.

Gauvain, Richard. "Ritual Rewards: A Consideration of Three Recent Approaches to Sunni Purity Law." *Islamic Law and Society* 12, no. 3 (2005): 333-393.

Gerner, Debbie J. "Roles in Transition: The Evolving Position of Women in Arab-Islamic Countries." In *Muslim Women*, 71-99. Beckenham, UK: Croom Helm Ltd., 1984.

Ghadially, Rehana. "A Hajari (Meal Tray) for Abbas Alam Dar: Women's Household Ritual in a South Asian Muslim Sect." *The Muslim World* 92, no. 2 (2003): 309-322.

Handayani, Dwi. "Veiled: Muslim Women in Modern Mission Strategies: Response 1." In *When Women Speak...*, 19–23. Oxford: Regnum Books, 2018.

Hatem, Mervat. "A'isha Taymur's Tears and the Critique of the Modernist and Feminist Discourses on Nineteenth Century Egypt." In *Remaking Women. Feminism and Modernity in the Middle East*, 73-87. Cairo: The American University in Cairo Press, 1998.

Hegland, Mary Elaine. "Shi'a Women's Rituals in Northwest Pakistan: The Shortcomings and Significance of Resistance." *Anthropological Quarterly* 76, no. 3 (2003).

Helminski, Camille Adams. *Women of Sufism: A Hidden Treasure, Writings and Stories of Mystic Poets, Scholars and Saints*. Boston: Shambhala Publications, 2003.

Hermansen, Marcia. "Introduction: The New Voices of Muslim Women Theologians." In *Muslima Theology*, 11-34. New York: Peter Lang, 2013.

Hidayatullah, Aysha A. *Feminist Edges of the Qur'an*. New York: Oxford University Press, 2014.

Islam, Sarah. "The Qubaysiyyat: The Growth of an International Muslim Women's Revivalist Movement from Syria (1960-2008)." In *Women, Leadership, and Mosques: Changes in Contemporary Islamic Authority*, 11:161-183. Leiden: Brill, 2012.

Jardim, Georgina L. *Recovering the Female Voice in Islamic Scripture: Women and Silence*. London: Routledge, 2014.

Jaschok, Maria, and Jingjun Shui. *The History of Women's Mosques in Chinese Islam*. Richmond, UK: Curzon Press, 2000.

Khattab, Huda. *The Muslim Woman's Handbook*. 2nd ed. London: Ta-Ha Publishers, 1994.

Klingorová, Kamila, and Tomáš Havlíček. "Religion and Gender Inequality: The Status of Women in the Societies of World Religions." *Moravian Geographical Reports* 2 (June 30, 2015) https://doi.org/10.1515/mgr-2015-0006.

Krause, Wanda. *Women in Civil Society: The State, Islamism, and Networks in the UAE*. New York: Palgrave Macmillan, 2008.

Lamrabet, Asma. *Women and Men in the Qur'ān*. Translated by Muneera Salem-Murdock. New York: Palgrave Macmillan, 2018.

———. *Women in the Qur'an: An Emancipatory Reading*. Translated by Myriam Francois-Cerrah. Place of publication not identified: Kube Publishing, 2016.

Lane, E. W. *Manners and Customs of the Modern Egyptians*. 3rd ed. London: Everyman's Library, 1860.

Lindsay, James E. *Daily Life in the Medieval Islamic World*. Wesport, CT: Greenwood Press, 2005.

Maghen, Ze'ev. "Close Encounters: Some Preliminary Observations on the Transmission of Impurity in Early Sunni Jurisprudence." *Islamic Law and Society* 6, no. 3 (1999): 348-392.

Maher, Bridget. *Veiled Voices*. DVD, Documentary. Typecast Releasing, 2010.

Mahmood, Saba. "Feminist Theory, Embodiment, and the Docile Agent: Some Reflections on the Egyptian Islamic Revival." *Cultural Anthropology* 16, no. 2 (2001): 202-237.

———. *Politics of Piety. The Islamic Revival and the Feminist Subject*. Princeton: Princeton University Press, 2005.

———. "Rehearsed Spontaneity and the Conventionality of Ritual: Disciplines of Salat." *American Ethnologist* 28, no. 4 (2001): 827-853.

Malina, Bruce J. *The New Testament World: Insights from Cultural Anthropology*. 3rd ed. Louisville: Westminster John Knox Press, 2001.

Malti-Douglas, Fedwa. *Woman's Body, Woman's Word. Gender and Discourse in Arabo-Islamic Writing*. Princeton: Princeton University Press, 1991.

Meltzer, Julia, and Laura Nix. *The Light In Her Eyes*. DVD, Documentary. Clockshop and Felt Films, 2012. www.TheLightInHerEyesMovie.com.

Mernissi, Fatima. *Women's Rebellion & Islamic Memory*. London: Zed Books, 1996.

Nadwi, Mohammad Akram. *Al-Muhaddithat: The Women Scholars in Islam*. Oxford: Interface Publications, 2007.

Padwick, Constance E. *Muslim Devotions: A Study of Prayer-Manuals in Common Use*. Oxford: One World, 1961.

Philips, Abu Ameenah Bilal. *Islamic Rules on Menstruation and Post-Natal Bleeding*. Kuala Lumpur: A. S. Noordeen, 1995.

Pormann, Peter E. "Female Patients and Practitioners in Medieval Islam." *The Lancet* 373, no. 9675 (May 9, 2009): 1598-1599. https://doi.org/10.1016/S0140-6736(09)60895-3.

Rasmussen, Anne. *Women, the Recited Qur'an, and Islamic Music in Indonesia.* Berkley, CA: University of California Press, 2010.

Rinaldo, Rachel. "Women and Piety Movements." In *The New Blackwell Companion to the Sociology of Religion,* 584–605. Blackwell Companions to Sociology. Chichester, UK: Wiley-Blackwell, 2010.

Roded, Ruth, ed. *Women in Islam and the Middle East: A Reader.* 2nd ed. New York: I. B. Tauris, 2008.

Saqib, Muhammad Abdul Karim. *A Guide to Salat (Prayer).* Riyadh: Darussalam, 1997.

Sardar, Ziauddin. *Desperately Seeking Paradise: Journeys of a Sceptical Muslim.* London: Granta Books, 2005.

Shannon, Jonathon H. "The Aesthetics of Spiritual Practice and the Creation of Moral and Musical Subjectivities in Aleppo, Syria." *Ethnology* 43, no. 4 (2004).

Shaarawi, H., *Harem Years: The Memoirs of an Egyptian Feminist (1879-1924).* Cairo: The American University in Cairo Press, 1998.

Shehadeh, Lamia Rustum. *The Idea of Women in Fundamentalist Islam.* Gainesville: University Press of Florida, 2003.

Silvers, Laury. "Representations: Sufi Women, Early Period, Seventh-Tenth Centuries." In *Encyclopaedia of Islam,* 5:541–43. Leiden: Brill, 2007.

Sowayan, Saad Abdullah. "'Tonight My Gun Is Loaded': Poetic Dueling in Arabia." *Oral Tradition* 4, no. 1-2 (1989): 23.

Wadud, Amina. *Qur'an and Woman: Rereading the Sacred Text from a Woman's Perspective.* Oxford: Oxford University Press, 1999.

Wagner, Daniel A. *Literacy, Culture and Development: Becoming Literate in Morocco.* New York: Cambridge University Press, 1993.

Wilks, Ivor. "The Transmission of Islamic Learning in the Western Sudan." In *Literacy in Traditional Societies,* 161-197. Cambridge: Cambridge University Press, 1968.

Zeidan, Joseph T. *Arab Women Novelists: The Formative Years and Beyond.* Albany, NY: State University of New York Press, 1995.

MAKING OF A MISSIONARY: THE DA'IYYA[1]

Moyra Dale[2]

Introduction

In restricted social environments, Muslim women have always used religious occasions in the home, such as Qur'anic recitations or *dhikr*[3] to gain blessing and enjoy the religiously-sanctioned opportunity to gather and talk together over a glass of tea or a meal. Now women's homes and special gatherings are increasingly being used as sites for *da'wa*, encouraging women to conform their lives and dress to prescribed Islamic norms. So a birthday party becomes a place to urge the claims of *hijab* on all the young women attending. At the same time, women are moving into more public (albeit restricted) space, such as using women's areas in mosques, or giving exhortatory sermons in the women's carriage on the train system.

This paper draws on research over a period of about eighteen months in a Middle Eastern city, when I attended the women's programme in a Sunni mosque in an upper middle-class area, and on interviews with the leader or *da'iyya* who had founded the programme, whom I will call Eman.

Da'wa

The word *da'iyya* comes from the root *du'a* meaning 'to call' or 'to invite'. In Islamic religious terms, *da'wa* is "the invitation, addressed to men *(sic)* by God and the prophets, to believe in the true religion, Islam." It determined the Muslim community's relationship

---

[1] This paper was delivered at a day conference held at the Australian Catholic University, Melbourne, on 4 August, 2010. It was first printed in the *CSIOF Bulletin,* no 3, 2010 and has been reprinted here with permission

[2] Moyra Dale (Ph.D, D.Th) spent over two decades in the Middle East including work in education and ethnographic research. She now writes and teaches on Islam and Cultural Anthropology.

[3] Meditation on God, usually through reciting his names or songs of praise.

to non-Muslims: "Those to whom the *da'wa* had not yet penetrated had to be invited to embrace Islam before fighting could take place."[4] The contemporary piety movement relates *da'wa* not only to non-Muslims, but also to the duty of every practising Muslim to urge fellow Muslims to correct Islamic practice. Emerick puts *da'wa* alongside enjoining/forbidding[5] and jihad as the three fundamental duties for Muslims.[6]

Mahmood connects the recent growth of Muslim women teachers with the development of the concept of *da'wa*:

> In many ways the figure of the *da'iya* exemplifies the ethos of the contemporary Islamic Revival, and people now often ascribe to this figure the same degree of authority previously reserved for religious scholars.[7]

Eman described the role of the *da'iyya* in even higher terms: "the *da'iyya* is the ambassador of God to people and the successor of the Messenger."[8]

Through the role of *da'iyya* women are now ascribed a role of authority and implicit leadership (*khalifat al-nabi*) that was generally reserved for men. How they take up that role is shaped by their personal context, and the competing forces of opportunity, or access to education and patronage, and opposition, whether gender-based or political.

Support
Women teachers in history

The history of Islam has included women who were leaders[9] and teachers at different times throughout its history. Aisha and

---

[4] M. Canard, "Da'wa," in *Encyclopaedia of Islam* (Leiden: Brill, 1965), 2:168-170.

[5] Al-Imran, 104, 110 specifically links *da'wa* and enjoining / forbidding: (and let there be from you people *inviting* to the good, enjoining what is right and forbidding what is wrong.), whereas al-Taubah, 71 addresses men and women equally, 'the believing men and believing women' to be engaged in enjoining and forbidding, along with prayer and alms-giving.

[6] He lists the seven beliefs, five faith practices and three duties: *da'wa* (calling others to Islam), *jihad* (striving in God's cause) and encouraging good while forbidding wrong. Yahiya Emerick, *What Islam is All About* (Kuala Lumpur: A.S. Noordeen, 1997), 50-51.

[7] Saba Mahmood, *Politics of Piety* (Princeton: Princeton University Press, 2005), 58.

[8] Lecture handout, Thursday Lecture, 2007.

[9] Fatima Mernissi, *The Forgotten Queens of Islam*, trans. Mary Jo Lakeland (Cambridge: Polity Press, 1993).

Fatima are among those commonly mentioned from the time of Muhammad, but there are also examples of women teachers as well as hadith transmitters through Islamic history. Such women had to have access to education. Usually from the *ulama*[10] class, these women were often taught by a male relative such as their father, and sometimes also had access to private tutors. Traditionally female religious scholars were often relatives of male clerics. Education, a male patron, and often class, were crucial qualifications.[11]

Increased education and resources

However, the recent growth in women *da'iyyas,* or missionaries, is enabled by two major factors. The first is the increase worldwide in women's literacy and education. More recently, religious material has become widely available in popular media such as books, tapes and DVD's, and satellite channels. This has given women more access to information and debate around theological issues and faith duties.

Alongside these developments has been the growth in conservative Islamic movements across the Muslim world. This is both enabled by and in turn contributes to the growth of religious material in popular media. These movements prioritize religious education, including for women. Some women preachers are self-educated, but increasingly religious institutions are offering training to women. Al-Azhar University in Cairo began training women preachers in 1999.[12]

---

[10] Religious scholars.

[11] Zaynab al-Ghazali (1917-2005), a famous Islamist activist in Egypt, had a father who was an Al-Azhar-educated independent religious teacher as well as cotton merchant. He encouraged al-Ghazali to become an Islamic leader citing the example of Nusaybah bint Ka'ab al-Maziniyah, a woman who fought alongside Muhammad in the Battle of Uhud. Al-Ghazali divorced her first husband because she claimed that he interfered with her 'struggle in the way of God' (*jihad fi sabil lillah*), and married her second husband with the condition that he would not stand in the way of her work of *da'wa.* Her ability to enforce such stipulations in her marriage, together with her inability to have children, freed her to take a leading role with the work of the Muslim Brotherhood in Egypt - this while teaching that Muslim women's energies should be focused on home and family. Mahmood, *Politics of Piety*, 180-184;
http://www.islamicthinkers.com/index/index.php?option=com_content&task=view&id=273&Itemid=26 and http://www.answers.com/topic/zaynab-al-ghazali

[12] Lara Deeb, "Arab States," Margaret Rausch, "Egypt" and "North Africa," Maimuna Huq, "South Asia," Souad T. Ali, "Sudan," Yucel Demirer, "Turkey," Sabine Kalinock, "Iran," in "Religious Practices: Preaching and Women Preachers," in *Encyclopaedia of*

Eman's own role as *da'iyya* is enabled by support from her family. Growing up, her father combined his business trips with doing *da'wa* in local mosques. At home he called his children together for daily prayer and teaching, and encouraged them to attend the mosque programmes, including over the long summer breaks. Eman's mother also gave her daughters freedom to spend long hours at the mosque, instead of the more traditional role of staying at home and helping with domestic work. Eman's socio-economic background and family links give her the freedom to be able to invest her time in the mosque programme. Now married to an engineer, she ably combines her role as wife and mother with a busy teaching schedule.

A Muslim woman's role as *da'iyya* is dependent on a home and social context that give her access to education; and it is also validated by prior fulfilment of her domestic responsibilities.

Opposition
Home duties and *da'wa*

Women find their piety defined primarily in domestic terms. So they may encounter family resistance to involvement in a programme of religious learning and teaching that takes them outside the home and domestic responsibilities. Opposition from family, especially from the husband or his female relatives, was sometimes discussed at the mosque programme. Provided women can show they are adequately carrying out home duties, they can claim moral high ground in giving attention to religious duties. Arguments from religious sources can sometimes give women more freedom to challenge traditional cultural gender restrictions.[13]

Cultural practices

The role of women in leadership is still controversial. In many Muslim women's gatherings around the world, the teaching is still given by a man. Particularly controversial is the practice of a woman leading women in prayer in a mosque when there is a man present. While this is supported by three of the four schools of Islamic law (Shafi'i, Hanafi and Hanbali), Mahmood describes the opposition

---

Women and Islamic Cultures, ed. Suad Joseph (Leiden: Brill, 2007), 5:335-354. Also an interview with Eman.

[13] Haleh Afshar, Rob Aitken, and Myfanwy Franks, "Feminisms, Islamophobia and Identities," *Political Studies* 53 (2003): 262-283.

faced by an Egyptian woman *da'iyya* who didn't interrupt her lesson to allow women to join the male imam at the call to prayer, but waited until the end, and then led the women herself in prayer.[14] Eman also follows this practice, but the imam in the mosque is supportive of her.

Kalmbach describes how a *da'iyya* in Damascus adopts conservative behavioural and teaching practices which give her the space to teach more radical interpretations of Islam.[15] So Eman generally follows very conventional norms of deportment. Her dress outside the home or in front of non-related men[16] is always conservative, with long dark overcoat and headscarf, showing only her face. She is careful to always defer to the male leadership of the mosque and ensure that the women's voices are not heard in the male-occupied main body of the mosque. By keeping her practice conservative she avoids censure, even while disputing the teaching of the four schools of law on men as imams in mixed gatherings through a tradition[17] which defends the right of women to lead a mixed group of men and women in prayer.

Women gain the right to challenge traditional social norms of religious leadership by showing their conformity to religious social practices of dress and general behaviour, and by supporting their challenge from within the authoritative religious texts and traditions.

Political pressures
Muslim groups have an ongoing dance of engagement and restriction with the governments of the Muslim countries in which they operate. Increasingly such governments are adopting an Islamic

---

[14] Mahmood, *Politics of Piety*, 87-88.

[15] Hilary Kalmbach, "Social and Religious Change in Damascus: One Case of Female Islamic Authority," *British Journal of Middle Eastern Studies* 35, no. 1 (2008): 37-57.

[16] This includes anyone not in immediate family relationship (that is, father, brothers, nephews, husband, sons).

[17] This Hadith is to be found in Musnad Ahmad ibn Hanbal, Sunan Abi Dawud and other Hadith sources. It presents the following narration:

"(Umm Waraqah) requested permission from the blessed Messenger (peace and blessings of Allah be upon him) that if someone could perform the Adhan in her home... Eventually, the noble Messenger (peace and blessings of Allah be upon him) appointed an old man as a Mua'dhdhin (caller to the Prayer) for her and also granted Umm Waraqah (ra) permission to lead her household in Prayer."

http://www.mihpirzada.com/articles/canwomanbecomeimam.html, accessed August 8, 2010. Some people argue that this only gives a woman permission to lead mixed prayer in her home, but not in the mosque.

stance, which requires validation from religious authorities within society. In restrictive political environments, however, opposition has tended to find expression within mosques and conservative Islamicist groups.

For a while women *da'iyyas* attracted less attention than male religious leaders, but as their number and influence grows, they are coming under increased attention and surveillance. In Egypt, women *da'iyyas* now have to have the state-issued preaching licence.[18] For a long time in Syria, the secretive women's Qubaysi movement met in houses, but with their rapid growth in numbers and influence (they are said to focus on women from wealthy or influential families), the government now has opened a number of mosques to them where their teaching can be more easily observed.

During the time I was attending the mosque, there were some months when the government ordered mosque gates to be shut for some of the time, and activities in the mosque restricted, as part of a clamp-down aimed at restricting opposition. When I recently went to visit Eman, she told me that foreign women were no longer allowed to attend the mosque programme, but only local women from near the mosque. Even the classes she had held in her home for foreign women were no longer allowed. She indicated that her home was watched and reported on, concluding that the government was nervous of international Islamic links.

Mahmood points out that the piety movement doesn't directly confront governments. However, its insistence on seeking to apply Islamic norms in every area of life challenges an implicit secular position that seeks to restrict Islam to matters of religious practice and family law[19], thereby refusing a separation into matters of *'ibaada* (worship) and *'amalaat* (works).

The perceived opposition of the west to Islam also shapes *da'wa*. The call, or *da'wa*, is to the Muslim community, so that by being renewed and true to their faith they will be able to resist western incursions. And *da'wa* is also to the west, inviting them to acknowledge Islam as the truth rather than opposing it.

---

[18] Mahmood, *Politics of Piety*, 84.
[19] Ibid., 46-47.

The Mission

The *da'wa* to women attending the mosque programme called them to:

- move beyond ritual to knowledge,
- fulfil their home responsibilities appropriately as Muslim women,
- be involved in *da'wa* themselves to their own society and beyond.

Beyond ritual to knowledge

The emphasis on knowledge was a constant theme. Eman exhorted the women to undergird devoted practice with understanding, telling them, 'An hour's thought is better than a year's worship.'

This teaching is not challenging the practice of the fundamental religious duties. Nor does Eman generally question the popular practice of accruing of merit or blessing through the multiple repetition of particular verses, or recitation of the whole Qur'an, in what could be seen as a semi-magical or mechanical use of text. When she teaches on "*aql* (mind) as being as or more important than *din* (religion) – Muslims throughout the community are very good at practising their religion, less good at using their mind,"[20] Eman is not placing knowledge in opposition to faith practice. Rather, in a religious framework, knowledge is presented as one of the religious duties, which may have priority over other duties. "If you need learning, take the time you spend in *dhikr* to learn."[21]

Similarly, the teaching in the mosque programme does not oppose religious teachers, nor does it encourage choice outside an Islamic framework. The women should be aware of the options for choice and how to exercise them: "People were free to agree with a given judgment or not, even as they were free to take from any of the four different schools of interpretation: and they could choose different schools for different times or subjects."[22]

Dīn and domestic duties

---

[20] Comment from a Muslim mosque teacher (Da'iyya), from my notes taken on Eid al Adha, 2006.

[21] Thursday lecture, Notes 55.

[22] Private lecture on Women and Islam, 2005.

Women were encouraged to attend the mosque programme. At religious feasts women would give testimonies about how the programme had helped them. Such times almost always had a discussion of family problems that made it difficult to attend, with vigorous discussion around the right of women to come to the mosque in the face of opposition from husband or mother-in-law. Eman was careful not to subvert the priority of domestic duties, which also counted as part of a woman's proper worship. "There are different kinds of worship. There is the service of the home and children, teaching the children, caring for their food and cleaning."[23] "Education and worship in the home is more important than attending the mosque," but in the same breath she reminded the women that, "mosques and religion are for men and for women."[24] So she also insisted that the husband had no right to forbid his wife to attend the mosque, and if he did so, she wasn't wrong to resist him. "For him to order her in her prayers and her worship, he doesn't have the right in this, there are boundaries he doesn't cross."[25]

While this is accepted within Islam, it is an important shift to locate a woman's prayers and worship in the mosque. Traditionally women have always prayed at home.[26] Eman's focus is on the lectures and acquiring knowledge as a necessary part of women's

---

[23] Tuesday lecture, notes 25.

[24] Thursday lecture, notes 13.

[25] Interview.

[26] "For the woman, it's not required of her that she pray the obligatory five prayers in the mosque. This is inconvenient for her because the woman in Islam has to dress and it's not possible in every place and time of prayer to dress completely and go out, then return and remove the clothes, and this is a problem for her, so Islam doesn't require the woman to go out to pray in the mosque." Interview.
For men at least, congregational prayer is always preferable to individual prayer: "The Blessed Prophet said, 'Prayer in a congregation is worth more than twenty-seven prayers said alone' (Emerick, *What Islam is All About*, 138). However, Khattab quotes the following Hadith to say: "The Islamic recommendation to offer prayers on congregation in the mosque applies to men only. The Prophet (SAAS) advised women to offer their prayers at home, in the most secluded corner of the house."
"Umm Humayd Sa'idiyyah (RA) said: O Prophet of Allah, I desire to offer prayers under your leadership'. The Holy Prophet (SAAS) said: 'I know that, but your offering the prayer in a corner [of your house] is better than your offering it in a closed room, and your offering it in a closed room is better than your offering it in the courtyard of your house; and your offering it in the courtyard of your house is better than your offering it in the neighbouring mosque, and your offering it in the neighbouring mosque is better than your offering it in the biggest mosque of the town' (Imam Ahmad and al-Tarbarani; similar Hadith in Abu Da'ud)." Huda Khattab, *The Muslim Woman's Handbook* (London: Ta-Ha Publishers, 1994), 2.

worship, rather than the *dhikr* and Qur'anic recitation which also take place at the mosque.

All called to do *da'wa*

Eman encouraged the women to take any opportunity to be involved in *da'wa*. A series of lectures and handouts told women the appropriate behaviour and words to use at times like weddings, births, and funerals. They could copy good teaching tapes and give them away, or leave pamphlets in public places for people to pick up. Those who travelled overseas for work or study, whether to the Gulf or the West, were given contacts of other graduates from the mosque, and encouraged to think about how they might contribute. Eman urged the women to respond if they saw negative comments on Islam on the internet, and to consider learning another language so that they could engage more effectively with the west. I knew other young people learning English with missionary intent in order to relate to westerners.

However, although everyone is encouraged to be involved in *da'wa*, not everyone can be a *da'iyya*. Eman offered special training for some: "We will teach girls for free, in English and computers, the outstanding girls to become well-informed *da'iyyas*, like the prophets, the best representation, circumspect, diplomatic, neat. No prophet has flaws. There are special characteristics for a missionary – not all people can be one."[27]

Conclusion

Contemporary *da'wa* movements offer women opportunity to move beyond domestic spheres to new physical and textual spaces. For these *da'iyyas,* the domestic is not left behind, but becomes part of an expanding sphere of involvement.

Smith discusses the shift from domestic to public sphere: "Of course, for centuries and still today, here and globally, women care for children, cook, do housework, and make other contributions to survival. It isn't that we weren't conscious or that we ceased to be subjects when we were at home doing the work of caring and cleaning. The extraordinary moment came when we saw that this was a place from which we could speak to and of the society at large,

[27] Thursday lecture: Notes 54.

moving into a terrain of public discourse that somewhere along the line had been appropriated by and ceded to men."[28]

Eman is involved in teaching local women and sometimes expatriates, as well as lecturing in the Gulf states. She draws on the traditional texts of Qur'an and Hadith, books of *tafsir* (commentaries), alongside CD recordings and satellite programmes. And the content of her teaching moves between the everyday and everynight responsibilities of women's worlds, and global discussions of the nature of Islam and the place of women within it.

References

Afshar, Haleh, Rob Aitken, and Myfanwy Franks. "Feminisms, Islamophobia and Identities." *Political Studies* 53 (2003).

Canard, M. "Da'wa." In *Encyclopaedia of Islam*. Vol. 2. Brill: Leiden: Brill, 1965.

Deeb, Lara. "Arab States." In "Religious Practices: Preaching and Women Preachers." In *Encyclopaedia of Women and Islamic Cultures*. Vol. 5. Edited by Suad Joseph, 335-336. Leiden: Brill, 2007.

Demirer, Yücel. "Turkey." In "Religious Practices: Preaching and Women Preachers." In *Encyclopaedia of Women and Islamic Cultures*. Vol. 5. Edited by Suad Joseph, 347-349. Leiden: Brill, 2007.

Emerick, Yahiya. *What Islam is All About*. Kuala Lumpur: A. S. Noordeen, 1997.

Huq, Maimuna. "South Asia." In "Religious Practices: Preaching and Women Preachers." In *Encyclopaedia of Women and Islamic Cultures*. Vol. 5. Edited by Suad Joseph, 343-346. Leiden: Brill, 2007.

Kalinock, Sabine. "Iran." In "Religious Practices: Preaching and Women Preachers." In *Encyclopaedia of Women and Islamic Cultures*. Vol. 5. Edited by Suad Joseph, 339-340. Leiden: Brill, 2007.

---

[28] Dorothy E. Smith, *The Conceptual Practices of Power: A Feminist Sociology of Knowledge* (Boston: Northeastern University Press, 1990), 199.

Kalmbach, Hilary. "Social and Religious Change in Damascus: One Case of Female Islamic Authority." *British Journal of Middle Eastern Studies* 35, no. 1 (2008).

Khattab, Huda. *The Muslim Woman's Handbook*. London: Ta-Ha Publishers, 1994.

Mahmood, Saba. *Politics of Piety*. Princeton: Princeton University Press, 2005.

Mernissi, Fatima. *The Forgotten Queens of Islam*. Translated by Mary Jo Lakeland. Cambridge: Polity Press, 1993.

Rausch, Margaret. "Egypt." In "Religious Practices: Preaching and Women Preachers." In *Encyclopaedia of Women and Islamic Cultures*. Vol. 5. Edited by Suad Joseph, 337-339. Leiden: Brill, 2007.

Souad, T. Ali. "Sudan." In "Religious Practices: Preaching and Women Preachers." In *Encyclopaedia of Women and Islamic Cultures*. Vol. 5. Edited by Suad Joseph, 346-347. Leiden: Brill, 2007.

Smith, Dorothy E. *The Conceptual Practices of Power: A Feminist Sociology of Knowledge*. Boston: Northeastern University Press, 1990.

http://www.islamicthinkers.com/index/index.php?option=com_content&task=view&id=273&Itemid=26

http://www.answers.com/topic/zaynab-al-ghazali

http://www.mihpirzada.com/articles/canwomanbecomeimam.html

RABI'A AL-'ADAWIYYA:

The Model of a Pious Woman

Ruth Nicholls[1]

Over the centuries, many women—be they Jewish, Hindu, Buddhist, Christian or Muslim—have chosen to adopt a life of asceticism. Choosing a strictly disciplined life has usually been in conjunction with a search for a meaning beyond themselves, and/or to experience the 'ultimate reality'. For those associated with the Abrahamic religions, that ultimate reality is usually referenced in the English language as *God/god*. When comparing the Abrahamic religious derivatives of Judaism, Christianity and Islam, the undergirding theology for that word in terms of its meaning, character and impact on thought and practice has resulted in significant differences between those religions giving rise to issues which are at times contradictory and conflicting. Moreover, how life is understood and practiced based on the understanding of 'that ultimate reality' results not only in diverse, contrasting and often conflicting worldviews but also in dissimilar social and cultural behaviours which also impact and are impacted by religious (theological) interpretations. Since the focus of this article is Islam, I will use the Arabic word for god, *Allah,* wherever possible to distinguish the Muslim understanding of god from that which undergirds either the Jewish and/or Christian concepts. Also, within the context of Islam, it is the Sufis who have primarily sought to express their faith through ascetic and mystical lifestyles.

While anecdotally, it may be claimed that women are more likely to be practitioners of religion, women's spirituality and the probability of its uniqueness, except possibly since the rise of

---

[1] Ruth Nicholls is an adjunct research fellow with the Arthur Jeffery Centre for the Study of Islam. Ruth spent many years in an Asian country with an Islamic majority. Her special interests are in Sufism and folk Islam.

125

feminism, appears to have been ignored both from a scholarly perspective as well as by academic levels of scholarship. Not surprisingly, the feminists will proclaim, for men have not only populated the halls of scholarship but have also considered themselves superior to women, so women's issues and their perspectives have basically been overlooked. Added to that, women's inherent sexuality has deemed them (by men) to be 'weaker', more emotionally inclined than rationally able while at the same time more 'sinful'. In effect, while women constitute some 50% of the population, they are essentially ignored and, to a large degree, 'invisible'.

Within the original early Islamic context, it is the Qur'an, Hadith and the *sunna* of the Prophet that impacted how women and their spirituality have not only been conceptualized, but also expressed both verbally and practically. The sayings and practice out of which the Qur'an, Hadith and *sunna* were developed initially emerged within the recognized historical period of the late 7th to early 8th centuries CE from within the distinct social and cultural context of the Arabian Peninsula.[2] Both the historical period, the social context and the Prophet's own worldview automatically undergird his visions and his understandings as well as his interpretations of his revelations from Allah and his subsequent pronouncements concerning women. Further, Allah's revelations primarily appear to be in response to the prevailing conditions of the time.[3] In Islamic terminology they are characterized as the times of ignorance requiring a return to the true Islam as expressed by obedience to Allah.

---

[2] While the traditional context is claimed to be Mecca and Medina, both of which are located in the Arabian Peninsula, Mark Durie cogently argues for a different context for the emergence of the Qur'an from those desert locations: the language of the Qur'an is not that of the Bedouins and the geographical references (earthquakes; agrarian lifestyle; and the location of ruins) all suggest a very different location. "Problems with the Qur'an Origin Story," in *Understanding and Answering Islam,* ed. Ruth Nicholls (Melbourne: Melbourne School of Theology Press, 2018), 45-63.

[3] Andy Bannister's work on the oral-formulaic character of the Qur'an (Andrew Bannister, *An Oral-Formulaic Study of the Qur'an* [Lanham: Lexington Books, 2014]) indirectly raises issues regarding the 'eternal nature' of the Qur'an as does placing the Qur'an within its historical and cultural context which it reflects. Equally, one must ask, "how does a book which is claimed to be 'eternal' refer to such specific time determined events/issues such as the Prophet's marriage to Zayd (Zeinab)?"

Central to the Prophet's message in relation to Islamic spiritual practice are two generic commands which are closely related: one demands obedience, the other service. With respect to obedience the command is to "obey God and the Apostle; that ye may obtain mercy" (Q3:132).[4] Such a command appears to apply equally to both men and women (cf. 4:124; 5:16, 97; 9:17, 72; 16.97; 33:36, 59, 73; 40:40; 57:12; 85:10), with Q24 including various directives for believing women. However, the Islamic view of creation appears contradictory. According to some Qur'anic verses, men and women share the same creation process as is recorded in Q4:1 (cf. also Q53:45, 46):

> O mankind! reverence your Guardian-Lord, who created you from a single person, created, of like nature, His mate, and from them twain scattered (like seeds) countless men and women...

While Q78:8 refers to Allah creating male and female:

> He did create in pairs, male and female, from a seed when lodged (in its place).

Likewise, Q22:5 reads,

> O mankind... (consider) that We created you out of dust, then out of sperm, then out of a leech-like clot, then out of a morsel of flesh, partly formed and partly unformed... whom We will to rest in the wombs for an appointed term, then do We bring you out as babes...

Assumedly *mankind* refers to both males and females, as does the word *babes*. So, if men and women share the same creation process shouldn't that mean that they would share the same spirituality? Certainly, in terms of observing the five pillars, they do share the same spirituality. However, according to Q23:12-14, the reference appears to focus on the creation of the male with the women being referred to as 'another creature'.

> Man we created from a quintessence (of clay); then we placed him (as a drop of sperm) in a place of rest, firmly fixed: then

---

[4] All English quotations of the Qur'an are taken from that of Yusaf Ali as is found on the *al Tafsir* website, https://www.altafsir.com. Some other references include 4:13, 59; 5:92; 8:1, 20, 24, 46; 11:123. Cited January 21, 2019.

we made the sperm into a clot of congealed blood; then of that clot we made (a foetus) a lump; then we made out of that lump bones and clothed the bones with flesh; and then we developed out of it another creature. So blessed be God, the best to create.

Is there here then the suggestion that men are created differently and therefore their spirituality will be different? According to one Muslim source on the procreation of the human race, the female is said to be "secondarily important".[5] So, one might well ask, then, is the spirituality of women also only of secondary importance? In terms of practical expression and attitudes, it appears to be the case.

Certainly, the Prophet's comments about women as reported in the Hadith not only question a woman's intelligence but also her spirituality.[6]

> Narrated Abu Said Al-Khudri and reported in Sahih Bukhari 1:6:301 (cf. also 2:24:541).
> Once Allah's Apostle went out to the Musalla (to offer the prayer) o 'Id-al-Adha or Al-Fitr prayer. Then he passed by the women and said, "O women! Give alms, as I have seen that the majority of the dwellers of Hell-fire were you (women)." They asked, "Why is it so, O Allah's Apostle?" He replied, "You curse frequently and are ungrateful to your husbands. **I have not seen anyone more deficient in intelligence and religion than you** (emphasis added). A cautious sensible man could be led astray by some of you." The women asked, "O Allah's Apostle! What is deficient in our intelligence and religion?" He said, "Is not the evidence of two women equal to the witness of one man?" They replied in the affirmative. He said, "This is the deficiency in her intelligence. Isn't it true that a woman can neither pray nor fast during her menses?" The women replied in the affirmative. He said, "This is the deficiency in her religion."[7]

---

[5] Cf. Hak Dini Kur'an Dili, 2:1274. As reported by Mehmet Paksu, https://questionsonislam.com/article/how-was-first-woman-created, cited January 21, 2019.

[6] Can it be argued that this verse only refers to giving 'witness' and to the fact that a women's impurity is a limiting factor for religious practise? However, the mention of 'cursing' and 'ingratitude', together with 'leading astray', suggests that the hadith applies more broadly which has been the case.

[7] https://islam.stackexchange.com/questions/41314/why-islam-claims-women-are-deficient-in-religion-and-intelligence-when-in-reali, cited January 21, 2019.

It should be noted that al-Khudri, the reporter of this hadith, was a member of the 'bench'—that is, one of Muhammad's close companions (*sahāba*)—and as a consequence, his recollections would be considered reliable. Further, it should be noted that there were others who have also added their testimony to such a comment.[8] In another Hadith the Prophet is reported as saying that the majority of the inhabitants in hell were women (Sahih al-Bukhari 3241; Sahih Muslim 2736, 2737), meaning that "among the inmates of Paradise women would form a minority" (Sahih Muslim 49).[9] However, it needs to be acknowledged that a considerable number of these hadith were recorded many years after the death of the Prophet. Not surprisingly then, as Power writes, "As Muslim scholars gathered the accounts of Muhammad's life and early Islamic history, they found that discerning real traditions from fictitious accounts was no straight forward task."[10] Yet, given the fact that these hadith appear to have an early origin because they are narrated by one of the Prophet's wives and by at least one who sat on his 'bench' or belonged to his 'companions', then it would appear that this understanding of women finds its origin at the very beginning of Islam.

Given the conflicting nature of the stance regarding women as found in the Qur'an, Hadith and *sunna,* how then might women respond? Some uncritically accept that which they have been told, living within the confines of those boundaries. At the other end of the continuum of response are those who find their own way of expressing their spirituality within the confides of their culture and the codes of their religion while at the same time questioning those boundaries and seeking to move beyond the perceived restrictions placed upon them. Rabi'a al 'Adawayya is one of the earliest (recorded) women outside of the Qur'anic circle of women whose spirituality moved beyond mere mechanical obedience to the sayings of the Prophet while seeking to serve *Allah* out of the conviction of her heart.

---

[8] Cf. Narrated by 'Imran bin Husain: al-Bukhari 3241, https://sunnah.com/bukhari/59/52; Sahih al-Bukhari 3241, https://www.sunnah.com/urn/30280; Usama b. Zaid (one of the Prophet's wives) reported in Sahih Muslim 2736, https://sunnah.com/muslim/49; Imran b. Husain reported in Sahih Muslim 2738a, https://sunnah.com/muslim/49.

[9] https://sunnah.com/bukhari/59/52 Sahih al-Bukhari 3241; https://sunnah.com/muslim/49; all cited January 21, 2019.

[10] Bernie Power, *Challenging Islamic Traditions: Searching Questions about the Hadith from a Christian* Perspective (Pasadena, CA: William Carey Library, 2016), 6.

Other than the wives of the Prophet and the women of the Prophet's days, Rabi'a al 'Adawayya al Kaysiyya (also known as Rabe'a bint Esma'il al-'Adawiya, or Rabi'a al Basri[11] – d. 185/801) is the first named (Sufi) woman who has gained a significant place within the world of Islam. This Rabi'a was a contemporary of the famed Al-Hasan ibn Abi'l Hasan al-Basri (d. 110/728). Not surprisingly both their tombs are located in Basra.[12] This Rabi'a is not to be confused with other pious women who have shared the same name.[13] So while Rabi'a al 'Adawayya has been the first to have gained a significant named reputation she is not the only woman to have been recognized for her spirituality. Islamic writers[14] from the early years of Islam refer to women who in their estimation have become spiritual exemplars: some are mentioned by name, others unnamed are referred to in passing.[15] As-Sulami (d. 412/1021)[16] recorded some 82 women in his book *Dhikr an-Niswas al-Muta 'abbidat as-Sufiyyat* in which Rabi'a's is not only the first entry but also one of the longer ones. Another writer ibn al-Jawzi (d. 597/1201) referred to some 16 women: some of whom he describes as 'elect among the female worshippers'.[17] However, given that these women have achieved a recognized and significant level of spirituality, this then poses a problem. These women are obviously not 'spiritually deficient', nor are they 'lacking in intelligence', which then suggests (to these males [writers]) that these women are unique. In trying to come to terms with this phenomenon, some of their male counterparts recognize them as 'honorary males'[18] – that is, within

---

[11] An alternative spelling for Basri is Basra.

[12] This Rabi'a al-Adawayya is not the Rabi'a al Adawiyya whose tomb is located on the Mount of Olives in Jerusalem. Steven Oiello, "Rabi'a 'l-'Adawiyya: Legend or woman?" https//papers.ssrn.com/sol13/papers.cmf?abstract-id+2852872, cited October 15, 2016. However, it would appear that at least in countries such as Malaysia that the account of Rabi'a Basri has been conflated with the accounts of others who bear the name Rabi'a.

[13] For example: As Sulami referred to a Rabi'a al Azdiyya whom 'Abd al-Wahid ibn Zayd asked to marry' (128) and Rabi'a bint Isma'il of Damascus (63). 'Abu 'abd ar Rahman as-Sulami, "Dhikr an-Niswa al-Muta'abbidat as-Suffiyyat," in *Early Sufi Women*, ed. and trans. Rkia Elaroui Cornell (Lahore: Suhail Academy, 2005).

[14] These include as-Sulami, Farid al-Din Attar.

[15] Cf. Dhu an-Nun is said to have encountered a pious (Sufi) woman on the coasts of Syria (cf. Cornell, *Early Sufi Women*, 15; Arberry, *Muslim Saints*, 11).

[16] As-Sulami, "Dhikr."

[17] Ibid., 264, 298, 310, 322, 326.

[18] Tarayn Ryan in an article "The Masculinization of Christian Holy Women" writes: "...men had difficulty imagining a woman who was simultaneously fully feminine and fully holy. Male authors used the *vitae* of saintly women to attempt to resolve the cognitive dissonance in imagining holy women, but in doing so they ascribed masculine characteristics to some women." *Journal of Theta Alpha Kappa* 37, no 2. (2013): 13-27.

the spiritual arena they are given 'male status'. According to Helminski, quoting Margaret Smith, who quoted Attar, Hasan al Basri is reported to have said,

> I passed one whole night and day with Rabi'a speaking of the Way and the Truth, and it never passed through my mind that I was a man nor did it occur to her that she was a woman, and at the end when I looked at her, I saw myself a bankrupt... and Rabi'a as truly sincere.[19]

Indeed, in order to justify Rabi'a's inclusion in his *Tadhkirat al-Auliya* Farid al-Din Attar wrote,

> If anyone says, "Why have you included Rabe'a in the rank of men?" My answer is, that the Prophet himself said, "God does not regard your outward forms." The root of the matter is not form, but intention, as the Prophet said, "Mankind will be raised up according to their intentions." Moreover, if it is proper to derive two-thirds of our religion from A'esha, surely it is permissible to take religious instruction from a hand maid of A'esha. When a woman becomes a "man" in the path of God, she is a man and one cannot anymore call her a woman.[20]

Here, Attar turns to the Prophet who it appears in terms of his statement does not distinguish between male and female, at least in terms of outward form! This then allows Attar to come to the conclusion that, because of Rabi'a's 'intentions', she has been 'raised up'. However, he fails to consider the possibility that a 'female' can be 'raised up' so proceeds to give Rabi'a 'male status'. Obviously for these men there was no alternate explanation. Even the intensity and the quality of these women's spirituality was not able to dislodge or transform their pre-existing worldview which was further confirmed by an unquestioning attitude to the Prophet's pronouncements that women were spiritually inferior. Even though Attar goes on to note that 'two-thirds of our religion derives from A'esha' and considers that this makes it possible for men to take instruction from a woman, his worldview remains unchallenged. This is also in spite of his own record of Rabi'a which goes on to demonstrate not only the quality of her spirituality but also how she gave instruction to those who visited her and did so ably. At least one of those who visited her was

---

[19] Camille Adams Helminiski, *Women of Sufism: A Hidden Treasure* (Boston: Shambala, 2003), 25.

[20] Farid al-Din Attar, *Muslim Saints and Mystics: Episodes from Tadhkirat al-Auliya (Memorial of the Saints)*, trans. A. J. Arberry (London: Routledge, 1966), 40.

her contemporary, the famous Sufi, Al-Hasan ibn Abi'l Hasan al-Basri. In fact, from Attar's account most of the men who came to visit her appear to have deliberately done so. Attar also recounts an occasion when a party of men visited Rabi'a basically with the purpose of trapping her. Her reply, however, shows the sharpness of her mind and her perceptiveness.

> "All the virtues have been scattered upon the heads of men," they said. "The crown of prophethood has been placed on men's heads. The belt of nobility has been fastened around men's waists. No woman has even been a prophet.
> "All that is true," Rabe'a replied. "But egoism and self-worship and 'I am your Lord, the Most High' have never sprung from a woman's breast. No woman has even been a hermaphrodite. All these things are the speciality of men."[21]

In Attar's *Memorial of the Saints*, Arberry notes that he focuses on "the words" of the Sufis as his overriding preoccupation: that is, he is concerned with their knowledge (gnosis) and its transmission.[22] On the other hand, Cornell comments that as-Sulmani has several aims in his work. One of those Cornell identified as a "hermeneutic of remembrance"[23] (cf. Q48:25). As-Sulmani then uses the Islamic form of historiography known as *tabaqat* which 'assess[es] the backgrounds of hadith transmitters and the bearers of tradition'[24] in considering the women he includes. That is, as-Sulmani was concerned that these women whose identity was verifiable should not be forgotten. His other focus of servitude (service to God – *abbidatas*) was 'so central to as-Sulmani's understanding of women's spirituality that he enshrines the concept in the title... *Dhikr an-niswa al-muta' abbidatas-sufiyyat.*'[25]

Interestingly, as far as is currently known, it would appear that Rabi'a al 'Adawayya is also the first (Muslim/Sufi) woman to have left a written record. While the origins of that record have been

---

[21] Arberry, *Muslim Saints*, 48. However, a translation of this same passage by Paul Smith in *Rabi'a al-Adawiyya: Life and Poems*, New Humanity Books, 14. www.newhumanitybooks.com) reads as follows, "What you say is true... but on the other hand , women have never been so infatuated with themselves as men, nor have they ever claimed Divinity."

[22] Arberry, *Muslim Saints*, 14.

[23] Cornell, *Early Sufi Women*, 48-49.

[24] Ibid., 49.

[25] Ibid., 54.

disputed, the early writers such as as-Sulami and Farid Attar have no hesitation in attributing various words (works) to her.[26]

One must then ask, what is it about this Rabi'a and other Sufi women that has meant that they have not only been recognized for their spirituality but also in many cases have become mentors and advisors (*sheikha/pirana*) to others: both women and men.[27] Indeed, some of those men are the very ones who are writing about these women. Like those women, these men were also desiring to follow the injunctions of the Prophet not merely as rote observance to a series of rules, but also out of an inner desire to please God and meaningfully follow his commands.

About 100 years after the death of Rabi'a, in an attempt to justify the Sufi position following al-Hallaj's execution because of his esoteric claim of "I am the truth" and the distinct possibility that Sufism would be outlawed,[28] al Kalabadhi (d. 385/995) "musters all his forces to prove that the true doctrine of the Sufis, so far from being heretical, is actually conformable with the strictest standards of orthodoxy."[29] Al Kalabadhi, after providing an introduction, then goes on to justify the Sufi position in some eighty aspects where Sufism might be considered to be at variance with formal orthodox theology. Some of the areas he included were: gnosis (knowledge) of Allah, miracles of the saints, revelation of thoughts, abstinence, patience and poverty. Although al Kalabadhi appears to follow the accepted premise that women were deficient in intelligence and religion, he refers in passing to the unnamed woman who encountered Dhu 'i-Nun as well as Rabi'a al 'Adawiyya. In so doing, he implies at least by implication that women too can, in certain circumstances, and do meet the criteria that he outlined.

Rabi'a al-'Adawiyya's Spirituality

What was it then about Rabi'a's spirituality that 'raised her up', to use the Attar phrase, and has given her an honoured place in

---

[26] For the purposes of this article, I am assuming that the works attributed to Rabi'a are her works.

[27] As-Sulmani notes that Sufyan ath-Thawri "sought her advice on legal matters and referred such issues to her. He also sought her spiritual advice and supplications." Cornell, *Early Sufi Women*, 74.

[28] Abu Bakr al-Kalabadhi, *The Doctrine of the Sufis*, trans A. J. Arberry (Cambridge: Cambridge University Press, 1979), xiv.

[29] Ibid., xiv-xv.

Islamic spiritual history? This is especially remarkable since little is actually known about Rabi'a though as-Sulmani endeavoured to verify his sources noting the persons from whom he gained his information. According to Arberry, Attar also used a number of sources, some of which are now no longer extant, when writing his account.

Even from the few details that are known of Rabi'a's life, she takes her place among the ascetics of Islam. While asceticism has a long history (Hinduism and Buddhism also have their ascetic practices), Christianity had also bred its own ascetics who were scattered throughout the Middle Eastern area during the years when Rabi'a was alive. Yet, Islamic asceticism and its almost seamless emergence into mysticism has its own history and distinctives. According to Arberry,[30] the initial ascetic movement was a reaction to the "worldly considerations," "decline in piety" and the "extravagance of the early years after the death of the Prophet."[31] Arberry, then, quotes from al-Hasan al-Basri, a contemporary of Rabi'a, himself an ascetic who advised poverty and abstinence,[32] but there was more to the ascetic life. It was a life of devotion (meditation and recollection of Allah), prayer and fasting, as well as a life of service, particularly service to Allah through rigorous obedience to his requirements as well as one's fellow humans:

> Serve God, and join not any partners with Him; and do good-to parents, kinsfolk, orphans, those in need, neighbours who are near, neighbours who are strangers, the companion by your side, the wayfarer (ye meet), and what your right hands possess: For God loveth not the arrogant, the vain glorious (Q4:36; cf. 10:3; 21:92; 29:56).

All the accounts of Rabi'a's spirituality comment on her poverty and the austerity of her lifestyle. Attar indicates that she had no lantern, no knife, but only a reed mat, a broken pitcher from which she drank and performed her ablutions. It is reported that Rabi'a and her servant girl often just ate bread. In Ibn al-Jawzi's account, Rabi'a was visited by a Muhammad ibn 'Amr who said:

---

[30] A. J. Arberry, *Sufism: An Account of the Mystics of Islam* (London: Unwin Paperbacks, 1950), 31-44.
[31] Ibid., 32.
[32] Ibid., 32-33.

134

I visited Rabiʻa when she was an old woman of eighty years of age. She looked like a shrunken, old water-skin, and appeared to be on the verge of collapsing. In her house I saw a worn, rectangular mat and a clothes rack made of Persian reeds ... . The door to the house was covered by a skin ... . There was also a jar, a mug and a piece of felt that served as her bed and her prayer rug.[33]

Yet when she was sick she refused a purse containing gold. Interestingly, it would also seem that Rabiʻa may have followed an example that her own father had adopted, for when Rabiʻa was born, although the family was in dire circumstances, her father refused to ask for assistance until he had a dream advising him as to what he should do. In fact, according to Attar, Rabiʻa had made a covenant with the Almighty Allah not to ask for anything but to depend on Allah alone.[34]

Was extravagance an issue for Rabiʻa that she felt that she needed to renounce it? Hardly. Rabiʻa's lot in life was hard. She was born in poverty; orphaned at an early life; then during a famine she was kidnapped and forced into cruel servitude. After her master heard her praying and apparently seeing a light above her head, he offered her freedom. From that point onward, not only did she adopted an austere lifestyle, first going to the desert and a hermitage, but she also came to believe that a life of poverty was her estate. Attar retells incident when Malik-e Dinar[35] visited Rabiʻa and offered to get help for her from his rich friends. Rabiʻa replied:

> "Malek, you have committed a grievous error... Is not my Provider and theirs one and the same?"
> "Yes," [Malek] replied.
> "And has the Provider of the poor forgotten the poor on account of their poverty? And does He remember the rich because of their riches?"...
> "No," [Malek] replied.

---

[33] Reported in Cornell, *Early Sufi Women*, 276.

[34] Attar, *Muslim Saints and Mystics*, 44

[35] Author's comment. In Arabic it is possible to play on words. Do we have such an instance here? Malek can be translated 'king' and 'dinar' coin. Was Malek himself wealthy but personally not prepared to help Rabiʻa? A thought to ponder! Attar in his *Muslim Saints* recounts a hagiography in which Malek miraculously is given two dinar when his life was in danger. (Attar, *Muslim Saints and Mystics*, 26.27)

"Then... since He knows my estate, how should I remind Him. Such is His Will, and I too wish as He wills."[36]

Rabi'a's comments here also reflect another aspect of the ascetic lifestyle: that of submission to the will of Allah. "Such is His Will, and I too wish as He wills," she said. Early on in her life when she was running from a stranger, she fell and broke her arm. Even on that occasion her prayer revealed that same submissive attitude.

> Lord God... I am a stranger, orphaned of mother and father, a helpless prisoner fallen into captivity, my hand broken. Yet for all this I do not grieve: all I need is Thy good pleasure, to know whether Thou are well-pleased or no.[37]

However, there was another dimension to Rabi'a's poverty as is reflected in this prayer that is also recorded in Attar's account.[38]

> O God, whatsoever Thou hast apportioned to me of worldly things, do Thou give that to Thy enemies; and whatsoever Thou has apportioned to me in this world to come, give that to Thy friends: for Thou sufficest me.

Rabi'a accepted poverty on the basis that Allah was all that she needed. However, her 'sufficiency' in Allah was much deeper and many faceted.

As an ascetic one would anticipate that Rabi'a led a life of prayer and fasting which is indeed reflected in the various accounts of her life. It is said that she would spend the night praying often standing while maintaining a fast. One account recalls that she fasted, prayed and stayed awake for seven days and nights.[39] Following one such occasion when she prayed all night, it is reported that she had a dream.

> After an all-night vigil, I prayed to God at dawn and slept. In my dream I saw a tree: green, bright, vast, of indescribable beauty: and on this tree were three kinds of fruit, such as I had never seen among all the fruits of this world. They shone like the breasts of maidens, red, white, and yellow; they

---

[36] Ibid., 50.
[37] Ibid., 41.
[38] Ibid., 51.
[39] Helminski, *Women of Sufism*, 29.

shone like globes and living suns in the green hollows of the tree. I marveled at them, and asked: Whose tree is this?

A voice replied, "This is your tree, sprung from the seed of your prayers." Then I began to walk around it, and as I did so I counted eighteen fruits the color of gold, lying on the ground beneath it.

I said, "It would have been better if these fruits hadn't fallen but were still on the Tree."

And a voice answered, "They would be there still except for the fact that while you were praying you kept worrying: 'Did I remember to add the yeast to the dough?' And so they fell, and there they lie."[40]

Of her own prayers she wrote:

O God, another Night is passing away,
Another Day is rising –
Tell me that I have spent the Night well so I can be at peace,
Or that I have wasted it, so I can mourn for what is lost.
I swear that ever since the first day You brought me back to life,
The day You became my friend,
I have not slept –
And even if You drive me from your door,
I swear again that we will never be separated.
Because You are alive in my heart.[41]

In addition, as is also reflected in this poem, Rabi'a's importance stems primarily from her own understanding of Allah and her relationship with Him: "You became my friend," "You are alive in my heart." It was this knowledge (revelation) which in turn impacted how she related to those who came to her for teaching, instruction and guidance. It was this role which resulted in her becoming a *sheikha/pirina* in her own right. It is primarily in this latter role that Attar's accounts frame her. One occasion two 'notables' visited her and were hungry. Rabi'a only had two loaves which she placed in front of them, at which they were satisfied. Just then a beggar came, so Rabi'a took the two loaves and gave them to the beggar, much to the quiet displeasure of the visitors. Not long after a maid arrived with 18 warm loaves of bread which Rabi'a refused. A little later the maid returned with 20 warm loaves which

[40] Ibid., 32.
[41] Ibid., 33.

she accepted. The men then questioned her about her actions. This was Rabi'a's reply:

> I knew when you arrived that you were hungry... I said to myself, How can I offer two loaves to two such notables? So when the beggar came to the door I gave them to him and said to Almighty God, 'O God, Thou has said that Thou repayest tenfold, and this I firmly believed. Now I have given two loaves to please Thee, so that Thou mayest give twenty in return for them.' When eighteen were brought me, I knew that either there had been some misappropriation, or that they were not meant for me.[42]

This is an interesting account from several angles. It reflects Rabi'a's understanding of Allah in that He is pleased with gifts to beggars (an act of service) so much so that those who please Him will receive a tenfold return (this also reflects a theology of reciprocity). The account also implies that Rabi'a had 'added knowledge' or even a revelation (the men were hungry) and that the arrival of the gift of the 20 loaves was a miracle. So, by implication, Attar is confirming that she not only reflects the qualities of a Sufi but that she has also achieved a significant level of spirituality. While this incident is not recorded by Al Kalabadhi it certainly reflects a number of aspects of Sufism to which he refers.

In several of Attar's accounts, Rabi'a's spirituality is shown to 'exceed' that of males, even that of her fellow Sufi, the famous Hasan. On one occasion Rabi'a was surrounded by animals who ran away as Hasan approached. Hasan indicated his surprise at which Rabi'a commented, "You eat their fat. Why then should they not flee from you?"[43] On another occasion she found Hasan weeping and chastised him, saying, "Master, this weeping is a sign of spiritual languor. Guard your tears." Not surprisingly, Hasan was offended by her comments. Later when they were near a lake, Hasan threw his prayer mat on the water and invited Rabi'a to pray. Rabi'a's response was, "...when you are showing off your spiritual goods in this worldly market, it should be things that your fellow-men are incapable of displaying." Rabi'a then threw her prayer mat into the air and it flew (another miracle!?). Attar comments Hasan had not attained that station and that he felt it. Rabi'a, in an attempt

---

[42] Attar, *Muslim Saints and Mystics*, 44.
[43] Ibid., 45.

to console him, said, "...what you did fishes also do, and what I did flies also do. The real business is outside both these tricks. One must apply one's self to the real business."[44]

As-Sulmani's account of Rabiʻa focuses much more on her understanding of Allah and her relationship with him which grew out of her experiences of him. For example, Rabiʻa is reported to have said:

> For everything there is a fruit (*thamara*), and the fruit of the knowledge of God (*ma'rifa*) is in orientating oneself toward God at all times (*iqbal*).[45]

It is also reported that someone asked her,

> "How is your love for the prophet (may God bless and preserve him)?" To which she replied, "Verily I love him. But love for the Creator has turned me away from love for created things."[46]

Smith[47] reports on a similar question:

> "O Rabi'a... do you love the Lord?"
> "Truly," she replied, "I love Him."
> "And do you regard Satan as an enemy?"
> "I love the Lord so much," she answered, "that I do not trouble myself about the enmity of Satan."

That is, Rabiʻa's understanding of Allah was such that He became the total focus of her life and her thinking which in her mind was expressed in terms of love which is reflected in this incident as is also recorded by as-Sulmani:

> "One day, Rabiʻa saw Rabah... kissing a young boy. "Do you love him?" she asked.
> "Yes," he said. To which Rabiʻa replied, "I did not imagine that there was room in your heart to love anything other than God, the Glorious and Mighty!" Rabah was overcome at this and fainted. When he awoke he said, "On the contrary, this is

---

[44] Ibid., 45.
[45] As-Sulmani, *Early Sufi Women*, 76.
[46] Ibid., 78.
[47] Smith, *Rabi'a al-Adawiyya*, 11.

a mercy that God Most High has put into the hearts of His slaves."[48]

Notice that this record reflects the Sufi intention of being focused on *Allah* to the point of being 'absorbed' in him, though here it is being 'absorbed by him'. Indeed, it was Rabi'a's prayer that she be "so absorbed in [Allah's] love that no other affection may find room in [her] heart."[49]

The above mentioned incident also supports as-Sulmani's contention that Rabi'a, "his slave," had achieved the level of sainthood through her service to *Allah*. On one occasion when she was asked, what was the best way for a slave to come to God, she wept. Here's her reply,

> How can the likes of me be asked such a thing? The best way for the slave to come close to God Most High is for him to know that he must not love anything in this world or the Hereafter other than Him.[50]

Rabi'a's desire was to worship God out of love, not out of fear of Hell or hope of Paradise.[51] Her unswerving commitment of love ("O my hope and my rest and my delight, the heart can love none other but Thee," which is said to reflect *Sura* 5:54, "He will love as they will love Him"[52]) has given her an elevated place in Islamic saintly history.

Reports of Rabi'a's spirituality also reflect another aspect of her spiritual perfection as understood by the Sufis. Al-Kalabadhi refers to it in his *Doctrines of the Sufis* as the state of "intoxication" which led to the use of a gamut of imagery, especially in Sufi poetry, relating to wine and drunkenness. As-Sulmani reported that someone found Rabi'a "staggering like one inebriated," a further example of the level of her Sufic spirituality.

"What causes you to stagger?" he asked.

---

[48] As-Sulami, "Dhikr," 78.
[49] Smith, *Rabi'a al-Adawiyya*, 14.
[50] As-Sulami, "Dhikr," 80.
[51] Attar, *Muslim Saints and Mystics*, 51.
[52] Annemarie Schimmel, *The Mystical Dimensions of Islam* (Chapel Hill: University of North Carolina Press, 2011), 39-40.

"Last night I became intoxicated with love for my Lord and woke up inebriated from it," she replied.[53]

Another of her poems also reflects this aspect of her devotion.

> My cup, my wine, and the Friend make three,
> And I, full of love and longing... I, make four.
> Cup of joy, and happiness that never ends, is
> Given by Winebringer to one, after one before.
> And, if I am looking, I look only for that One,
> If I am without that One I can't see anymore.
> Don't blame me... I love beauty of that One,
> And, by God... my ears cannot hear your furor.
> How often from desire and bitter attachment
> I have made many streams from my eyes to pour.
> My tears never stop and being with that One
> Is not lasting, and my sore eyes sleep no more.[54]

In Islamic understanding Allah is one, and this poem reflects that emphasis by its frequent use of the word "one". But the poem also refers to another aspect of spiritual devotion: that of weeping. Earlier it was mentioned that Rabi'a encountered Hasan weeping but rebuked him for it, yet Rabi'a herself would often be found weeping, for weeping was considered a sign of spiritual progression. "I have made many streams from my eyes to pour. My tears never stop,"[55] said Rabi'a. In fact, Helminski devotes a whole chapter to Sufi women noted for their weeping.[56] Such was Sufic devotion that the accusation of madness was often cast in their direction. Rabi'a too recognized this aspect which is recorded in one of her poems.

> The devotees and the ascetics of God,
> to please Him the flesh were starving;
> Throughout every night they kept vigil,
> Their swollen eyes they weren't closing.
> They were so confused, by loving God,
> The people them as made were thinking.
> They're wise, of course... they know so
> Much... though stress is from knowing![57]

---

[53] Ibid., 78.

[54] Smith, *Rabi'a al-Adawiyya*, 101.

[55] Ibid., 101.

[56] Helminski, *Women of Sufism*, 40-42.

[57] Ibid., 102.

Indeed, Rabi'a speaks with glowing words about her Allah as reflected in the language of her poems, as is found in this example:

> O my happiness and my desire and refuge too,
> And my Friend and my sustainer and my Goal;
> O my Beloved, longing for you sustains me...
> If it wasn't for You, my Friend, life of my soul,
> I'd have been mad on the earth wherever I was:
> Such gifts, grace, You gave to make me whole.
> Your love is now my only desire and bliss and
> Is known to heart's eye, thirsting, like my soul.
> I've none but You, who makes deserts bloom,
> You're my joy, deep inside me, Whom I extol.
> I am now bound to You my whole life through,
> in the blackness of my eyes You are an aureole.
> And so, if You are satisfied with me, well then
> O my heart's desire, my joy has become whole.[58]

Yet, while she uses words such as 'my Beloved', 'Beauty', 'my Healer', 'my Joyfulness' and 'my life',[59] there also seems to be a harshness about Rabi'a's Allah. To misquote Milton in his sonnet "On his blindness," Rabi'a's Allah does seem to demand "day labour, light denied." For example, on her trip to Mecca, her donkey died. She then remonstrates with Allah,[60]

> "O God... do kings so treat a woman who is a stranger and powerless? Thou hast invited me unto Thy house, then in the midst of the way Thou has suffered my ass to die, leaving me alone in the desert?"

However, it does seem that Allah heard her prayer and the donkey revived and she continued on her way. During the course of her journeying, Rabi'a became very weary and cried out that she was merely clay and Allah's house (Kaaba) was a stone and that she needed him. Allah's reply was, "Be content with my name."[61] Obviously a spiritual reply to a physical need which she took as a demand to greater asceticism. On another occasion when she was weak from fasting, someone brought her food, only for a cat to spill it while she went to fetch a lamp. She then went to fetch a jug to

---

[58] Ibid., 99.
[59] Ibid., 89.
[60] Attar, *Early Saints and Mystics*, 41.
[61] Ibid., 42.

break her fast but in the meantime the lamp died. It seems that as she went to drink the jug slipped from her hand and was broken. "O God," she cried and lamented extremely loudly, "what is this that Thou art doing with Thy helpless servant?"

> "Have a care', a voice came to her ears, 'lest thou desire Me to bestow on thee all worldly blessings, but eradicate from thy heart the care for Me. Care for me and worldly blessings can never be associated together with a single heart. Rabe'a, thou desirest one thing, and I desire another; My desire and thy desire can never be joined in one heart."[62]

Once again, Rabi'a took this as a call to greater abstinence, more devotion in terms of prayer and fasting and in her service to Allah. Indeed, from the perspective of Sufic asceticism, Rabi'a's response is said to reflect her growing spiritual perfection. On one occasion when Rabi'a looked out of her dwelling, her servant invited her to come outside and see what the Creator had done. Rabi'a's reply reflects her 'absorption' with Allah.

> "Do you rather come in," Rabe'a replied, "and see the Maker. The contemplation of the Maker preoccupies me, so that I do not care to look upon what He has made."

Also, it seems that Rabi'a is insecure in her relationship with Allah. "If you are satisfied with me"; or "tell me that I have spent the Night well so I can be at peace"; or "all I need is Thy good pleasure, to know whether Thou are well-pleased or no". Sadly, a great lover, but did she also wonder if her love was returned?

Conclusion

This quotation from Annemarie Schimmel provides a fitting summary to Rabi'a's life.[63]

> ...the great lover Rabi'a al-'Adwiyya certainly helped to shape the image of the ideal pious woman who can be praised in the most glowing terms (just because of her difference from the ordinary representatives of her sex!)... To call a virtuous

---

[62] Ibid., 47-48.

[63] Annemarie Schimmel, *Mystical Dimensions of Islam* (Chapel Hill: University of North Carolina Press, 2011), 426.

woman "a second Rabi'a" was and still is, quite common among the Muslims.

By making her "differen[t] from the ordinary representatives of her sex," however, is to deny the uniqueness of Muslim women's spirituality. Devoted women follow the pillars of Islam, often outstripping some of the male members of their household in the regularity and fervour of their performance, despite the limitations that their religion has placed on them. In terms of seeking to live lives in accordance with the demands of Allah, many women find their way to Sufi Sheikhs for advice, guidance and blessing and often leave with a deeper commitment to prayer and religious practice. Other women, like Rabi'a al-'Adawiyya and those who followed her example, chose the ascetic pathway, seeking to reach the heights of Islamic devotion, only to have their femininity dismissed and be given 'male status' for their spirituality. Yet, that is in spite of the fact that even several of the wives of the Prophet were known to have followed their husband's ascetic practices and have been recognized as devout women, not only within the Sufi community but also among those who would consider themselves more orthodox in their practice.

Indeed, do not these devout women call into question the assumption that women are "deficient in intelligence and religion"? If women indeed share the same creation process as that of the male, surely they too on the basis of their 'intention' as the Prophet proclaimed can be 'raised up' as Attar deduced? Sadly Attar, though, was unable to allow such understanding to redefine his understanding of women and succumbed to giving them a 'nominal male status'. Schimmel, though, sees it otherwise.

> One should not be misled by the constant use of the word "man' in the mystical literature of the Islamic languages: it merely points to the ideal human being who has reached proximity to God where there is no distinction of sexes.[64]

Yet, for many Muslim women, the challenge they still face is being considered "deficient in intelligence and religion," though they are devout and dedicated in their devotion to Allah and his will.

---

[64] Schimmell in Helminski *Women of Sufism, A Hidden Treasure,* p108

Further Reading:

Rabi'a al Adawiyya or Rabi'a al Qaysiyya
www.contemplative
spirituality.org/media/ifaith2010rabia.pdf   cited   23
August 2018
https://pdfs.semanticscholar.org/b3af/711260ed74a2d
84033e71ba65e99186075fa.pdf

Piela, Anna, "Women are Believers in Their Own Right: One Muslim Woman's Challenge to Dominant Discourses Shaping Gender Relations in Islam," Hartford Seminar, DOI: 10.111/muwo.12021 cited 23 August 2018

Silvers, Laury. "'God loves Me': The Theological Content and Context of Early Pious and Sufi Women's Saying on Love." *Journal for Islamic Studies* 30 (2010): 33-59.

WOMEN AND FATWAS

Women Negotiating Living in an Islamic Context

Ruth Nicholls[1]

Women using a cell phone will have acid thrown in her face.
It is forbidden for girls to receive degrees and certificates.
(Maulana Abdul Haleem)

These are just two of the fatwas that have been issued against women in Pakistan in recent times.[2] Similarly in India the chief cleric of the Dar al-Uloom, a Deobandi Islamic college and the most important in India, issued a fatwa on April 4, 2010, which reads,

> It is unlawful for Muslim women to do job in government or private institutions where men and women work together and women have to talk with men frankly and without veil.

In reporting on the fatwa the associated commentary was as follows:

> In other words, what the fatwa suggests is that Muslim women can work only in such places where they can fully veil themselves and where they cannot 'frankly' (whatever that might mean) talk with men. These would, presumably, be women-only jobs, which involve entirely women staff and clients and which hermetically seal off women from any contact with males that require 'frank' conversation with the latter. The fatwa also effectively bans Muslim women from a whole range of jobs in the private sector as well.[3]

---

[1] Ruth Nicholls is an adjunct research fellow with the Arthur Jeffery Centre for the Study of Islam. Ruth spent many years in an Asian country with an Islamic majority. Her special interests are in Sufism and folk Islam.
[2] Anna Mahjar-Barducci, "Pakistan: Fatwas Against Women," published June 12, 2012, http://www.gatestoneinstitute.org/3105/pakistan-fatwas-against-women.
[3] Yoginder Sikand, "Deoband's Fatwas on Women," *Economic and Political Weekly* 45, no. 21 (2010): 15-17; https://www.outlookindia.com/website/story/unveiling-deobands-

These recently issued fatwa have obviously been delivered in relation to women and will have a significant impact on their lives. The fatwa regarding women working outside the house is not a new one but in the case of India has been re-issued. For all Muslims, though for Muslim women in particular (and also for women who wish to adopt Islam), *fatwas*[4] basically determine their life, how they live and what they can and not do. Therefore, it is important to understand the significance and role of fatwas. So, what are they? Who has the power to issue them? What authority do they carry?

UNDERSTANDING FATWAS
What are fatwas?

A recent statement by the Islamic Supreme Council of America defined a fatwa as follows:

> A fatwa is an Islamic legal pronouncement, issued by an expert in religious law (*mufti*), pertaining to a specific issue, usually at the request of an individual or judge to resolve an issue where Islamic jurisprudence (*fiqh*) is unclear. Typically, such uncertainty arises as Muslim society works to address new issues.[5]

According to the Encyclopaedia Iranica, a fatwa

> is the authoritative ruling of a religious scholar on questions of Islamic jurisprudence that are either dubious or obscure in nature or which have newly arisen without known precedent.[6]

Essentially then a fatwa is an answer to question.

The person asking the question is a *mostafti*, the process of creating the fatwa is termed *istafta*; the person who issues the fatwa is a *mufti* who can be either a male or female, though they are

---

fatwas-on-women/265579, cited October 23, 2018. See also "The Critical Analysis of Fatwas Issued on Muslim Women in India,"
http://in.boell.org/sites/default/files/downloads/Microsoft_Word__Synopsis_of_Fatwa1_web(1).pdf.
[4] The Arabic plural of *fatwa* is *fatawa*, but the accepted English plural is *fatwas*.
[5] Shaykh Muhammad Hisham Kabbani, "What is a fatwa?"
http://www.islamicsupremecouncil.org/understanding-islam/legal-rulings/44-what%20is%20a%20fatwa.html, cited November 1, 2018.
[6] "Fatwa," *Encyclopaedia Iranica*, http://www.iranicaonline.org/articles/fatwa, cited November 1, 2018.

predominantly male, and the actual delivery is termed *ifta.*[7] The delivery can either be done orally or in written form. The practice is said to issue from the days of the Prophet when he was "asked to give a ruling" (cf. Q4:127, 176), though according to these verses it is Allah himself who gives it. This has had at least two consequences: a fatwa often contains the phrase "Allah knows best" (or its equivalent) and has meant that the decision given is often without supportive evidence.

Given that Islam has no inherent legislative authority and is dependent upon the Qur'an, the hadith and *sunna* of the Prophet to reveal the divine will, it has developed a detailed legal system called the *shari'a* which regulates all aspects of life: public and private; political and personal; and especially religious. In fact, nothing is considered outside of its jurisdiction. Also, because there is such a strong insistence on obeying the law and doing the will of Allah, it is not surprising that questions arise, such as "How do I follow Allah's will or obey the Shari'a in such and such a situation?" In addition, as time has passed, Islam has spread and encountered new cultures and customs which has also led to queries and questions as to what obedience entails. The effects of industrialism and modernization, often considered western innovations, have also given rise to new issues, challenges and problems—many of which are not specifically dealt with in the Qur'an—that have called for a 'ruling'. As a result, religious scholars with the skill of interpreting the law have become the exponents of the law and regulators of behaviour.

However, within Islamic jurisprudence, there are at least three levels at which fatwas are operational. On occasions, in order to make a legal decision the judge (*qazi/qadi*) may require further (religiously based) information for the particular case and so will seek an *opinion* (*fatwa*) from the religious scholars in relation to it. A fatwa is also sought when a case does not already appear in the law (*fiqh*) books.[8] The judge's decision is only applicable to those who are named in the case, though later it might be applied more widely.

The second level at which fatwas are issued is in relation to public behaviour whereby the *mufti* issues a declaration which will

---

[7] See above. Also note that the spelling of these terms can differ.
[8] "Fatwa," in *The Oxford Encyclopaedia of the Modern Islamic World*, ed. John L. Esposito (Oxford: Oxford University Press, 1995), 2:8.

determine public conduct. In fact, one could say that almost every aspect of life in an Islamic context, requires an opinion. How does one wash for prayers? Can a baby be vaccinated?[9] How should one mourn? How does one dress? The list is endless and so the number of fatwas are also virtually innumerable. Indeed, on some of the internet sites that offer fatwas, they are numbered (cf. Al-Islam: https://www.al-islam.org; Islam questions and answers: https://islamqa; and Quora: https://www.quora.com/).

At the public level, fatwas are issued by the constituted body within that country that has been granted the authority to issue fatwas. In Saudi Arabia it is The Council of Senior Scholars, while in Indonesia one of the bodies is the Indonesian Council of Ulama (MUI) which is semi-official, though there are several others.[10] In Egpyt, the Dar al-Ifta al Masrriyah[11] was established in 1895 by official decree and is closely associated with the Al-Azhar University. When these bodies issue a fatwa it usually becomes law and must be obeyed. In such situations obedience is monitored by the 'religious police' where these have been constituted a formal body. In Saudi Arabia, this is through 'the Committee for the Promotion of Virtue and the Prevention of Vice' while in Iran it is the 'Guidance Patrol'. In countries where there are no formal religious police it is the duty of the regular police to enforce obedience. If one is caught, it can result in rough treatment, beating, arrest and jail including death. Questions regarding what is acceptable Islamic practice arise not only in countries where Islamic rule operates but perhaps even more so in countries where Muslims constitute a minority. As has been evidenced in the UK and Europe, Muslim communities often strive to have these fatwas instituted as law – as has been the case with the instigation of halal requirements.

---

[9] On October 15, 2019, it was reported by the United Nations Vaccination Project that Clerics in Pakistan via the Council of Islamic Ideology ratified 100 fatwas relating to the polio vaccination project. Islamic extremists, who rejected the project, were using violence against those involved. While women and children will benefit it seems that the acts of violence were the main reason for the pronouncements.
https://www.theaustralian.com.au/world/the-times/clerics-issue-fatwas-to-end-pakistan-polio-vaccine-panic/news-story/0707bd01f361dee963dc0b46d81bf77d.
See also https://www.dawn.com/news/1510879, cited November 18, 2019.
[10] Cf. Nico J. G. Kaptein, "The Voice of the 'Ulama': Fatwas and Religious Authority in Indonesia," *Arch.de Sc. Soc. Des Rel.* 125 (2004): 115-130.
[11] "Foundation of Dar al Iftaa al Misriyyah,"
www.dar-alifta.org/Foreign/Module.aspx?Name=aboutdar, cited December 3, 2018.

The third level at which fatwas are sought is by individuals who are wanting to understand what they should do or how they should act in a given situation. Strictly speaking, since a *fatwa* is only an opinion, though a legal one, the person receiving it is not obliged to follow that ruling. Each of the internet websites mentioned above offer *fatwas* in response to individual questions. Some of the questions appear to be new issues; some older ones on which fatwas have been previously issued. The following is an example from the *Islam Question and Answer* site:

(Response) 259422

Question

We are living in [a particular country] and my wife is six months pregnant. My wife is suffering from varicose veins in both legs because of pregnancy, so the doctor told her to wear compression stockings, which are sheer and the skin can be seen through them. He told her to wear them all day long, except at night time. Please note that the stockings are complete, and are like pants at the top; they do not cover the feet only. How can she do wudoo'? Can she wipe over the stockings only, and if that is the case, how should she wipe over them, noting that putting the stockings on and taking them off is difficult because they are compression stockings.

Answer

Praise be to Allah.

The view of the majority of scholars is that it is not allowed to wipe over sheer socks or stockings, and that this concession is allowed only in the case of thick socks.

See the answer to question no. 228222.

If these stockings are light and what is beneath them can be seen, then the more correct view is that it is not permissible to wipe over them.

But if they are needed for medical purposes, and it is difficult to take them off every time one does wudoo', then the individual may do wudoo' before putting them on, then he or she should put a thick socks over them, then when needing to do wudoo', he or she may wipe over the thick socks until he or she takes them off, or the period during which wiping over the socks is allowed comes to an end.

If he or she is not able to do that, and taking off the compression socks is something that will cause harm or delay recovery, then the matter comes under the ruling on wearing a cast, so he or she should wipe over all of it from top to bottom, which is the place which is required to be washed.

See the answer to question no. 192736.

If your wife takes the stockings off at night, she should do wudoo' when she wants to pray Fajr, then put the compression stockings on, then put on thick socks over them, then wipe over the socks, as the ruling on wiping will apply to the socks and not to the stockings that are worn under them. Then when night comes, she may take off both the stockings and the socks, then when she wants to do wudoo' for Fajr (on the following day), she should do the same thing, and so on.

I put this question to our Shaykh, 'Abd ar-Rahmaan al-Barraak, may Allah preserve him, and he said that these stockings come under two rulings:

In one way they resemble a cast, because they are worn for an essential need, and in another way, they resemble socks. In my view, she may wipe over the part of the foot that it is required to wash, and regard them as being like the khuffayn (leather socks or slippers) in terms of the time-frame (within which it is permissible to wipe over the socks). They should also be put on when in a state of purity (i.e., after doing wudoo').

And Allah knows best.

Comments on the Fatwa

Obviously, the person who is requesting the information is married, living overseas and is requesting an opinion in relation to his wife and her ability to wash her feet which is a ritual requirement prior to observing each of the ritual pray cycles. 'Washing the feet' becomes an issue because of the 'new' situation relating to 'compression stockings'. The situation is also 'new' in that it has no direct reference in either the Qur'an or the Hadith. Therefore, the reply is based on deduction and inference from verses in the Qur'an and/or statements made in the Hadith, as well as prior understanding and existing modes of thinking. In this case, the response has been numbered, and within the reply, several other fatwas are mentioned. Clearly the person to whom this is addressed has computer access and would be able to view them.

The fatwa follows the prescribed format. There is the obligatory salutation at the beginning, followed by a brief answer, which is then qualified by referring to another authority. It ends with the customary statement: "Allah knows best."

Officially, it is only a *mufti*, who has been trained to issue *fatwas*, who has the right to pronounce such an opinion which is required to follow a format that has been established over the centuries. Theoretically, a *mufti* can either be male or female. In the past *muftis* have been predominantly male, though females are increasingly taking on this role,[12] even in Saudi Arabia.[13] However, in practice, since some *fatwas* are issued without due authority, some countries such as Bangladesh have made it an offence to issue an unauthorized fatwa.[14] A statement entitled *Amman Message* issued by a conference organized by the King of Jordan, which included representatives from both Sunni and Shi'ite scholars, reads:

> Acknowledgement of the schools of Islamic jurisprudence (*Mathahib*) within Islam means adhering to a fundamental methodology in the issuance of fatwas: no one may issue a 'fatwa' without the requisite personal qualifications which each school of Islamic jurisprudence determines [for its own adherents]. No one may issue a 'fatwa' without adhering to the methodology of the schools of Islamic jurisprudence. No one may claim to do absolute 'Ijtihad' and create a new school of Islamic jurisprudence or to issue unacceptable 'fatwas' that take Muslims out of the principles and certainties of the 'Shari'ah' and what has been established in respect of its schools of jurisprudence.[15]

However, the degree to which the *Amman Message* is universally accepted within the Islamic community is difficult to assess.

Creating fatwa

The three primary areas which give rise to a fatwa have been outlined above. The first is a judge in a court of law who needs to understand that issue more clearly. Since that is a technical issue, it will not be pursued further in this article. The second most important source of fatwas has been an individual, usually a mufti, though an

---

[12] Rachel Rinaldo, "How a growing number of Muslim women clerics are challenging traditional narratives," *The Conversation*, published June 7, 2017, 1, https://theconversation.com/how-a-growing-number-of-muslim-women-clerics-are-challenging-traditional-narratives-77932.

[13] Note a number of websites refer to this development: https://www.washingtonpost.com/news/monkey-cage/wp/2017/10/10/women-will-soon-be-issuing-fatwas-in-saudi-arabia-this-isnt-as-groundbreaking-as-youd-think/?noredirect=on&utm_term=.ef873f2b0a04, and http://www.arabnews.com/node/1169376/saudi-arabia, as well as https://www.khaleejtimes.com/region/saudi-arabia/saudi-women-can-now-issue-fatwas-report, all cited November 1, 2018.

[14] N. Hosen and A. Black, "Fatwas: Their Role in Contemporary Secular Australia," *Griffith Law Review* 18, no. 2 (2009): 405n2.

[15] Amman Message, http://ammanmessage.com, cited December 3, 2018.

imam may also take on that role. Overtime, organisations have arisen or have been constituted for the purpose of issuing fatwas or have been granted authority to issue fatwas. Consequently, there is no one single name for the issuing authority. In Saudi Arabia the issuing authority consists of 21 religious scholars who have been appointed by the King and are paid by the Government and is called the Council of Senior Scholars. Historically, Saudi Arabia has been the centre for issuing fatwas for those of a Sunni persuasion. In the mid-nineteenth century, Egypt became an additional centre for pronouncing fatwas. However, in most countries where Islam has spread, centres for issuing fatwas have emerged. In addition, particularly with the growth of education, religious scholars (*ulema)* have also issued fatwas based on their own reasoning and interpretations. Consequently, fatwas have been issued by those whose legal and religious understanding is extensive compared to those which have been issued by a local less well-trained individual. Not all fatwas that have been issued have been recorded, though with modern technology, this has been made easier. In Australia, it appears to be the Grand Mufti who issues fatwas. He is elected by the Australian National Imans Council (Sunni) which was created in 2006 and which currently has some 95 members.[16]

The third group who request fatwas are individual, ordinary Muslims living their daily lives. They may be seeking information about something new, such as the use of cell phones, or it may be an issue for which there is an already established fatwa though they may not be aware of it.

In these days of the internet, fatwas can be obtained through various sites. In earlier times and still today, a person can go to a *dar-al-ifta* office in person and present their question to one of the members of the fatwa council, who will register the inquirer's details and then answer the question. These days the question and answer can be added to a database. A similar process is involved for those who submit questions in writing or via the internet. According to the *Dar al-Ifta al Misriyyah* web site, they have issued about 50,000 fatwas.

Initially all fatwas were issued in Arabic. In these days, depending on the country where the fatwa is being pronounced and

---

[16] Cf. https://en.wikipedia.org/wiki/Australian_National_Imams_Council, and https://en.wikipedia.org/wiki/Grand_Mufti_of_Australia, cited December 3, 2018.

the medium in which the fatwa is issued, it may be presented in Arabic with a translation into the local language or it may be in the local language only, especially if it is being printed in a newspaper or published on the internet.

Fatwas are based on Islamic scholarly principles using the science of Islamic jurisprudence. According to the Dar-al-Iftaa al Misriyyah, "It is necessary that a fatwa include a ruling based on the surrounding reality and that it change according to difference in the place, time, people, and circumstance." However, in reality, many of the fatwas that are issued appear merely to repeat the fatwa as it was given earlier and quote previous explanations without any consideration to "difference in place, time, people, and circumstance." Nevertheless, over time there has been a change in the way fatwas are presented. Originally an individual *mufti* had the right to issue the fatwa. More recently fatwas have been issued through a fatwa issuing body. Initially the legal method followed for issuing a fatwa was that of *taqlid*, which followed the accepted opinions of earlier scholars without the application of independent reasoning.[17] The response may or may not include appropriate references to the Qur'an, the Hadith and previous fatwas. They may also refer to other scholars, as seen in the fatwa example above. It must be remembered that fatwas are considered to be an expression of God's will and are usually concluded by the phrase indicating that Allah knows best. As such they are presumed to be definitive for practise and unquestionable.

More recently, particularly where there is a fatwa issuing *organization*, a different process can be used to come to a conclusion. It is the result of a collective effort, which in Arabic is known as the "The Study of [Religious] Issues" (*bahth al-masâ'il*) that is a type of collective decision making (*ijtihad*).[18] A third way of developing a fatwa is "weighing different opinions and choosing from among them the one which is regarded as most suitable to the circumstances and closest to the sources of law."[19]

Fatwas are also announced in the public domain. One of the most famous is that which was issued from Iran in response to Salman

---

[17] Cf. Kaptein, "The Voice of the 'Ulama'," 118.
[18] Ibid., 120.
[19] Ibid., 121.

Rushdie's book *Satanic Verses*, and which condemned him to death. Following the United Nations Fourth World Conference on Women: Action for Equality, Development, and Peace Beijing, 1995, a fatwa was reported on the official site of the Kingdom of Saudi Arabia: Portal of the General Presidency of Scholarly Research and 'Ifta,' issued by Ibn Baz, stating:

> The Council of Senior Scholars and the Constituent Assembly for Muslim World League issued a decision that condemns this conference. I was a participant and chairman of those two boards at that time. This conference contradicts Islam and deviates from Allah (Exalted be He) and His Messenger (peace be upon him) because it contains the spread of pornography and the disgrace of honor. It aims at rendering human societies to be like herds of beasts. Therefore, it was obligatory to boycott this conference. [20]

Another of Ibn Baz's fatwas is as follows:

> The ruling on women studying engineering and chemistry
> Q: Is it permissible for women to pursue some scientific fields such as chemistry, physics, etc.? (Part No. 24, Page 40).
> A: Women should not specialize in fields that are not appropriate for them. There are many areas of study that is [sic] more suitable for them to pursue, such as Islamic studies, Arabic language, and so on. As for chemistry, engineering, architecture, astronomy and geography, they are not suitable specialties for them. They should rather choose what is beneficial for them and the society, such as obstetrics and gynecology and similar specialties.[21]

---

[20] Ibn Baz was the Grand Mufti of Saudi Arabia from 1993-1999. Against the World conference, Beijing,
http://www.alifta.net/Fatawa/fatawacoeval.aspx?languagename=en&View=Hit&HajjEntryID=0&HajjEntryName=&RamadanEntryID=0&RamadanEntryName=&NodeID=4660&PageNo=1&SectionID=14.

[21] Alifta,
http://alifta.net/Search/ResultDetails.aspx?languagename=en&lang=en&view=result&fatwaNum=&FatwaNumID=&ID=4708&searchScope=14&SearchScopeLevels1=&SearchScopeLevels2=&highLight=1&SearchType=exact&SearchMoesar=false&bookID=&LeftVal=0&RightVal=0&simple=&SearchCriteria=allwords&PagePath=&siteSection=1&searchkeyword=099104101109105115116114121#firstKeyWordFound, cited January 10, 2019.

Interestingly, neither of these fatwas have any reference to the Qur'an, the Hadith or the Sunna. Rather, they are the reflections of the (male) scholars of that particular issuing body. Since there are no Qur'anic verses that directly apply to this situation, nor are there references in the Hadith or *sunna*, the conclusion is reached on the basis of deduction and inference of Qur'anic injunctions and hadith reports. Issues of innovation (*bida)* and blasphemy (*shirk*) would also have been included in considering the response. Obviously, any fatwa that is pronounced will reflect the stance of those who constitute the council issuing the fatwa. Not surprisingly, then, the above fatwas which were issued by the Council of Senior Scholars in Saudi Arabia reflect the Salafi position. Fatwas issued by the council in Iran will reflect a Shi'ite interpretation.

In 2017 at Cirebon, Indonesia, more than 500 people from Indonesia and female *ulema*[22] from 15 other countries including Saudi Arabia, Pakistan and Malaysia attended the Indonesian Women's Ulama Congress.[23] At that congress they "issued fatwas on three major issues, namely sexual violence, child marriage, and destruction of nature."[24] In relation to the fatwa on child marriages, Badriyah Fayumi the Congress [Chairperson] commented:

> ...that preventing child marriages is mandatory because child marriages cause more damage than bring benefits and goodness... parents, family, community, and government are the leading actors who must prevent child marriages. If child marriage has occurred, then the obligation of all parties to ensure the protection of children's rights, especially the right to education, health, parental care, and protection from all forms of violence, exploitation and discrimination.[25]

According to that same report there had been discussions with religious leaders and Islamic organisations to avoid friction if the

---

[22] The word *ulema* is used for scholars who are knowledgeable in Islamic shari'a law and are recognised as being able to speak on it and interpret it. From the report, it suggests that there were female scholars from a number of countries present at the conference.
[23] Yuli Saputra, "Kongres Ulama Perempuan Indonesia 2017,"
https://www.rappler.com/indonesia/berita/168188-rekomendasi-kongres-ulama-perempuan-indonesia-2017, cited December 10, 2018.
[24] Fathiyah Warday, "Kongres Ulama Perempuan Indonesia Hasilkan Tiga Fatwa,"
https://www.voaindonesia.com/a/kongres-ulama-perempuan-indonesia-hasilkan-3-fatwa-/4005416.html, cited December 10, 2018.
[25] Ibid.

Indonesian Women's Ulema Congress produced a fatwa.[26] In another report, The Religious Minister of Indonesia Lukman Hakim Saifuddin is quoted as saying,

> ...this congress succeeded in fighting for justice through awareness of the roles and relations of men and women. This congress was able to carry out not only recognition but also the revitalization of the role of female ulama since the time of Siti Aisyah to the present.[27]

Fatwas and Women

On any of the internet fatwa websites, one can scroll through the contents. Not surprisingly one finds a section relating to women. On the sites, however, there is no corresponding section of fatwas which appear to apply exclusively for men. Maybe it is assumed that unless the fatwa is specifically for women (who constitute approximately 50% of any population) it automatically applies to men (and possibly women, unless there is a particular fatwa for them on that issue). As mentioned earlier, in Muslim societies, fatwas are needed to regulate life, to tell people how they should obey Allah's will and observe the Qur'an and the Hadith.

There are at least two books in English that have been printed for women, enumerating many of the fatwas that relate to them. One of the books is by Ibn Taymyah, *Fatwas of Muslim Women*, translated by Sayed Gad and published by Dar ul-Manarah, Egypt, Al-Mansoura, 1420/2000. It is available as an online PDF. It includes over 200 fatwa, most of which are very brief and without any major overriding structure, though the fatwas do appear to be grouped together. If the Qur'an is quoted or if there is reference to a Hadith, the details associated with the reference are not generally provided. In the *Islamic Fatawa Regarding Women,* compiled by Muhammad bin Adbul-Aziz Al Musnad, translated by Jamaal Al-Din Zarabozo, printed by Darussalam, Saudi Arabia, there are some 366 fatwas. According to the book, these are "Shariah Rulings given by the Grand Mufti of Saudi Arabia Sheikh Ibn Baz, Sheikh Ibn Uthaimin, Sheikh Ibn Jibreen and others on matters pertaining to Women."[28] It is

---

[26] Ibid.

[27] Yuli Saputra, "Kongres Ulama Perempuan Indonesia 2017."

[28] Inside title page of Muhammad Bin Abdul Aziz Al Musnad, *Islamic Fatawa Regarding Women*, trans. Jamaal Al-Din Zarabozo (Riyadh: Darussalam, 2008).

divided into 22 sections which are as follows: Each section begins with the words 'Questions related to'...

Aqidah (Faith)
Knowledge
Physical Purification
Menstruation and Post Partum (sic) Bleeding
Prayer
Funerals
Zakat
Fasting
Hajj and Umrah
the Sacrifice
Marriage
Relations Between Spouses
Breast-Feeding
Divorce
Waiting Period (Iddah) and Mourning
Oaths and Vows
Expiation for a Broken Oath
Injurious Crimes
Hijab Dress and Adornment
Being Dutiful to One's parents
Supplications (Du'a)
Miscellaneous Nature

In this book, the largest sections apart from the Miscellaneous section included 48 fatwas in relation to *Hijab* Dress and Adornment, 43 in relation to Prayer, and 40 in relation to Marriage. The section relating to 'Menstruation and Post Partum (sic) Bleeding' had 24 fatwas with 'Questions relating to Aqidah (Faith)' having 23. Given such breadth and so many pronouncements, it is not possible to study or analyse all of them.

The next question that arises is how to select some examples that will reflect a fair and unbiased selection. I have decided to select three examples basically chosen at random from each of the larger sections based on length: a short one, a medium length one and a longer one. The short one comes from 'Questions Related to *Hijab* Dress and Adornment,' entitled "Being Held Accountable for What one Wears." It reads as follows:

159

The Question 247: "Is it correct that a person will be held accountable on the Day of Resurrection for what clothing he wore?"

Response: Yes, the person will be asked about his wealth and where he acquired it from and what he spent it on. This is stated in a hadith. The issuer is stated as Ibn Baz.[29]

One might ask does this question just apply to women or is it applicable to both men and women. Certainly, in this context it is applied to women but in terms of the response, one might ask does this just refer to men (pronouns *his, he*) or is that a limitation of the translation? Even so, given that women should stay at home, how can women acquire wealth and are they able to spend it? If the answer is yes, then it could be assumed that the fatwa would apply to women also. Nevertheless, the inference is that even for women they will be held accountable for what they wear.

The second example is taken from the section relating to Prayer. The fatwa is in relation to a "Muslim woman praying without *Hijab*."

Question 73: If a woman who does not wear *hijab* is forced to pray or if her *hijab* is not in accord with the shariah, for example, some of her hair or her shin is exposed for some reason, what is the ruling?

Response: First, it is necessary that one realise that *hijab* is obligatory upon women. It is not allowed for her to abandon it or be lackadaisical towards it. If the time for prayer comes and the woman is not properly attired or properly covered, then her situation may be broken down in the following cases:

If she is not wearing *hijab* or is not properly covered due to circumstances forcing her to be in that state, then she prays in the situation that she is in. Her prayer will then be valid and there will be no sin upon her. This is based on Allah's statement,

لَا يُكَلِّفُ اللَّهُ نَفْسًا إِلَّا وُسْعَهَا   [al-Bukhari 286][30]
"Allah burdens not a person beyond his scope."

---

[29] Ibid., 270.
[30] www.islamawakened.com/Qur'an/2/286, cited December 10, 2018.

Allah also says

فَاتَّقُوا اللَّهَ مَا اسْتَطَعْتُمْ   [al-Taghabun 16]
"So keep your duty to Allah (and fear Him) as much as you can."

However, if the woman is not wearing *hijab* or is not properly covered out of a voluntary choice, such as following the customs or mode of the people, and the lack of *hijab* here means not covering her face and hands, then her prayer is correct. But she is committing a sin if she is doing that in the presence of men that she is not related to.

Furthermore, if she is uncovering her skin, forearms, hair on her head and so forth, then it is not permissible for her to pray in that state. If she prays in that state, her prayer is not valid. And she is committing a sin on two counts. First, she is sinful because she is not covering herself in general. Second, she is sinful for performing the prayer in that state.[31]

Since the question is somewhat complex one needs to consider the answer carefully. Note, the woman who is appearing in public is being 'coerced into praying,' and moreover, she is in public without a *hijab* or covering. Secondly, the issue relates to praying the ritual prayers publicly, though one would assume that that is in the female section of the mosque.

The reply indicates that the *hijab* is obligatory, but if not the *hijab*, there is the requirements of being 'properly attired or properly covered'. If she is 'properly attired', her prayer is accepted. If she 'voluntarily' chooses not to be 'properly attired', her prayer is correct but she has 'sinned'. Obviously *if she is uncovering her skin, forearms, hair on her head and so forth*, she is considered to be sinning on two accounts:

First, she is sinful because she is not covering herself in general. Second, she is sinful for performing the prayer in that state.

So, even a woman's prayer life is regulated by laws: do's and don'ts. In this collection of fatwa there are some 43 of them. How many of

---

[31] Al Musnad, *Islamic Fatawa Regarding Women*, 102-103.

161

these fatwas do women know? So one might equally ask, how many of the women are sinning when they pray?

The third fatwa example from this Council of Senior Scholars (Saudi Arabia) is in relation to marriage. It has the title "For the Father to Force His Daughter into Marriage is Forbidden."

Question 176:
I have a half-sister from my father. My father married her to a man without her approval and without taking her opinion. She is twenty-one years old. The witnesses made a false witness, stating that she had agreed to the marriage. Her mother signed instead of her on the marriage contract. This is how the marriage was finalized. Until now, she refuses this marriage. What is the ruling concerning that marriage contract and those who gave false testimony?

Response: If that sister were virgin and her father compelled her to marry that man, then according to some scholars, that marriage is valid. They are of the opinion that a father may compel his daughter to marry someone she does not want if he is suitable. However, the stronger opinion on this question is that it is not allowed for a father or anyone else to compel a young lady to get married to one she does not want, even if he is suitable. The proof for this is the Prophet's statement,

لاَ تُنْكَحُ الأَيِّمُ حَتَّى تُسْتَأْمَرَ وَلاَ تُنْكَحُ الْبِكْرُ حَتَّى تُسْتَأْذَنَ[32]

"A virgin must not be married until her permission is sought."
The statement is general and there is no exception to it for any of the possible guardians. In Sahih Muslim, it is recorded as

وَالْبِكْرُ يَسْتَأْذِنُهَا أَبُوهَا[33]

"A virgin's father seeks her permission."
This version makes specific mention of the virgin girl and the father. This is a clear text on this disputed issue and what it states must be followed. Therefore, it is forbidden for a man to compel his daughter to marry a man that she does not want to marry. And the act that is forbidden cannot be valid or implemented. This is because it is being considered valid or implemented flies in the face of it being prohibited. If the Lawgiver forbids something, it means that the people cannot do it. If we then say it is valid, this means that we are

---

[32] Note the reference was not given in the text. It is Sahih Muslim 8:3303.
[33] The reference is Sahih Muslim 8:3308.

162

accepting it, acting upon it and giving it the same status as a contract that is approved by the Shariah. Based on this stronger opinion, the marriage by your father of your sister to one she does not want is an invalid marriage. The contract is null and void. The case must then be to taken to a court of law... Shaikh ibn Uthaimin.[34]

It is important to note that at the beginning of the response it is mentioned that there is an opinion that the father has done no wrong and the marriage is valid. It also indicates that the case "must... be taken to a court of law." The question, however, is, "Will those who are asking the question be prepared to do take the case to court?" In addition, since there are the two opinions, which of the opinions will be upheld in the court? The response also indicates that those who have offered false witness must repent and withdraw their statement in the presence of a *Shariah* judge. While falsely signing a marriage contract is considered 'sinful', the fatwa only asks for repentance and gives the admonished to "not repeat such an act ever again" One has to ask is that just punishment for being a false witness? In this case, it would appear that leniency is being offered to the 'mother' (that may indeed be fair because she may have been coerced into signing the document and may not have even known the true nature of the document she was signing). From personal observation and from the many stories I have heard and read, it would seem that the first opinion – that a father can force a daughter to marry is the *modus operandi*. This twenty-one year old woman might try to fight, but her chances of 'winning' are not good.

Women working the Fatwas

In a 2011 article, Mohamed Shahid Mathee reflected on how three women used their understanding of fatwas and Islamic law to gain their own ends while even "using the negative image men had of them to their advantage."[35] As Mathee notes in the abstract, these Muslim wives "clearly had their own idea of sexual rights and obligations, divorce and husbands." In other words, they understood the Islamic law that applied in their particular situation and were able to act independently as a result of that.[36] Obviously, this is in contradiction to Sahih Bukhari hadith 1:6:301, which is

---

[34] Al Musnad, *Islamic Fatawa Regarding Women*, 188-190.
[35] Mohamed Shahid Mathee, "Women's Agency in Muslim Marriage: Fatwas from Timbuktu," *Journal for Islamic Studies* 31 (2011): 86.
[36] Ibid., 75.

purported to quote the Prophet saying "that women are deficient in intelligence."[37] These women not only showed that they understood the system and were able to work it to their advantage, which, in effect, was in contradiction to the accepted understanding of the nature of women. Mathee also comments that "male *muftis* reformulate the questions (what is) and privilege their answers (what ought to be)."[38] Yet, he notes that even in the reformulation of the questions there is sufficient to "indicate Muslim women's agency" while the mufti would consider the women as being fickle and ignorant.[39] Mathee comments that the Timbuktu fatwas tell "not only what wives said and did, but also what they knew of Islamic law," while the muftis generally regarded "women as transgressors and ignorant of Islamic law."[40]

Of the three fatwas to which Mathee refers, one reports that, during an argument between a husband and a wife, the wife suddenly asks for a divorce. The husband did just that. In the second incident, which also occurred during an argument, the wife's words were: "You are forbidden to me as my father is." The question that arises is, "Can a wife be responsible for the repudiation of a marriage?" However, the wife's comment was dismissed since her "utterance" was considered "legally inconsequential." According to Mathee, "the mufti rejects her usage of this instrument [(*zihar*)]... and attempts to re-establish the hierarchic relation between a man and his wife." He adds, "Such women may be sinners (just as the men), but they were not ignorant of Islamic law and the Qur'an."[41] In a supporting example, Mathee refers to an incident where a woman went to a judge, claiming that her husband had divorced her. While the judge did not rule in favour of the divorce, he did allow her to refuse conjugal relations which was what she wanted. Apparently, she fabricated the story about her husband issuing a divorce. In the third case, a man told his wife that he was planning to travel and would be away for some extended time. The wife claimed that her husband said that if he was away for more than fifteen days she could divorce him herself. Since there were no witnesses her word was accepted, and she was granted a divorce.

---

[37] https://muflihun.com/bukhari/6/301 cited 13 December 2018
[38] Mathee, "Women's Agency in Muslim Marriage," 79. He also refers to Karin Miller in relation to this issue.
[39] Ibid.
[40] Ibid., 85-86.
[41] Ibid., 89.

After the appropriate length of time, she married again. When her husband returned a year later, she was pregnant, and her new husband refused to divorce her. Again, the woman knew Islamic law, was able to obtain fatwas in her favour herself and used her knowledge and skills to her advantage.

Women challenging Fatwas

Increasingly women are beginning to challenge fatwas as well as the thinking and understanding out of which the fatwas are being issued. This was evident during the recent women's conference in Indonesia. The fact that Saudi Arabia is giving women the right to issue fatwas is also a reflection of the growing influence of women's voices in the Islamic world. In fact, that Indonesian Congress (Cirebon 2017) went as far to claim:

> We wholeheartedly state that: Women are human beings who have all the potential of humanity as men through mind and body. All this is the gift of Allah SWT given to every human being that cannot be reduced by anyone in any name.[42]

In other words, the congress was claiming that female and male scholars are equal, which contradicts the Sahih Bukhari hadith quoted earlier that "women are deficient in intelligence."

Raheel Raza, a Pakistani Muslim now living in Canada who is an intercultural, Interfaith Diversity consultant and author, in her book *Their Jihad... Not my Jihad*, highlights many a fatwa issue, especially those which impinge on women's lives. In her book, she also records a number of incidents in which she herself experienced the impact of fatwas. Because she dared to host an event celebrating the Prophet's birthday, she received a fatwa condemning her for doing so.[43] According to the Saudi Arabian Council of Senior Scholars, because 'celebrating birthdays' has no source whatsoever in the pure *shariah'*, celebrating birthdays is considered an innovation, therefore to do so is unacceptable.[44] So because she dared

---

[42] http://www.rappler.com/indonesia/berite/168188-rekomendasi-kngres-ulama-perempuan-indonesia-2107.
[43] Raheel Raza, *Their Jihad... Not My Jihad* (Ingersoll: Basileia Books, 2005), 143.
[44] Al Musnad, *Islamic Fatawa Regarding Women*, 33.

to celebrate the event the next year, she was subjected to condemnation[45] and writes:

> Before people get their knickers in a knot and slap fatwa #2 on my head (I received fatwa #1 last year for celebrating the birth of my own Prophet), let me clarify that I indulge in celebrations of the cultural and non-alcoholic kind, keeping my feet firmly grounded in my own faith. In fact, it is because of my religious convictions that I feel it is important to greet others on their day of celebration.[46]

She also adds:

> Although this celebration is not an Islamic duty, it is a spiritual tradition developed by Muslims out of love and reverence for Prophet Mohammad and his family.[47]

Another fatwa that Raza condemns is the one that says "you shouldn't shake the hand of the person of the opposite sex."[48] Raza was attending a conference and reports this incident and her reaction,

> Next to me was a man, young enough to be my son, who made an excellent hi-tech presentation and at the end, when everyone was milling around, saying, "Good work," I held out my hand to congratulate him, as well. He pulled his hand back and said solemnly, with a straight face, "I don't shake hands with women." To say I was shocked would be an understatement. Not only did I find his attitude disrespectful, I wanted to challenge him and ask why he was there; was he was afraid of women or his own sexuality? But I held my tongue because that would mean making a mockery out of Muslims, which is exactly what we were there to discuss. As I fumed about this incident, someone kindly pointed out that certain restrictive misinterpretations of Islam condemn shaking hands with the opposite sex. I

---

[45] Note on November 21, 2018, a bomb blast in Kabul killed at least 50 people and injured some 80 others. The reason: they were celebrating the Prophet's birthday. https://www.dailymail.co.uk/news/article-6410311/At-50-killed-bomb-attack-gathering-mark-Prophet-Mohammads-birthday-Afghanistan.html; http://muslimnews.co.uk/news/middle-east/afghanistan-suicide-bombing-kills-43-people-celebrating-prophets-birthday, cited December 3, 2018.

[46] Raza, *Their Jihad... Not my Jihad*, 164.

[47] Ibid., 143.

[48] cf. Al Musnad, *Islamic Fatawa Regarding Women*, 343; see also https://www.al-islam.org/some-questions-related-womens-rights-islam-sayyid-rida-husayni-nasab/what-commandment-shaking-hands.

reminded them that people judging actions of Muslims without looking at the intention have a small view of moral and spiritual issues. Through our misinterpreted actions, we Muslims often create our own propaganda.[49]

Detractors of this position would point the finger at the negative influence of education, the decadent influence of the west and the evil suggestions flaunted by feminists. To her detractors, Raza is out of step with Islam. The traditional understanding is that Islam is the best of religions and that the place given to women in Muslim society is one of honour and freedom. Indeed, there are women within Muslim society who would agree with this sentiment and who would challenge those who seek to question the traditional narratives.

Conclusion

In this article we have considered fatwas and their significance for Muslim women. It is noted that Muslim society basically depends on fatwas to delineate how people are to obey the Shari'a and live according to God's will. Since some 50% of the population will be women, they too will be seeking how to obey the Shari'a and live according to God's will. Not surprisingly, the attitude imbedded in the Qur'an, Hadith and *Sunna* will have their impact on the interpretation that is given. Consequently, fatwas relating to women are innumerable. Some of those who are seeking a ruling are women themselves; sometimes it is the relatives of women who are seeking a ruling. In most cases fatwas have been thrust upon women without fitting consideration of their needs, without any consultation of their particular position and their perspective on living.

The Qur'an, in particular, offers confusing attitudes to women, while generally speaking, the Hadith reports appear to reflect a negative opinion of women. Nevertheless, since Islam is considered the 'best religion' *ipso facto*, women are said to be given the highest honour and place in society. Yet, even from within Islam there are voices questioning those interpretations. From the fatwas detailed above, the position given to women could be considered less than honouring. In spite of this, there are those within Islam who are seeking for a great voice for women. The fact that Saudi Arabia is considering allowing women to issue fatwas and the Indonesian

---

[49] Raza, *Their Jihad... Not my Jihad*, 140.

congress on Women reflect the fact that women are beginning to take a greater role within their society suggests that women's issues might be heard. There are also those like Raheel Raza who are observing Muslim society and its perspectives through a 'different lens' and offering comments and raising questions.

Given the fact that the foundation of Muslim society is living according to the will of Allah and obedience to the Shari'a, fatwas are going to remain a determinative issue within Islamic society whether one is male or female. With the constant tension between the traditional, liberal, modern and feminist interpretations of the bases of Islam, women will be subject to those who make the interpretations. Given the apparent inability of these groups to graciously accept that the others have a valid point of view and interpretation, the position of women and the pronouncement of fatwas in relation to their lives will constantly result in conflicting opinions and pronouncements, which, in some cases, will be diametrically opposed. Yet, as the article has shown, women are able to negotiate the system and work it to their own benefit.

Further References

Esposito, John L., ed. "Fatwa." In *The Oxford Encyclopaedia of the Modern Islamic World*. Vol. 2, 8-17. Oxford: Oxford University Press, 1995.

Lewis, B., Ch. Pellat, and J. Schacht, eds. "Fatwa." In *Encyclopaedia of Islam*. New Ed. Vol. 2, 866. Leiden: Brill, 1991.

THE TREATMENT OF WOMEN IN THE QUR'AN:

A Window into the Islamic Community in Singapore

Penelope Myra Tan[1]

Introduction

The stereotype of women in Islam worldwide being oppressed and marginalised is a common perception among non-Muslims. In a patriarchal Islamic system, the social status of these women has generally been portrayed as subordinate to that of her male counterpart. Klingorová and Havlíček, in their research findings entitled *Religion and Gender Inequality: The Status of Women in the Societies of World Religions*, conclude that amongst the highest levels of gender inequality observed are those who adhere to Islam.[2]

How does that compare with Muslims in Singapore's multi-racial and multi-religious population, where they make up 14.7%[3] of the nation's 5.6 million[4] people. In this country where the people pledge "regardless of race, language or religion, based on justice and equality,"[5] how equal does equal get? Before looking into the local context, it is necessary to first examine the Qur'an to determine how

---

[1] Writing under a pseudonym, Penelope Myra Tan is a part-time student with the Biblical Graduate School of Theology, Singapore, and she is on her way to completing a Graduate Diploma in Christian Studies. The original version of this paper was written in partial fulfillment for a module facilitated by BGST.

[2] Kamila Klingorová and Tomáš Havlíček, "Religion and Gender Inequality: The Status of Women in the Societies of World Religions," *Moravian Geographical Reports* 23 (2015): 2-11.

[3] Department of Statistics Singapore, "Key Indicators of Resident Population," Singapore Census of Population 2010, Statistical Release 1: Demographic Characteristics, Education, Language and Religion, last updated April 25, 2018, https://www.singstat.gov.sg/publications/cop2010/census10_stat_release1.

[4] Department of Statistics Singapore, "Latest Data," Population and Population Structure, last updated July 17, 2019, https://www.singstat.gov.sg/whats-new/latest-data.

[5] National Heritage Board, "National Pledge," Our Pledge, last updated November 5, 2018, https://www.nhb.gov.sg/what-we-do/our-work/community-engagement/education/resources/national-symbols/national-pledge.

Prophet Mohammad was instructed to treat women. As such, this essay will survey a limited number of topics within the Qur'an and selected Hadiths (Sahih Bukhari, Sahih Muslim, Sunan Abu-Dawud, and Malik's Muwatta) that concern women; namely, status, hijab, marriage, polygyny, domestic abuse, and divorce.

Depending on the sects or schools to which they belong, to a certain extent, Muslims are by and large shaped by their communities which in turn are guided by their country's constitutions and advocacy of Syariah laws. The Singapore government together with the Islamic religious authorities, *Majlis Ugama Islam Singapura* (MUIS) and *Persatuan Ulama dan Guru-Guru Agama Islam (Singapura)* (PERGAS),[6] clearly advocate the practice of moderate Islam. How does Singapore's dual court system affect the lives of Muslim women in these areas? How do the women themselves feel about their social status in the community? Do the Syariah laws practiced in Singapore protect the women? Are there any institutions in place to support and empower the Muslim women here? This paper will also attempt to answer these questions by looking at the programmes and services of various non-profit organisations and associations that work with Muslim women in Singapore.

Created Equal?
Several translations[7] of *Sura al-Nisa* 4:34 suggest that men have authority over women because Allah has made one superior to the other. Q2:228 shows that although women have similar rights accorded to them, men have a degree of advantage over them.[8] Elsewhere in the Qur'an, women are seen as "treacherous"[9] and "forgetful"[10] and as such a woman's testimony[11] is only half that of a man's. This contradicts Q35:28 which implies that both men and women are credited with equal capacity for learning, understanding,

---

[6] Islamic Religious Council of Singapore (MUIS) and Singapore Islamic Scholars and Religious Teachers Association (PERGAS).
[7] Q4:34, English Translation, accessed February 19, 2019,
http://corpus.Qur'an.com/translation.jsp?chapter=4&verse=34.
[8] Diana L. Owen, "The Qur'an, The Hadith, and Women," in *Voices Behind the Veil: The World of Islam Through the Eyes of Women*, ed. Ergun Mehmet Caner (Grand Rapids, MI: Kregel Publications, 2003), 67.
[9] Q12:28.
[10] Q2:282.
[11] Ibid.

and teaching.[12] In *Sura al-Nahl* (The Bee) verse 58, the birth of a baby girl is described as bringing shame to the father such that he chokes with suppressed agony.[13] Al-Bukhari, the most revered of Muslim traditionist scholars,[14] records in his Hadith Chapter 62 (*Nikaah*) report 124 that the majority of those who entered through the gates of Hell are women.[15] Elsewhere in *Sahih Muslim*, Eve is the reason for women's unfaithfulness towards their husbands.[16]

Muslims who believe that the Qur'an teaches that men and women are created equal often quote verses Q4:1 and Q49:13. They claim that the latter shows that man and woman originate from one being and so are equal.[17] Others claim that in being "children of Adam,"[18] neither one gender is favoured over the other but that both are equally honoured[19] as long as they are devoted[20] to Allah. Referring to Q33:35, Rosemary Sookhdeo believes that the passage places, regardless of sex, an "absolute identity of the human moral condition and identical spiritual and moral obligations" on all individuals.[21] She notes, however, that even though many Muslims believe that the Qur'an teaches gender equality, it is not lived out in reality. Sookhdeo goes on to say that in practice, the values being attached to women are degrading and humiliating, one which accords her a lower position in society.[22]

In Singapore, where 98.7% of the total Malay population are professing Muslims,[23] a look at education opportunities reveal that

---

[12] Aisha B. Lemu and Fatima Heeren, *Woman in Islam* (London: International Islamic Publishing House, 1978), 15.
[13] Q16:58.
[14] Encyclopaedia Britannica, s.v. "Hadith," accessed July 15, 2019, https://www.britannica.com/topic/Hadith#ref68899.
[15] *Sahih Bukhari* 62:124. "Wedlock, Marriage (Nikaah)," Sahih Bukhari, accessed July 15, 2019, https://www.searchtruth.com/book_display.php?book=62&translator=1&start=120.
[16] *Sahih Muslim* 8:3471. "The Book of Marriage (Kitab Al-Nikah)," Sahih Muslim, accessed July 15, 2019, https://www.searchtruth.com/book_display.php?book=8&translator=2&start=240.
[17] Jamal A. Badawi, "Gender Equity in Islam," WhyIslam.org, published December 15, 2014, https://www.whyislam.org/social-issues/gender-equity-in-islam/.
[18] Q17:70.
[19] Rosemary Sookhdeo, *Secrets Behind the Burqa* (McLean, VA: Isaac Publishing, 2008), 36-37.
[20] Q33:35.
[21] Sookhdeo, Secrets Behind the Burqa, 38.
[22] Ibid., 37.
[23] Department of Statistics Singapore, *Key Indicators of Resident Population*.

Muslim women and men have equal access. In the 2010 Population Census, the survey for 'Resident Polytechnic Graduates Aged 15 Years and Over by Field of Study, Ethnic Group and Sex'[24] show that 44.4% of all Malay graduates were female. This figure is significant when compared to only 40.6% of the total graduates surveyed being females. More interestingly, a similar survey conducted for 'Resident University Graduates Aged 15 Years and Over by Field of Study, Ethnic Group and Sex'[25] reveal that Malay female graduates were the only females across the different ethnic groups (Chinese, Malays, Indians, and Others) that outnumbered their male counterparts, and that by a whopping 13.69%.

There are many Muslim women in Singapore's academia, like Associate Professor Noor Aisha binte Abdul Rahman, who fervently advocates the elimination of discrimination against Muslim women in Singapore. She maintains that the weight of conservatism as a dominant mode of thinking of the law has diminished the prospects for potential revaluation and reform of the Muslim law that undermines gender equality.[26] In a subtler way, the Head of Asian Languages and Cultures at the National Institute of Education, Singapore (Nanyang Technological University), Associate Professor Hadijah binte Rahmat, believes that it is her duty as a Malay and Muslim person to do something for her community, religion, and country. In an interview posted on the *Persatuan Pemudi Islam Singapura* (PPIS) Facebook webpage,[27] Dr. Rahmat says she always sees herself as a human being and never as a woman, especially when she writes about the community or world issues. She speaks with the voice of a human being where there is no gender. She insists that she does not let any perspective of women stand in her way and that is what she wishes to change in terms of the community's perspective and mindset towards women.

In the field of politics, we find amongst the Singapore Ruling Party's 'Women's Wing,'[28] two female Members of Parliament who

---

[24] Ibid., Table 35.

[25] Ibid., Table 37.

[26] Noor Aisha Binte Abdul Rahman, "Convention on the Elimination of Discrimination Against Women and the Prospect of Development of Muslim Personal Law in Singapore," *Journal of Muslim Minority Affairs* 34, no. 1 (2014): 62.

[27] Hadijah Rahmat, "Aura Hawa," Facebook, October 8, 2015, https://www.facebook.com/ppis.sg/videos/1016836388355360/.

[28] "Women Members of Parliament," Women's Wing, People's Action Party, accessed July 15, 2019, https://www.pap.org.sg/womens-wing/members-of-parliament.

are veiled in the traditional Muslim headscarf. They are Mdm. Rahayu Mahzam and Dr. Intan Azura Mokhtar who are a part of a team taking care of the electoral divisions of Jurong and Ang Mo Kio, respectively. In 2017, Madam Halimah Yacob became the very first female President of Singapore and first Malay head of state in 47 years since the death of Yusof Ishak, Singapore's first president.[29] Considering that the incumbent president of Singapore is a Muslimah, we can safely conclude that the position adopted by the Muslim community on women and even women leadership in Singapore is an open and equal one.

Hijab

Surprisingly, there is no mention at all in the Qur'an about women having to veil their hair or faces in the way the more conservative Muslims of today do. In Q3:59, Allah tells Mohammad to instruct the women to ensure their outer garments are worn long so as to be recognised and not insulted. Q24:31 suggests that believing women's headscarves should cover their necklines so as not to reveal their cleavage. Hjärpe maintains that the "wearing of the veil has no, or at best, questionable, support in the Koran"[30] and that though proper dress is obligatory, it does not also imply veiling the face.[31] Sookhdeo sees no injunction in the Qur'an requiring a Muslim woman to veil her face or head but she believes that this practice drew its influence from the upper classes of Byzantine Christians of the day.[32]

However, there are many Hadith reports that instruct women to cover their bodies and veil their heads. In Sunan Abu-Dawud, the unveiled black-haired Ansar women were described as having crows on their heads.[33] Instead, when a woman reaches the age of maturity, she should have her bosom[34] and all parts of her body except her face

---

[29] "Singapore Presidents," Personalities, National Library Board Singapore, accessed February 14, 2019. http://eresources.nlb.gov.sg/infopedia/articles/SIP_808_2004-12-28.html.
[30] Jan Hjärpe, "The Attitude of Islamic Fundamentalism Toward the Question of Women in Islam," in *Women in Islamic Societies: Social Attitudes and Historical Perspectives*, ed. Bo Utas (London: Curzon Press, 1983), 19.
[31] Ibid., 20.
[32] Sookhdeo, *Secrets Behind the Burqa*, 47.
[33] Sunan Abu-Dawud 32:4090. "Clothing (Kitab Al-Libas)," Sunan Abu-Dawud, accessed July 15, 2019, https://www.searchtruth.com/book_display.php?book=32&translator=3&start=50.
[34] Ibid., 32:4091.

and hands[35] covered. In fact, it is in Sahih Bukhari that the origins of the Hijab were documented. Anas bin Malik tells of how the Verses of Al-Hijab (the veiling of ladies) were revealed on the night of the Prophet Mohammad's marriage to Zainab bint Jahsh.[36]

According to Wu, there is a confusion in the terminology used for "hijab."[37] "Hijab" describes the veil in the sense of a screen or curtain, while "khimar" is the veil that is worn over the head known as the "tudung" in Singapore. However, many Muslims and non-Muslims have come to accept the use of "hijab" and "tudung" interchangeably.

Although the *tudung* was originally intended to facilitate modesty, it does not appeal to every Muslim woman in Singapore because of the very hot and humid weather.[38] Says an anonymous ex-Muslim in a testimony on the webpage of the Council of Ex-Muslims of Singapore: "It didn't help that Singapore is SO humid. Each time I was out, I just wanted to rip off my hijab and feel the wind in my hair."[39] Some women choose to wear the hijab only for special and solemn occasions such as the Eid, weddings and funerals, much to the displeasure of their mothers and sisters who threaten them with the fear of hellfire for being dressed immodestly.[40] Dr Suratman in her research with five women discovered that they found the *tudung* "inhibiting" and that "the experiences of the women in the study show that expressions of Malay Muslim identity in Singapore are not necessarily shared by all members of the ethnic community."[41] These women choose to assert their self-identity rather than a collective Malay Muslim identity.

---

[35] Ibid., 32:4092.

[36] Sahih Bukhari 62:95. "Wedlock, Marriage (Nikaah)."

[37] Ridzuan Wu, "The Confusing Use of Terminology," in *Tudung: Beyond Face Value*, ed. Salinah Aliman (Singapore: Bridges Books, 2002), 19.

[38] "Of Tudungs and Attempts at Salvaging My Faith." Council of Ex-Muslims Singapore, accessed February 14, 2019, http://cemsg.org/ex-muslim-testimonies-006-of-tudongs-and-attempts-at-salvaging-my-faith/.

[39] Ibid.

[40] Filzah Sumartono and Margaret Thomas, eds., *Growing Up Perempuan* (Singapore: AWARE Singapore, 2018), 69.

[41] "Tudung Girls: Unveiling Muslim Women's Identity in Singapore," Singapore Research Nexus, Faculty of Arts and Social Sciences, Singapore National University, published May 8, 2018, http://www.fas.nus.edu.sg/srn/archives/56663.

On the other hand, while acknowledging that the debate of donning of the *tudung* among Singaporean Muslim women is a complex one, local poet and playwright Alfian Sa'at attempts to explain the reasons why.[42] For one, the issue of whether or not women should be allowed to wear the *tudung* for front-line public service vocations has become a tussle for legitimacy in representing the concerns and rights of the Muslim community. He notices with regret that the debate has shifted from the real concern to instead focus on how the debate should be conducted. Next, he opines that the wearing of the *tudung* is not just the putting on of an extra headscarf. If public service frontline uniforms are to conform to *tudung* standards, then the entire uniform will have to be changed to include long sleeves for tops and ankle-covering lengths for bottoms. Sa'at then goes on to suggest three reasons as to why Muslim women choose to wear the *tudung*. Firstly, he states that it is for their own comfort and freedom: freedom from prying and roving lecherous eyes and freedom from being the cause of tempting another into sin. By covering up in accordance with this dress code, a Muslimah is also acting in obedience to her religious beliefs which in turn bestows upon her psychological and spiritual assurances. Secondly, the *tudung* also presents the young Muslim woman's suitability for marriage to a conservative Muslim man. Lastly, he suggests that it is perfectly acceptable for a Muslim woman to be wearing a brightly coloured headscarf and even use cosmetics, and be part of both the "people of the world" as well as the "people of God".

In his conclusion, Sa'at maintains that covering up for a Muslimah allows her the freedom to go out of the house, work and contribute in greater ways to the household's needs and yet remain faithful to her religious beliefs. He challenges the rest of us Singaporeans with this food for thought: "What can we do, as a multicultural, multi-religious society, to respect that choice and ensure their wellbeing?"

Marriage

According to *Sura* Al-A'rāf (7:189), woman is created from man so that he may find comfort in her. Allah created spouses from amongst the people so that they may live with each other in

---

[42] Jeanette Tan, "Playwright Alfian Sa'at Explains Quite Perfectly the Complexity of the Tudung/Hijab Issue in Singapore," *Mothership*, published April 6, 2017, https://mothership.sg/2017/04/playwright-alfian-saat-explains-quite-perfectly-the-complexity-of-the-tudunghijab-issue-in-spore/.

tranquillity, love, and kindness.[43] The "love of desirable things" made alluring for men include women, children, gold, silver, treasures, horses, livestock, and farmland.[44] With the exception of those listed in Q4:22-23, "other women are lawful to you, so long as you seek them in marriage, with gifts from your property, looking for wedlock rather than fornication."

Diana Owen suggests that the true status of women in terms of marriage is anything but that painted above. She insists that the "denigration of women, who allegedly are genetically inferior to men, continues within the context of marriage. A woman is an object, a possession, which is coveted by man (Q3:14). She is likened to a field, and her husband, as landowner, is permitted to approach her at his leisure in order to satiate his appetite (Q2:223)."[45] *Sura al-Nisa* 4:20 does tell us that if a man should wish to replace one wife with another, he should not take her bride-gift back, even if he had given her a great amount of gold.

The local term for bride-gift is the "Mahar."[46] Given by the groom after the solemnisation ceremony, the Mahar symbolises the start of the husband's responsibility in fulfilling the wife's everyday needs. The Mahar is the bride's right and she is the owner of the gift which can be in cash or kind, such as gold or silver. In an affluent society like Singapore, one would expect the minimum rate for the Mahar to be much more than the SGD100 stipulated by the Registry. It seems rather belittling for the bride to be only worth as much as that, but on second thoughts, she would only have to return that amount to secure her release in a divorce. Then again, Prophet Mohammad was said to have paid the price of only one sheep (the highest amongst the Mahars for his wives) on marrying Zainab bint Jahsh and only two mudds (1.75 kilograms) worth of barley on marrying some of his other wives.[47]

Is the wife a commodity that can be easily replaced or is she just a play-thing? In Sahih Bukhari 62:172, we read of Prophet

---

[43] Q30:21.
[44] Q3:14.
[45] Owen, *Voices Behind the Veil*, 71.
[46] "Maskahwin and Marriage Expenses," Registrar of Muslim Marriages, last updated April 2, 2015,
https://www.romm.gov.sg/about_marriage/romm_maskahwin_expenses.asp.
[47] Sahih Bukhari 62:100-101. "Wedlock, Marriage (Nikaah)."

Mohammad's asking Jabir bin Abdullah if he was married. Jabir replied that he was married to a matron. To that, the Prophet asked Jabir why he was not married to a virgin (young girl) instead so that he "may play with her" and she with him. In terms of the woman's right to choose her own husband, Asghar Ali Engineer in his article on "The Status of Muslim Women"[48] observed that most women are not consulted before a marriage as it is the father's right to marry her off to whomever he so chooses. She is not allowed to lay down any conditions whatsoever. According to the regulations stipulated by the Registry of Muslim Marriages (Singapore), there is no mention of the consent of the bride, but instead the consent of the bride's parents or guardians and *Wali*[49] is compulsory. In fact, the *Wali* must accompany the bride when she makes her registration at the Registry.[50] Serious consequences leading to annulment of the marriage await the couple should the bride's *Wali* be found unlawful. This regulation averts forced marriages and also prevents children secretly getting married without their parents'/guardians' and *Wali's* knowledge.

The Registry of Muslim Marriages (Singapore) promotes marriage as the Islamic way of life based on *Sura al-Rum* verse 21. The Registry regards marriage as a life-long journey and that the couple should make every effort towards building and maintaining a strong and long-lasting marriage.[51] As such, they work with non-profit social welfare organisations such as Persatuan Pemudi Islam Singapura (PPIS) and Association of Muslim Professionals (AMP) to provide support and assist couples in their marital journeys. According to the regulations of the Registry, all marriages involving partners under the age of 21 will have to attend and complete a marriage preparation programme.[52] Designed to equip young couples with the necessary information for a successful new phase in life together, marriage enrichment and consultation services are also available. Though not compulsory, other programmes for first marriages and remarriages are highly recommended.

---

[48] Asghar Ali Engineer, "Status of Muslim Women," *Economic and Political Weekly* 29, no. 6 (1994): 298.
[49] "Wali," Registrar of Muslim Marriages, last updated May 10, 2019, https://www.romm.gov.sg/about_marriage/romm_wali.asp.
[50] Ibid.
[51] "Marriage Preparation Programmes," Registrar of Muslim Marriages, last updated May 10, 2019, https://www.romm.gov.sg/resources/marriage_preparation.asp.
[52] Ibid.

Polygyny

A Muslim man may marry up to four wives[53] and has full control[54] over which wives he wishes to lay with. However, Q4:129-130 suggests that the man will never, however hard he tries, be able to treat all four wives with equal fairness. Hadith report 2128 in Kitab Al-Nikah of Sunan Abu-Dawud warns the man who has two wives that if he should be more inclined to one wife, he will have one side of his body hanging down as punishment on the Day of Resurrection. In a polygamous marriage, the husband must not neglect any one wife leaving her suspended between marriage and divorce.[55] However, if they should choose to divorce, it is allowed by Allah and he will provide for each of them out of his plenty.

In Singapore, where polygamous marriages are almost unheard of, a check surprisingly revealed that polygyny is indeed allowable.[56] However, the Registry of Muslim Marriages (Singapore) has put in place stringent criteria for men who wish to marry a second, third, or fourth wife. Besides having to prove that he has the capability to provide for his wives financially, physically, and emotionally, he must be in good standing with his current wife/wives and furnish specific reasons for the need of another marriage. Additionally, the application will first be reviewed by the *Kadi* (state appointed solemnizer), then following separate interviews of all parties involved, he will make a judgment with reference to the Syariah Law. Due to these rigorous measures, there were only ten such officially registered marriages in 2017.[57]

The mention of polygyny in Singapore will most likely bring about contentious discussions because of its rarity and the stigma attached to it. As such, polygamists are careful to guard their domestic lives and keep it as private as possible.[58] In her article,

---

[53] Q4:3.

[54] Q33:51.

[55] Q4:129-130.

[56] "Polygyny," Registrar of Muslim Marriages, last updated May 10, 2019, https://www.romm.gov.sg/about_marriage/romm_polygyny.asp.

[57] Department of Statistics Singapore, "Statistics on Marriages and Divorces, 2017," accessed February 15, 2019, https://www.singstat.gov.sg/publications/population/marriages-and-divorces.

[58] Nabilah Mohammad, "More Than One: A Look At Polygamy In Muslim Marriages In Singapore," *Research on Islamic and Malay Affairs*, published January 17, 2019,

Nabilah Mohammad believes that polygamy may be an option for consenting spouses whose intent is to maintain the social welfare of the family, to preserve happiness, protect and raise children, and to stave off illicit affairs and marriage disunion.[59] She also suggests that polygyny is a viable solution to the wife's illness or infertility.

In spite of the stringent criteria set by the Registry of Muslim Marriages (Singapore), men have been known to circumnavigate the law by getting married outside of Singapore. "Zahid was earning a meagre income as a technician. It was unlikely that the *tok kadi* would allow him to take on multiple wives."[60] So, Chahaya became his third wife in Indonesia. On hindsight, she is totally convinced that polygamy is not an option. She says: "Those who practise polygamy these days *buat untuk puaskan nafsu dengan menggunakan alasan sunnah Nabi.*"[61] Mr. Hasan, a general manager of a big company, married a second wife outside Singapore. Not needing to furnish legitimate grounds for this second marriage, he had only this reason to give: "I want to avoid sins. I do not want to commit adultery."[62]

What do the first wives have to say about their husbands marrying another? Mr. Azri's two wives, Mdm. Wani and Mdm. Liza, live under the same roof with their seven children and his aged parents. While Mdm. Wani struggled to accept the second wife initially, she eventually acquiesced; convinced that the benefits of this newfound sisterly-female support outweighed the cons.[63] They live harmoniously together helping each other out with household chores and child rearing. Mr. Azri insists that his second wife is an "add-on" and not a "replacement" for the first wife.

Social activist and family lawyer Ms. Halijah Mohamad firmly believes that the practiced state of polygyny does not adhere to what Islam actually intends and that it should be subject to strict conditions to secure fair treatment for the women.[64] She maintains that a careful

---

http://www.rima.sg/commentary/more-than-one-a-look-at-polygamy-in-muslim-marriages-in-singapore/#.XS7X8C2p18V.

[59] Mohammad, "More Than One."

[60] Firqin Sumartono, "Poligami – Ikut Sunnah Atau Nafsu? In Conversation with Chahaya," in *Growing Up Perempuan* (Singapore: AWARE Singapore, 2018), 213.

[61] "Anyway, those who practice polygamy these days do it to satisfy their own lust using the excuse that they are following the Prophet's way." Ibid., 216.

[62] Mohammad, "More Than One".

[63] Ibid.

[64] Ibid.

reading of the Qur'an will show that Islam supports polygyny for the protection of widows and orphans and not for lust.

Whether good or bad, a polygamous life and its domestic scene is one that demands, besides the financial means, a lot of patience, tolerance, negotiating, and compromise. It is a decision the men, together with their wives, must carefully deliberate upon. If lived out properly, polygyny can be a blessing for the family, but if not, it can become a nightmare leading to a failed marriage and distressing consequences.

Domestic Abuse

Q4:24 states that, "If you fear high-handedness from your wives, remind them [of the teachings of God], then ignore them when you go to bed, then hit them." When coupled with Q2:223, "Your wives are your fields, so go into your fields whichever way you like," makes one wonder if the Qur'an sanctions abuse within marriage. Report 2142 in Sunan Abu-Dawud's Kitab Al-Nikah records the Prophet saying that "a man will not be asked as to why he beat his wife." However, in report 139 of the same chapter, the Prophet says regarding wives: "Give them food what you have for yourself, and clothe them by which you clothe yourself, and do not beat them, and do not revile them." With contradictions such as these, how do practitioners of Islam reconcile them?

Though there seem to be more reported incidences of maid abuse than wife abuse in Singapore, the number of organisations dedicated to dealing with domestic violence in Muslim households tells us otherwise. Organisations such as Singapore's pioneer family violence specialist centre (PAVE), Association of Women for Action and Research (AWARE), and Persatuan Pemudi Islam Singapura (PPIS) actively provide support services for victims and perpetrators of domestic violence. These organisations also run programmes to educate the public in promoting, maintaining, and developing the well-being of family units. In a talk organised by AWARE, the audience shared that it was not enough to work with the women, but engaging the abusers was also necessary to tear down the concept of toxic masculinity.[65] In her article, "A Perspective on Domestic

---

[65] Shafeeqah Ahmad Rosli, "Ramadan Talk with Women and Law in Islam (WALI): Violence in Muslim Marital Homes – What is to be done?" *Association of Women for Action and Research*, published June 13, 2018,

Violence in the Muslim Community," Salma Elkadi Abugideiri believes that the way to curb this taboo trend is to increase public education on the dynamics of domestic abuse and its impact on the family for both community leaders and their members.[66] Likewise, Filzah Sumartono, a Project Coordinator with AWARE, believes that the "community must continue to recognise and consistently reject attitudes that excuse and enable violence."

Q4:24 appears to give the license to men to beat their wives into submission. PAVE has seen cases where Muslim men believe that it was their right to beat their wives and where women believe their husbands were allowed to.[67] A controversial article published on October 13, 2017 in the local Malay language newspaper, *Berita Harian*, caused an uproar within the Malay community. Written by Ustaz Mohd Zaid, Islamic scholar and Head of Dakwah Division and Imam Executive of Al-Mawaddah Mosque, the article teaches "How to Handle a Stubborn Wife." Although he suggests limits to the extent of the beating, damage was duly done. Muslim Member of Parliament (MP) and the Parliamentary Secretary for the Ministry of Education and the Ministry of Social and Family Development, Associate Professor Muhammad Faishal Ibrahim, was quick to refute the article. He said:

> We do not condone spousal abuse or violence in any form, whether within or outside of the family context. Marriage is a life-long partnership between man and wife built on mutual love and respect, and thus our duty as husbands is to love and respect our wives, in the same way we ask them to love and respect us. It is common for couples to have conflicts and disagreements from time to time. If couples are unable to resolve these issues, they should seek help rather than resort to violence.[68]

---

https://www.aware.org.sg/2018/06/ramadan-talk-with-women-and-law-in-islam-wali-violence-in-muslim-marital-homes-what-is-to-be-done/.
[66] Salma Elkadi Abugideiri, "A Perspective on Domestic Violence in the Muslim Community," *Working Together* (Fall 2005): 4.
[67] Adisti Jalani, "Clear Statements on Islam's Position on Marriage and Violence Welcomed," *The Straits Times*, published October 21, 2017, https://www.straitstimes.com/forum/letters-in-print/clear-statements-on-islams-position-on-marriage-and-violence-welcomed.
[68] Nur Asyiqin Mohamad Salleh, "Violence not acceptable in any form, says Senior Parliamentary Secretary Faishal Ibrahim," *The Straits Times*, published October 15, 2017, https://www.straitstimes.com/singapore/violence-not-acceptable-in-any-form-says-senior-parliamentary-secretary-faishal-ibrahim.

Similarly, Ustaz Irwan Hadi (Deputy Director, Religious Policy and Regulation of the Office of Mufti, MUIS) quoted Tabi'in[69] Atho' bin Abi Rabah whose interpretation he believed was the closest to the example of the Prophet. According to Ustaz Hadi, the Tabi'in's interpretation of the term "wadhribuhunna" only expresses displeasure and anger (yaghdab 'alaiha) instead of physically hitting.[70] This interpretation in his opinion is the most appropriate for that Qur'anic verse.

Divorce

Divorce is allowed only twice according to Q2:229 on the condition that each time the wives are taken care of in an acceptable manner until released. Additionally, the man is not to take back any bride-gift in a divorce, but if the woman is the initiator, she may opt to give something for her release. The woman shall be paid fair maintenance;[71] however, she will lose custody of all the children to the father[72] after they have been weaned.[73]

Asghar Ali Engineer argues that the triple *talak* (instant and irrefutable divorce) was strictly prohibited by the Prophet Mohammad and it became known as the *talaq-i-bid'a* (innovated form of divorce) or even as 'sinful form of divorce'.[74] However, he notes that it is still the most practised form of divorce in India and elsewhere. He goes on to explain that, although the Islamic revolution had abolished this practice, it crept back into the male dominated Islamic system. On the other hand, Engineer is confident that the *talak* pronounced in the Qur'an is a very fair one for the woman as it prescribes independent arbiters for both the woman and the husband. Unfortunately, he concedes, it is never practised.

---

[69] Considered amongst the best generations after the "Sahāba" (companions of Prophet Mohammad), a "Tabi'in" is one who has seen a "Sahāba" and was a rightly guided Muslim who also died as one. Accessed July 18, 2019,
http://www.mailofislam.com/tabieen.html.
[70] Irwan Hadi, reply to "My spouse is hitting me as he says I am not obeying him. I heard the Qur'an permit this. Is it true?" Facebook, October 14, 2017,
https://www.facebook.com/awaresg/posts/last-friday-an-advice-column-written-by-ustaz-mohammad-zaid-isahak-was-published/1679549372057495/.
[71] Q2:241.
[72] Q65:6-7.
[73] Q2:223.
[74] Engineer, "Status of Muslim Women," 298.

In Singapore, a man may pronounce *talak* on his wife in the presence of two witnesses. The man has the unilateral right without needing any proof for grounds of divorce. The Syariah Court will take this pronouncement into consideration when they initiate divorce proceedings. On the other hand, the woman may initiate divorce in one of three ways: *khuluk* (divorce by compensation), *taklik* (divorce by breach of marriage condition) or *fasakh* (annulment of marriage). Should the wife be unable to invoke a divorce via any of the three ways, the couple may seek the court's arbitration.

Pronouncing *talak* upon wives caught off-guard causes them much emotional distress. In August 2017, the Singapore Parliament amended the Administration of Muslim Law Act (AMLA) with the addition of a clause for men to be able to apply for divorce without first pronouncing *talak*. Though AMLA has no provisions against the triple *talak*, lawyer Halijah believes that Singapore's legal infrastructures protecting wives have served as a deterrent for men to abuse the triple *talak*.[75]

The stigma of being a divorcee still runs deep within the Malay community. Known as a *janda,* she "is still viewed with suspicion and sometimes contempt."[76] Seen as one who has failed in a previous marriage or as one who is entering upon the new marriage not a virgin, she is only valued as a used product. Programmes for remarriage and stepfamilies facilitated by the PPIS Vista Sakinah Centre are highly encouraged.[77] These programmes aim at helping to nurture stepfamilies towards harmony, tranquility, and stability. Personalised couple consultation sessions aid couples in getting to know their strengths, needs, and goals with the focus on building a "resilient stepfamily that lasts a lifetime." There are also workshops for children to help prepare them for the remarriage and new stepfamily dynamics.

---

[75] Melody Zaccheus and Janice Tai, "Getting Muslim Men to Think Twice About Divorce," *The Straits Times*, published September 19, 2017, https://www.straitstimes.com/singapore/getting-muslim-men-to-think-twice-about-divorce.

[76] Sumartono and Thomas, *Growing Up Perempuan*, 267-268.

[77] "Remarriage Preparation Programmes," Registrar of Muslim Marriages, last updated May 10, 2019, https://www.romm.gov.sg/resources/remarriage_preparation_programme.asp.

In Singapore, it is mandatory to attend marriage counselling programmes before couples are allowed to file for divorce. This new initiative aimed at strengthening marriages within the Muslim community has paid off.[78] 2017 saw the number of Muslim divorces fall to a 5-year low with 1587 couples throwing in the towel. This is 3.8% lower than 2016's 1637 divorces. Besides this new initiative, another possible reason for the positive result may be the Singapore government's increased support for couples in their marriages in terms of marriage preparation and marriage counselling sessions. Sadly, though, 23.5% of the total Muslim divorces filed were because of a cheating spouse.[79]

Conclusion

After considering the Qur'an and the position of Muslim women in Singapore in terms of their status, hijab, marriage, polygyny, domestic abuse, and divorce, it is fair to conclude that these women enjoy an equality that is reasonable within the confines of moderate Islam. From the many Muslim women in positions of political power and academia, the Singapore Government and the Singapore Muslim community have done well to support gender equality that is clearly guided by the country's constitutions and advocacy of the Syariah laws.

However, more can be done to improve harmony within the family units and to protect the women. To do this, government agencies and religious bodies must continue to recognise the context of Singapore's diverse society and Islam within that context. Norshahril opines that to progress, Muslims must look beyond theological arguments to understand contemporary problems.[80] If it is to be believed that Allah has indeed created men and women to be equal, then it is as much a woman's responsibility as a man's to take up the study of religious doctrines so as to be able to participate in reasonable and acceptable interpretations.

Promoting gender equality through educating both Muslim men and women is vital. It is an endeavour that must not be limited to only women. Men must learn and understand their roles and

---

[78] Cara Wong, "Muslim Divorces at 5-year Low," *The Straits Times*, published July 11, 2018, https://www.straitstimes.com/singapore/muslim-divorces-at-5-year-low.
[79] Ibid.
[80] Norshahril Saat, *Faith, Authority and the Malays: The Ulama in Contemporary Singapore* (Singapore: Select Publishing, 2015), 36.

responsibilities in their family nucleus as both loving husbands and doting fathers. Women on the other hand must continue their pursuit of learning and finding what it means for her to be a Muslim woman: her worth, her position, and her place in the family as well as in society. She must be given the opportunity to be empowered and valued as an equal created by Allah as a child of Adam. Filzah Sumartono suggests that more conversations with Muslim women about their roles are much needed.[81] She proposes that they will need that revolutionary courage to give a voice to injustices that lie hidden behind closed doors. She advocates a need for a paradigm shift in the ideas and gender roles so that the potential of Muslim women will not be hindered and that they will be able to enjoy a greater freedom. Only with these positive influences, religious institutions, and government support will the treatment of Muslim women in Singapore undergo even more favourable reforms towards true gender equality.

Bibliography

Abugideiri, Salma Elkadi. "A Perspective on Domestic Violence in the Muslim Community." *Working Together* (Fall 2005): 4.

Amal, C. M. "Current Issues Affecting Muslim Women." In *Ministry to Muslim Women: Longing to Call Them Sisters*, edited by Fran Love and Jeleta Eckheart, 11-20. Pasadena, CA: William Carey Library, 2000.

Badawi, Jamal A. "Gender Equity in Islam." WhyIslam.org, https://www.whyislam.org/social-issues/gender-equity-in-islam/.

Council of Ex-Muslims Singapore. "Of Tudungs and Attempts at Salvaging My Faith." Accessed February 14, 2019, http://cemsg.org/ex-muslim-testimonies-006-of-tudongs-and-attempts-at-salvaging-my-faith/.

Department of Statistics Singapore. "Latest Data." Population and Population Structure. Last updated July 17, 2019, https://www.singstat.gov.sg/whats-new/latest-data

—— "Key Indicators of Resident Population." Singapore Census of Population 2010, Statistical Release 1: Demographic

---

[81] Filzah Sumartono and Firqin Sumartono, "How the Role of Malay Women Has—or Hasn't—Evolved." *Association of Women for Action and Research*, published July 27, 2017, https://www.aware.org.sg/2017/07/how-the-role-of-malay-women-has-or-hasnt-evolved/.

Characteristics, Education, Language and Religion. Last updated April 25, 2018, https://www.singstat.gov.sg/publications/cop2010/census10 _stat_release1.

—— "Religion." Singapore Census of Population 2010, Statistical Release 1: Demographic Characteristics, Education, Language and Religion. Last updated May 9, 2018, https://www.singstat.gov.sg/publications/cop2010/census10 _stat_release1.

—— Statistics on Marriages and Divorces, 2017, https://www.singstat.gov.sg/publications/population/marri ages-and-divorces.

Encyclopaedia Britannica. "Hadith." Accessed July 15, 2019, https://www.britannica.com/topic/Hadith#ref68899.

Engineer, Asghar Ali. "Status of Muslim Women." *Economic and Political Weekly* 29, no. 6 (1994): 297-300.

Hadi, Irwan. "My spouse is hitting me as he says I am not obeying him. I heard the Qur'an permit this. Is it true?" Facebook, October 14, 2017. https://www.facebook.com/awaresg/posts/last-friday-an-advice-column-written-by-ustaz-mohammad-zaid-isahak-was-published/1679549372057495/.

Hjärpe, Jan. "The Attitude of Islamic Fundamentalism Toward the Question of Women in Islam." In *Women in Islamic Societies: Social Attitudes and Historical Perspectives,* edited by Bo Utas, 12-25. London: Curzon Press, 1983.

Jalani, Adisti. "Clear Statements on Islam's Position on Marriage and Violence Welcomed." *The Straits Times,* published October 21, 2017, https://www.straitstimes.com/forum/letters-in-print/clear-statements-on-islams-position-on-marriage-and-violence-welcomed.

Klingorová, Kamila, and Havlíček, Tomáš. "Religion and Gender Inequality: The Status of Women in the Societies of World Religions." *Moravian Geographical Reports* 23 (2015): 2-11, https://www.researchgate.net/publication 279526649_Religion_and_gender_inequality_The_status_of_ women_in_the_societies_of_world_religions.

Lemu, B. Aisha, and Fatima Heeren. *Woman in Islam.* London: International Islamic Publishing House, 1978.

Mohammad, Nabilah. "More Than One: A Look at Polygamy In Muslim Marriages In Singapore," *Research on Islamic and Malay Affairs*, published January 17, 2019, http://www.rima.sg/commentary/more-than-one-a-look-at-polygamy-in-muslim-marriages-in-singapore/#.XS7X8C2p18V.

National Heritage Board. "National Pledge." Our Pledge. Last updated November 5, 2018, https://www.nhb.gov.sg/what-we-do/our-work/community-engagement/education/resources/national-symbols/national-pledge.

National Library Board Singapore. "Singapore Presidents." Personalities. Accessed February 14, 2019, http://eresources.nlb.gov.sg/infopedia/articles/SIP_808_200 4-12-28.html.

Noor Aisha Binte Abdul Rahman. "Convention on the Elimination of Discrimination Against Women and the Prospect of Development of Muslim Personal Law in Singapore." *Journal of Muslim Minority Affairs* 34, no. 1 (2014): 45-65.

Owen, Diana L. "The Qur'an, The Hadith, and Women." In *Voices Behind the Veil: The World of Islam Through the Eyes of Women*, edited by Ergun Mehmet Carer, 61-92. Grand Rapids, MI: Kregel Publications, 2003.

Parshall, Phil, and Julie Parshall. *Lifting the Veil: The World of Muslim Women*. Waynesboro, GA: Gabriel Publishing, 2002.

People's Action Party. "Women Members of Parliament." Women's Wing. Accessed July 15, 2019, https://www.pap.org.sg/womens-wing/members-of-parliament.

Rahmat, Hadijah. "Aura Hawa." Facebook, October 8, 2015, https://www.facebook.com/ppis.sg/videos/10168363883553 60/. Registrar of Muslim Marriages. "Marriage Preparation Programmes." Marriage Info, Preparing for Marriage. Last Updated October 5, 2018, https://www.romm.gov.sg/resources/marriage_preparation. asp.

—— "Maskahwin & Marriage Expenses." Marriage Info, Preparing for Marriage. Last Updated April 2, 2015, https://www.romm.gov.sg/about_marriage/romm_ maskahwin_expenses.asp.

——— "Polygyny." Marriage Info, Other Types of Marriages. Last Updated October 5, 2018, https://www.romm.gov.sg/about_marriage/romm_polygyny.asp

Saat, Norshahril. *Faith, Authority and the Malays: The Ulama in Contemporary Singapore*. Singapore: Select Publishing, 2015.

Sahih Bukhari. "Haddith Books." Searchtruth.com. Accessed July 15, 2019 https://www.searchtruth.com/book_display.php?book=62&translator=1&start=120.

Sahih Muslim. "Haddith Books." Searchtruth.com. Accessed July 15, 2019, https://www.searchtruth.com/book_display.php?book=8&translator=2&start=240

Shafeeqah Ahmad Rosli. "Ramadan Talk with Women and Law in Islam (WALI): Violence in Muslim Marital Homes – What is to be done?" *Association of Women for Action and Research*. Published June 13, 2018, https://www.aware.org.sg/2018/06/ramadan-talk-with-women-and-law-in-islam-wali-violence-in-muslim-marital-homes-what-is-to-be-done/.

Singapore National University. "Tudung Girls: Unveiling Muslim Women's Identity in Singapore." Singapore Research Nexus, Faculty of Arts and Social Sciences, May 8, 2018, http://www.fas.nus.edu.sg/srn/archives/56663.

Sookhdeo, Rosemary. *Secrets Behind the Burqa*. McLean, VA: Isaac Publishing, 2008.

Sumartono, Filzah, and Margaret Thomas, eds. *Growing Up Perempuan* Singapore: AWARE Singapore, 2018.

Sumartono, Filzah, and Firqin Sumartono. "How the Role of Malay Women Has—or Hasn't—Evolved." *Association of Women for Action and Research*. Published July 27, 2017, https://www.aware.org.sg/2017/07/how-the-role-of-malay-women-has-or-hasnt-evolved/.

Sumartono, Firqin. "Poligami – Ikut Sunnah Atau Nafsu? In Conversation with Chahaya" in *Growing Up Perempuan*, edited by Filzah Sumartono and Maragret Thomas, 209-217. Singapore: AWARE Singapore, 2018.

Sunan Abu-Dawud. "Haddith Books." Searchtruth.com. Accessed July 15, 2019, https://www.searchtruth.com/book_display.php?book=32&translator=3&start=50.

Tan, Jeanette. "Playwright Alfian Sa'at Explains Quite Perfectly the Complexity of the Tudung/Hijab Issue in Singapore." *Mothership*, published April 6, 2017, https://mothership.sg/2017/04/playwright-alfian-saat-explains-quite-perfectly-the-complexity-of-the-tudunghijab-issue-in-spore/.

Wong, Cara. "Muslim Divorces at 5-year Low," *The Straits Times,* July 11, 2018, https://www.straitstimes.com/singapore/muslim-divorces-at-5-year-low.

Swartley, Keith, ed. *Encountering the World of Islam.* Colorado Springs, CO: Authentic Publishing, 2005.

Wu, Ridzuan. "The Confusing Use of Terminology." In *Tudung: Beyond Face Value*, edited by Salinah Aliman, 19. Singapore: Bridges Books, 2002.

Zaccheus, Melody, and Tai, Janice. "Getting Muslim Men to Think Twice About Divorce." *The Straits Times*, published September 19, 2017. https://www.straitstimes.com/singapore/getting-muslim-men-to-think-twice-about-divorce.

WOMEN AND SHARI'A LAW

The England and Wales Scene

Jane Wiseman[1]

Introduction

The purpose of this paper is to present a critical study of the debate surrounding *The Independent Review into the Application of Shari'a Law in England and Wales, presented to Parliament by the Secretary of State for the Home Department by Command of Her Majesty*, published in February 2018. In May 2016, Theresa May, the then Home Secretary, commissioned an Independent Review of Shari'a law in the UK. It set out to enquire whether the activities particularly of Shari'a councils in the UK are compatible with British law. The focus was on whether Shari'a law is being misused or misapplied, and more significantly, whether there were discriminatory practices against women who are the main users of Shari'a councils. This paper will include a consideration of the Independent Review, its membership, methodology, and findings. The paper will also include a consideration of Islam in the UK, Shari'a councils, Islamic law, and the views of women's rights groups before drawing some conclusions.

The Independent Review

The Independent Review was set up in 2018 to evaluate Shari'a law, particularly as used within Shari'a councils in England and Wales. The Review set out to consider whether Shari'a law is being misused or applied in a way "that is incompatible with the domestic law in England and Wales and particularly if there were discriminatory practices against women who use Shari'a councils."[2]

---

[1] Jane has a MA in Applied Theology and together with her husband has been in church leadership for fourteen years. She lives in Southampton and has three adult children.
[2] *The Independent Review into the Application of Sharia Law in England and Wales*, published February 2018, http://assets.publishing.service.gov.uk/government/uploads/system/uploads/attachment_d

191

The Review was set up to focus exclusively on the work of Shari'a councils in England and Wales and not to look at Shari'a practises in general. Shari'a is an all-encompassing term that includes not only "law in the western sense" of criminal law and judicial procedure but other aspects of life, including religious observance, fasting, prayer, and pilgrimages. Shari'a is a written body of law, which has "developed on the basis of a diversity of opinions among jurists in the classical period of Islam."[3] It dates from the 8th century and is rooted in the teachings of the Qur'an. The Review acknowledges that the councils are voluntary organizations with "no legal status and no legal binding authority under civil law," but accepts that they fulfil an important role for Muslims.[4] Shari'a is a source of guidance to many Muslims but the councils themselves have no legal jurisdiction in England and Wales. The Review defined Shari'a councils as a "voluntary local organisation of scholars who see themselves or are seen by their communities as authorised to offer advice to Muslims principally in the area of religious marriage and divorce."[5]

Mona Siddiqui, Professor of Islamic and Interreligious studies at Edinburgh University, chaired the Review. She was supported by a panel of experts that included an experienced family law barrister, a retired High Court judge, and a specialist family law solicitor. The panel was advised by two religious and theological experts. The Review collected evidence both written and oral from a wide variety of sources. This included users of Shari'a councils, the councils themselves, women's rights groups, academics, lawyers, and other interested parties. The review panel also visited a number of Shari'a councils across England to speak to both council members and men and women who use them.

The Review comments that one of the challenges was gathering evidence from the men and women who use Shari'a councils. It proved difficult to get many of the women who'd had negative experiences to come forward.[6] After the Review was launched, there was a boycott instigated by a number of women's

---

ata/file/678478/6.4152_HO_CPFG_Report_into_Sharia_Law_in_the_UK_WEB.pdf,accessed April, 2019.
[3] Ibid., 4.
[4] Ibid., 4.
[5] Ibid., 4.
[6] Ibid., 7.

organisations opposed to the Review's terms of reference and to the selection of some of its panel and advisers. [7]

The Report discovered that the vast majority of users were women, indeed over 90%, and most seeking an Islamic divorce. The Review was concerned that the "rise of extremism" was facilitated by a lack of social and political integration, and that the activity of Shari'a councils keeps Muslims isolated and separate from "wider British citizenship and life."[8] The Review's strategy was to encourage integration by "seeking out examples of best practice in relation to governance, transparency, and assuring compliance and compatibility with UK law."[9] The Review produced a number of findings and observations with recommendations.

Recommendations presented by the *Independent Review*
The principal recommendation of the Review was that Islamic marriages should be registered as civil unions. This would ensure that all Islamic marriages are civilly registered and recognised in the eyes of UK law. An Islamic marriage, as described by Dr Mark Durie, is not a religious ceremony solemnised by a celebrant, but a verbal contract (which may be written down) enacted between two men: the groom and the bride's *walī* or male guardian. It requires a payment of money or property, the *mahr*, by the groom to the bride.[10] It is also proposed that there should be minor amendments to legislation on divorce. By linking Islamic marriage to civil marriage, it ensures, says the Report, that a greater number of women will have the full protection afforded to them by UK family law and civil divorce.[11] Currently, religious marriages that take place in England and Wales, which are not accompanied by civil registration, are treated as non-marriages. A Muslim woman who is going through a divorce has no protection under UK family law. Couples who do not have a civil registration alongside an Islamic marriage do not have the same legal entitlements should the relationship end. A further impact of changing the marriage laws to ensure registration of Muslim

---

[7] Ibid., 7.
[8] Mark Durie, "Managing Shari'a Marriages in Britain," published March 9, 2019, https://interfaceinstitute.org/2019/03/09/managing-shariah-marriages-in-britain.
[9] Ibid.
[10] Ibid.
[11] *The Independent Review*, 6.

marriages would be to prohibit informal polygamy through multiple Islamic marriages.[12]

The second recommendation was to recognise that cultural change is required within Muslim communities so that they acknowledge women's rights in civil law, especially as regards marriage and divorce.[13] The Review panel acknowledged that women (and men) often face huge cultural barriers when seeking a divorce, and for this reason it is imperative that they are aware of their rights under domestic law and are not afraid to come forward.[14] This would require educational programmes to educate and inform women of their rights and responsibilities. The Review panel considered the best way of raising awareness of these issues would be through wide ranging campaigns, advice centres, NGOs (non-profit, voluntary citizens' group), and other women's groups. Alongside this is "the need to ensure that Shari'a councils operate within the law and comply with best practise, non-discriminatory processes and existing regulatory structures."[15]

Recommendations 1 and 2 of this Report aim to gradually reduce the use and need for Shari'a councils.[16] In the meantime, however, the Review panel recommended "regulation of Shari'a councils." The panel recognised that evidence from the review indicates that the practises and standards of services vary between and even within Shari'a councils. One member of the panel was not in agreement. Recommendation 3 proposed the creation of a body that would set up the process for councils to regulate themselves. That body would design a code of practice for Shari'a councils to accept and implement. The Review put it this way: "We propose the creation of a body by the state with a code of practice for Shari'a councils to accept and implement. This body would include both Shari'a council members and specialist family lawyers."[17] Amber Rudd responded in this way,

> Sharia law has no jurisdiction in the UK and we would not facilitate or endorse regulation, which could present

---

[12] Ibid., 17.
[13] Ibid., 18.
[14] Ibid.
[15] Ibid., 6.
[16] Ibid., 19.
[17] Ibid., 20.

councils as an alternative to UK laws... The Government considers that the proposal to create a State-facilitated or endorsed regulation scheme for Sharia councils would confer upon them legitimacy as alternative forms of dispute resolution. The Government does not consider there to be a role for the State to act in this way. Britain has a long tradition of freedom of worship and religious tolerance and regulation could add legitimacy to the perception of the existence of a parallel legal system even though the outcomes of Sharia Councils have no standing in civil law, as the independent review has made clear.[18]

Islam in Britain

In 2018, the Office for National Statistics estimated the Muslim population of the UK to be 3.3 million, or 5.5% of the population.[19] The growth rate is ten times that of the rest of British society. Islam cannot really be compared to other faiths. It is an all-encompassing system and way of life that impacts all areas of life from family to politics, to education. The Review was taken at a time when there were and continue to be heated debates on Shari'a law, concerns over the "Islamization of Britain," and the discriminatory nature of Islamic law.[20]

In a report written in 2017, Kern described some of the recent effects of his description of the "Islamisation of Britain" for the UK. He puts the Muslim population of Britain as exceeding 4.1 million in 2017 to be around 6.3% of the overall population of 64 million, according to a recent study on the growth of the Muslim population in Europe.[21] Kern believes the challenges of Islam and Islam related issues can be categorized into several broad themes including: extremism and security implications of British jihadists, the continuing spread of Islamic Shari'a law in Britain, sexual

---

[18] Amber Rudd, "Home Office to Consider the Report's Findings," https://www.familylawweek.co.uk/site.aspx?i=ed187811, accessed September, 2019.
[19] These UK statistics are taken from the Office for National Statistics, https://www.ons.gov.uk/aboutus/transparencyandgovernance/freedomofinformationfoi/muslimpopulationintheuk, accessed September, 2019.
[20] Soeren Kern, "The Islamization of Britain," https://www.gatestoneinstitute.org/11648/britain-islamization-2017, accessed April, 2019.
[21] Ibid.

exploitation of British children by Muslim gangs, Muslim integration into British society, and the failures of British multiculturalism.

He writes that, according to The Sunday Times, Muslim pupils outnumber Christian children in more than 30 church schools, including one Church of England primary school that has a "100% Muslim population." St. Thomas in Werneth, Oldham, is reported to have no Christian pupils, while at Staincliffe Church of England Junior School in Batley, West Yorkshire, 98% of pupils "come from a Muslim background."[22] The Church of England estimated that about 20 of its schools had more Muslim pupils than Christians and 15 Roman Catholic schools had majority Muslim pupils. The report also described how British security services had prevented 13 potential terror attacks since June 2013, according to Assistant Commissioner Mark Rowley, the UK's most senior counterterrorism police officer. He also said that there were 500 live counterterror investigations at any given time, and that investigators have been arresting terror suspects at a rate of close to one a day since 2014. The official threat level for international terrorism in the UK has stood at severe—meaning an attack is "highly likely"—for more than two years.[23]

In March 2017, the BBC announced that it would begin outsourcing production of Songs of Praise, a Sunday worship program that has been produced in-house for 55 years.[24] Critics of the move said they feared that Songs of Praise will lose its Christian focus in favour of Islam. Anglican priest Lynda Rose said a recent Songs of Praise episode featuring a segment about the Muslim faith, including Church of England children visiting a mosque, exemplified the "Islamization of the BBC." More than 6,000 people signed an online petition calling for MPs to investigate the BBC after it appointed Fatima Salaria as the BBC's head of religious programming – the second Muslim in a row to hold the post. Rev Lynda Rose, CEO of Voice for Justice UK, told Premier Christian Radio: "The UK is actually a Christian country, it's established as such by statue, all our laws, our traditions, our culture is founded on

---

[22] Ibid.
[23] Ibid.
[24] Ibid.

Christian values, so it would seem entirely right that Christianity be given priority air time."[25]

It is also a time when Muslim activists are demanding Shari'a law replace UK common law in a number of UK cities, and it is reported that there are now some 130 Shari'a law courts.[26] For the Review, "A crucial assumption is that the practice of Shari'a councils can be made compliant and compatible with British law."[27] There are many who would disagree with this statement.

Shari'a Law

In the Report, Shari'a is described as an all-encompassing term, which includes civil law, religious practises, and most areas of everyday life.[28] The word "Shari'a" (Way) is found once in the Qur'an (Sura 45:18), wherein Allah is speaking. Muslims therefore consider this to be divinely inspired and carries authority.[29] Thorneycroft explains that to the Muslim, Shari'a is the path to be followed and that Shari'a encompasses matters of criminal law, judicial procedure, and quasi-legal matters such as marriage and economics. It also regulates spiritual and moral matters.[30] She emphasises that Shari'a is viewed as a means to ensure the well-being of the Islamic community as a whole and concludes, "In traditional Islam there is no other kind of law apart from this revealed holy law. As such this law is considered immutable – it cannot be abrogated or altered."[31]

Chapman highlights the importance of law in Islam; "Islamic law is the epitome of Islamic thought, the most typical manifestation of the Islamic way of life, the core and kernel of Islam itself."[32] It is useful here to consider the background to Shari'a and Islamic law.

---

[25] Interview with Rev Lynda Rose, https://www.premier.org.uk/News/UK/Christian-group-hands-12-000-strong-petition-to-BBC-over-biased-religious-programming, accessed September, 2019.

[26] Kern, "The Islamization of Britain."

[27] Durie, "Managing Shari'a Marriages in Britain."

[28] *The Independent Review*, 3.

[29] Taken from the Qur'an online, https://www.quranexplorer.com/quran, accessed May, 2019.

[30] Charlotte Thorneycroft, *Islam and Human Rights: The Compatibility of Shari'a Law with the Declaration of Human Rights*. Occasional Paper No: 8 (Northwood: LST, 2007).

[31] Ibid., 3.

[32] Colin Chapman, *Cross and Crescent: Responding to the Challenges of Islam* (Nottingham: InterVarsity Press, 2007), 107.

Muslim Law Schools

Islamic Law is highly detailed and is drawn from a number of sources; the Qur'an and the Hadith (which clarifies and elaborates the teaching of the Qur'an). The *ijima* is the 'consensus' of scholars who formulate legal precepts and *qiyas* the considered opinion based on analogy. The four main schools of law developed over time and differ according to the emphasis placed on the interpretation of the four sources. They are named after the founder of the school and predominate in different areas, and vary in how conservative or liberal their construal of the law is. In the UK, because of the varying countries of origin of British Muslims, these different law schools are strongly represented by first generation Muslims, and in successive generations, there can be a tendency for secularisation or radicalisation.

Charlotte Thorneycroft highlights that a crucial principle in interpreting the Qur'an is that of abrogation. The Qur'an was revealed to Muhammad over a period of twenty years. During that time, many of the verses say different things on the same subject, which can lead to confusion and differences in interpretation of the same verses. To avoid any conflict, abrogation is the principle whereby the last verse revealed to Muhammad takes precedent over earlier revelations and hence carry more authority. There are different voices in Islam and hence different interpretations of the Islamic law.[33]

Islamic Law and Women

Shari'a law is drawn from the Qur'an and, if interpreted by a conservative scholar, will be discriminatory towards women. It has been interesting to look at the Qur'an and the hadith and some of the commentaries that are available online. It is important for Christians who are interested in understanding and connecting with local Muslims that they are conversant with the Qur'an, which plays such an integral role in the life of many Muslims. The Qur'an has some controversial views when it comes to women. If taken literally as the word of God and not disseminated through the lens of history and culture, some of the statements appear harsh and incompatible with today's western British ethos. Sura 4:3 states, whilst referring to orphans, "Marry women of your choice, two or three or four." This

---

[33] Thorneycroft, *Islam and Human Rights*, 3.

could be used to allow polygamy for a strict Muslim male.[34] Plus *Sura* 43:70, "Enter Paradise, you and your wives, in happiness."[35]

The Tafsir commentary elaborates on this and states, "no more than four" according to Al-Jalalayn. Sura 4:34 states that "Men are the caretakers of women as men have been provisioned by Allah over women." The Tafsir is clear that "Men are in charge, they have authority over women disciplining them and keeping them in check." Sura 4:34 then explains how to deal with women who are disobedient who are to be "scourged."[36] The Tafsir, Al-Jalalayn, writes, "strike them but not violently," others allow for slapping retaliation.[37] The Qur'an teaches that one male's portion equals two females and hence confers a lower status on women.[38] Thorneycroft explains that Muslim women are not allowed to marry non-Muslim men, but according to Bukhari, men are free to marry Muslim, Jewish, or Christian women.[39] It is knowledge and experience of the Qur'an that have caused some women's groups to react strongly, especially to the Review.[40]

The Work of Baroness Cox and her Private Member's Bills

Baroness Cox is a crossbench member of the British House of Lords and the founder and CEO of an organisation called Humanitarian Aid Relief Trust (HART). Since 2011, Baroness Cox has introduced two Private Member's Bills into the House of Lords. She believes that we are fortunate to live in a democracy that enshrines the principle of equality before the law but states that many women in the UK are not experiencing the rights to which they are entitled. She is behind a campaign, "Equal and Free," supported by a range of individuals and organisations concerned with the suffering of vulnerable women in the UK who experience religiously sanctioned gender discrimination.[41] The Campaign states that,

---

[34] https://www.quranexplorer.com/quran, accessed April, 2019.
[35] Ibid.
[36] https://www.altafsir.com/Tafasir.asp?tMadhNo=1&tTafsirNo=74&tSoraNo=4&tAyahNo=34&tDisplay=yes&UserProfile=0&LanguageId=2, accessed April, 2019.
[37] Ibid.
[38] Thorneycroft, *Islam and Human Rights*, 6.
[39] Ibid., 9.
[40] *The Independent Review*, 36-37.
[41] Equal and Free – the Campaign, http://equalandfree.org/about-the-campaign, accessed September, 2019.

although women from any faith tradition—or none—may suffer abuse and other problems associated with dysfunctional families, the plight of those in Islamic communities can be exacerbated by the application of established Shari'a law principles "which inherently discriminate against women and girls."[42] The Campaign is supported by a number of women's support agencies including the Muslim Women's Advisory Council, Muslims Facing Tomorrow and Basira (British Arabs Supporting Universal Women's Rights).

Baroness Cox has warned of the danger of a parallel legal system in the work of Shari'a councils. She was one of the first members of Parliament to alert the public to the problem of quasi-legal systems working in the UK and how they affect women negatively. In a recent email communication with Baroness Cox, in response to a question, she explained, "In a free society, individuals must be able to organise their affairs according to their own principles, whether religious or otherwise. Attempting to operate a parallel legal jurisdiction is another matter altogether."[43] She wrote that, although there are legitimate areas of operation for Shari'a councils in the UK, concerns remain that some are going well beyond their legal remit. There is also evidence that some of these tribunals are embedding discrimination against women in a way which conflicts with the principle of equality before the law. She said that such discrimination could take many forms, including inequality in access to divorce (for men often effectively free and unconditional), polygamy (practiced by men who have multiple 'wives' and numerous children), discriminatory child custody policies and inheritance laws, and the implicit sanctioning of domestic violence. Baroness Cox has, since 2011, introduced two Private Member's Bills into the House of Lords to draw attention to these concerns, having had experience of working alongside those affected by abuse, as well as a range of women's rights organisations and parliamentarians of all parties.[44] On Monday July 10, a new Bill was introduced into the House of Lords to protect vulnerable women from religiously sanctioned gender discrimination. The new Bill is entitled the Marriage Act (1949) (Amendment) Bill. Baroness Cox's Private Member's seeks to protect British women in polygamous households

---

[42] Ibid.

[43] Email received from Baroness Cox in response to a personal question, dated April 4, 2019.

[44] Information on the Bill introduced by Baroness Cox entitled the Marriage Act 1949 (Amendment Bill), http://equalandfree.org, accessed September, 2019.

or those who have had a religious-only marriage, and find upon divorce they have little or no rights in terms of finance or property.[45]

Baroness Cox is pushing for legal registration of Muslim weddings and states that almost two thirds of Muslim women are not legally married under UK domestic law and remain vulnerable and unprotected. The resulting suffering is worsened by the nature of the closed communities in which many of them live, where there is great pressure not to seek "outside" professional help, which might be deemed to bring "shame" on the family.[46]

In a speech to the House of Lords in February 2019, Baroness Cox reminded those present that she has introduced Private Member's Bills for the last eight years in an attempt to highlight the suffering from gender discrimination in the application of Shariʻa law of many Muslim women. She explained that many had come to her desperate, destitute, and even suicidal following asymmetrical divorce inflicted by their husbands.[47] In May 2019, Baroness Cox raised the question for debate, "what progress has been made in the prevention of grooming gangs in Rotherham and elsewhere; and what assistance they have offered to victims and their families?" There has as yet not been an answer. The Campaign states, "While consecutive debates within the Houses of Parliament have sought to expose the often deeply humiliating, and totally unacceptable cases of gender discrimination, the Government has so-far failed to provide an adequate response." There are atrocities involving Muslim grooming gangs that are now beginning to reach the media news. Baroness Cox has been involved in speaking up for some of these cases.[48] Baroness Cox will re-submit her Private Member's Bill

---

[45] Ibid.

[46] Speeches by Baroness Cox on impact of Shari'a, https://hansard.parliament.uk/search/MemberContributions?memberId=3364&startDate =2014-04-04&endDate=2019-04-04&type=Spoken&searchTerm=sharia%20law%20women&outputType=List&partial= False, accessed September, 2019.

[47] https://hansard.parliament.uk/Lords/2019-02-28/debates/9E6C7E1B-4462-47F4-A769-2546C5524403/IslamicCeremonyCivilMarriageRegistration?highlight=sharia%20law %20women#contribution-93960E93-1449-4124-863E-DEB09C5C66A0, accessed September, 2019.

[48] Rotherham Muslim grooming gangs, https://clarionproject.org/kidnapped-teenage-girl-held-for-12-years-by-sex-grooming-gang, accessed September, 2019.

(Marriage Act 1949 [Amendment] Bill) when Parliament returns on October 14, 2019.

In August 2018, Baroness Cox went to visit the Melbourne School of Theology, as described by Peter Riddell.[49] In her presentation, Baroness Cox highlighted the drift towards secular liberalism in western societies and the resulting challenges to minority groups, including Christians. She explained that one of the effects of aggressive secular humanism in the UK is that many Christians now suffer the feeling of discrimination and intimidation. She noted that whilst the majority of UK Muslims are law abiding and hospitable, there is however a "growth of militant Islamists who use the freedoms of democracy to achieve political change and try to destroy democracy and the freedom it enshrines." She drew attention to gender discrimination under Shari'a law. She explained that there are almost 100 unofficial Shari'a councils operating in the UK and she quoted from a human rights report, which stated that "for many British Muslims, Shari'a courts are in practice part of an institutionalised atmosphere of intimidation, backed by the ultimate sanction of a death threat."[50]

Other Opposing and Concerned Voices

A significant number of women's human rights groups and campaigners expressed their "profound concern and disappointment with the terms of reference and the people who were chosen to be part of the review panel."[51] They voiced concern over the existence of parallel and informal justice systems that do not represent women with justice and are discriminatory in effect and intent. They had serious concerns over religious codes of practise that they deemed to be discriminatory, taking place in Shari'a councils and that such a review would legitimise and endorse their existence. They expressed concern of the complete absence of voices of the victims themselves and of women's human rights organisations that have first-hand experience of the human rights violations that take place in Shari'a councils.[52] Maryam Namazie, is an ex-Muslim and British Iranian. She heads up the Council of Ex-Muslims and is a vocal critic of

---

[49] Peter Riddell, "Baroness Cox: Challenging Secularism and Militant Islamism," https://interfaceinstitute.org/2019/01/22/baroness-cox-challenging-secularism-and-militant-islamism-an-ongoing-task, accessed September, 2019.
[50] Ibid.
[51] *The Independent Review*, 29.
[52] Ibid.

areas of life.[64] Riddell further explained that any acceptance of Shari'a is likely to increase fragmentation in Britain and will open the door for demands for further adoption of Shari'a Law and hinted that Rowan Williams is by his own admission "no expert on this" and his "inclination to neatly equate Islamic Law with legal systems of other faiths is superficial and sloppy."[65] In the article, Rowan Williams did not take into account the views of British Muslims and demonstrated lack of expertise when it came to his own personal knowledge of the Qur'an, Islamic history, and diversity.

Ten years later, in February 2018, another Archbishop, Justin Welby, stated that Islamic laws are incompatible with British laws and should never become part of the British legal system. Islamic law has a different background of jurisdiction from the development of UK law.[66] The issue again became controversial when the British Law Society endorsed aspects of Islamic law for Shari'a compliant wills. These were later withdrawn because of inheritance discrepancies and inequality for women.[67]

Conclusion

Currently, there is a big debate in Britain over the whole aspect of accommodating Shari'a law and its compatibility with UK common law. Closer examination of the Qur'an and the writings about women, and listening to Muslim women with first-hand experience of Shari'a, there appears to be some significant areas that are not compatible, especially as regards the Islamic view of women. Baroness Cox includes much evidence from victims of abuse and, through her campaign "Equal and Free," engages with Muslim women who have suffered various forms of religiously sanctioned gender discrimination. These are included in the 2012 evidence booklet "Equal and Free?"[68] There is significant and growing evidence of inequality in the treatment of women through Shari'a councils.

---

[64] Peter Riddell, "The Archbishop and Shari'a: A Pas D'eux?" *The American Spectator* (2008), https://spectator.org/44096_archbishop-and-sharia-pas-de-deux, accessed April, 2019.

[65] Ibid.

[66] Michael Curtis, "Britain Confronts the Problem of Shari'a Law," *American Thinker*, published August 6, 2018.

[67] Ibid., 3.

[68] "Equal and Free? Evidence Booklet," http://equalandfree.org/case-studies, accessed September, 2019.

Thorneycroft notes that "there is a fundamental conflict between traditional Islamic law and international human rights standards... there are fundamental differences between traditional Shari'a law and international human rights law that prevent the two from coexisting."[69] She explains that one way forward is using progressive schools of thought. Some authors have pointed to a progressive theory of Muslim jurisprudence called the evolutionary principle.[70] This interpretation of the Qur'an distinguishes between the passages written during the Meccan and Medinan periods. The Medinan writings tend to be more hostile and aggressive. The Mecca suras should be the ones that are preferred for peaceful coexistence.

Study of Islamic law uncovers practices that are not compatible with UK common law and if taken to extreme interpretation could have serious implications for freedom and civil liberties. There are opportunities for change and to listen carefully to the voices of those who have been most impacted, alongside affected women's groups who have experienced first-hand what it is like to live under Shari'a. As part of her conclusion, Thorneycroft comments, "The weight of tradition and the powerful political interests served by the Shari'a will ensure that the road to reform of Islamic law will be a long and difficult one, but without it, international norms may never be fully integrated into the Muslim community."[71] The teaching of traditional jurists who claim that "the door of independent reasoning has been closed and the interpretation of the Qur'an and sunnah is complete," will keep communities closed and entrenched.[72]

Bibliography

An-Naim, Abdullahi Ahmed. *Towards an Islamic Reformation*. New York: Syracuse University Press, 1990.

Barnett, A., and M. Namazie. *Enemies Not Allies: The Far-Right*. London: One Law for All, 2011.

Caner, Emet, and Emir Fethi Caner. *Unveiling Islam: An Insider's Look at Muslim Life and Belief*. Grand Rapids, MI: Monarch, 2003.

---

[69] Thorneycroft, *Islam and Human Rights*, 9.
[70] Abdullahi Ahmed An-Naim, *Towards an Islamic Reformation* (New York: Syracuse University Press, 1990), 180.
[71] Thorneycroft, *Islam and Human Rights*, 10.
[72] Ibid.

Chapman, Colin. *Cross and Crescent: Responding to the Challenges of Islam*. Nottingham: InterVarsity Press, 2007.

Curtis, Michael. "Britain Confronts the Problem of Shari'a Law." *American Thinker*. Published August 6, 2018).

Daneshgar, Majid, and Walid A. Saleh. *Islamic Studies Today: Essays in Honour of Andrew Rippin*. Boston: Brill, 2017.

Kern, Soeren. "The Islamization of Britain," https://www.gatestoneinstitute.org/11648/britain-islamization-2017, accessed April, 2019.

Manea, Elham. *Women and Shari'a Law*. London: I. B. Tauris, 2016.

Musk, Bill. *Kissing Cousins? Christians and Muslims Face to Face*. Oxford: Monarch, 2005.

Namazie, Maryam. *Shari'a Law in Britain: A Threat to One Law for All and Equal Rights*. London: One Law for All, 2010.

Riddell, Peter. "The Archbishop and Shari'a: A Pas D'eux?" *The American Spectator* (2008), https://spectator.org/44096_archbishop-and-sharia-pas-de-deux, accessed April, 2019.

Siddiqui, Mona. *Christians, Muslims and Jesus*. Padstow: Yale University Press, 2013.

Solomon, Sam, and Atif Debs. *Not the Same God: Is the Quranic Allah the Lord God of the Bible*. London: Wilberforce publications 2018.

Sookhdeo, Patrick. *The Challenge of Islam to the Church and its Mission*. Pewsey: Isaac Publishing, 2009.

The Independent Review into the Application of Shari'a Law in England and Wales, https://assets.publishing.service.gov.uk/government/uploads/system/uploads/attachment_data/file/678478/6.4152_HO_CPFG_Report_into_Sharia_Law_in_the_UK_WEB.pdf.

The Qur'an: A New Translation by M. A. S. Abdel Haleem. Oxford: Oxford University Press, 2004.

Thorne, Clive. *Discovering Jesus through Asian Eyes*. London: Good Book Company, 2014.

Thorneycroft, Charlotte. *Islam and Human Rights: The Compatibility of Shari'a Law with the Declaration of Human Rights*. Occasional Paper No. 8. Northwood: LST, 2007.

MUSLIM WOMEN AND THE BUSINESS WORLD

The Connection between Women's Rights, Religious Freedom and Thriving Business Communities in the Muslim World

Shirin Taber[73]

In this article, I aim to explore the connection between women's rights, religious freedom and thriving business communities in the Muslim world. If we are serious about transforming the Muslim world in the 21st century though ensuring greater peace, innovation and religious freedom, then women are the most strategic solution. A growing number of governments, academic and faith organizations recognize that women are the key to transforming Muslim majority nations. An emerging modern generation is showing the world that Muslim women exhibit diverse desires, accomplishments and challenges. We need a robust perspective of Muslim women's roles in the development of healthy, thriving and religiously free societies with human rights at its core. While conservative Muslims embrace Sharia, holding on piously to their Islamist beliefs, there exists an increasing number who desire reform and democracy. Some women even leave the religion all together. Drawing on the examples of the Prophet's wife, Khadija, the Islamic feminist movement and Qur'anic texts, I argue that peace and prosperity in Muslim-majority nations depends on expanding women's rights in conjunction with religious freedom.

The Status of Women in the Muslim World

---

[73] Shirin Taber is Iranian-American and directs the Middle East Women's Leadership Network. She is the author of *Muslims Next Door* and the co-author of *Islam and North America*. Today she partners with NGOs and faith based organizations to produce media which promotes women's rights, peace building and religious freedom – www.mideastwomen.org.

While there is growing interest in the #METOO and #TIMESUP movements, one must not forget the women who are subjected to cultural and religious-based discrimination every day globally. Gender equality is not only defined by glass ceilings, pay raises, and workplace sexual harassment. No, there are millions of women subjugated to extremism all over the globe. These women are limited in their access to education, work, travel, healthcare, media, fashion, fitness and many other basic human developments. Millions face inequality in marriage, divorce, custody battles and inheritance laws.

A fundamental element of an inclusive, peaceful and prosperous society is reduced cultural and religious discrimination towards women. The expansion of women's rights and freedom of belief is crucial in order to advance toward sustainable peace and security around the world. However, a growing number of people report having experienced or witnessed discrimination in their workplaces and communities around the world. This is not surprising given that most leaders and institutions receive little to no education about the business significance of freedom of conscience and inclusion. Sadly, societies fail to build practices and protocols that reflect appropriate human rights, resulting in significant costs ranging from lower employee morale and productivity, which limit the growth potential of economies globally.[74]

In response to the tremendous need to highlight women's roles in peace-building solutions, leaders and stakeholders must focus on empowering Muslim women in business communities to achieve their fullest potential, giving them the visibility and platform to counter discrimination. In this following section I will explore the life of Khadijah, the Prophet's wife, a fearless and talented woman who utilized her business to expand her husband's impact. I will argue that for Muslim-majority nations to advance, they must allow the same independence, innovation and freedom of conscience that Khadija expressed during the early years of Islam.

Inspiration: Khadijah's Role in Muhammad's Life

---

[74] Brian Grim and Jo-Ann Lyon, "Religious Freedom Empowers Women," World Economic Forum Agenda, published May, 2016, https://religiousfreedomandbusiness.org/2/post/2016/05/religious-freedom-empowers-women.html.

According to Alfred Guillaume, the Professor of Arabic Studies and Head of the Department of Near and Middle East in the SOAS in the University of London, "Khadijah was a merchant woman of dignity and wealth." She was the richest and most respected woman in all of Quraysh. Prior to meeting Muhammad, she had already been married twice and had children. Because of her great affluence and power, many people sought to get close to her. She hired men from Quraysh to grow her business outside the country. When she heard about Muhammad's upright character, she sent for him to take her goods to Syria. Guillaume shares that "Khadijah was a determined, noble, and intelligent woman possessing the properties with which God willed to honor her."[75]

Muhammad was 25 and Khadijah was 40 when they met. She was his employer. When Khadijah heard of Muhammad's success on his business expedition and the claims that angelic beings attended to him, she proposed marriage to him. Soon after, Muhammad went with his uncle Hamza to take Khadijah's hand in marriage. Later they had 7 children together.[76] Muhammad and Khadija were married monogamously for twenty-five years. Clearly, he was devoted to her on many levels.

Today, Muslims revere Muhammad's first and cherished wife Khadijah; Khadijah is considered the mother of Islam. It is said that she fed and clothed the poor, assisted her relatives financially and provided marriage portions for poor relatives.[77] However, many fail to reflect upon the fact that Khadijah was Muhammad's boss and benefactor. Fifteen years older than he was, Khadija noticed Muhammad's good looks and pleasant demeanour, and inquired about him. Thus, she took the counter-cultural "first step" to begin a relationship with him.

After they were married, Khadija continued her business success, financing Muhammad's life and ministry. She allowed him the special privilege of spending countless hours alone meditating and developing his spiritual life. Once Muhammad began to have visions, she championed him, encouraging other leaders to listen to

---

[75] A. Guillame, *The Life of Muhammad* (Pakistan: Oxford University Press, 1982), 82-83, 106-113, 191, 313.

[76] Ibid.

[77] A. Christian Van Gorder, *Islam, Peace and Social Justice: A Christian Perspective* (Cambridge: Cambridge University Press, 2014), 162.

him and follow his new revelations. She was the first follower of Islam.

In contrast to many Muslim women today, Khadijah was no "housewife" or "help-mate" in the traditional sense. Once Muhammad became a Prophet, she used her platform to sponsor the growth of his new religion, Islam. One could easily imagine that without Khadija's great wealth, Muhammad would not have had the freedom to spend days hearing from God and growing his ministry. With the support of an empowering wife, Muhammad's ministry may have even died out. Khadijah allowed Muhammad a long leash, so to speak. Like some wives, she did not require her husband to work to help provide for the family. Although they sired seven children, she allowed him to take spiritual retreats, travel with his companions, lead a start-up ministry, and become an itinerant preacher. All of this existed under her benevolent umbrella.

As one carefully examines Khadija's life, a central question arises: why does the average Muslim woman's experience today look so different to that of Khadija's time? Why are millions of Muslim women "shut in," not allowed to express their gifts and talents freely? Why has the Muslim world lost touch with Khadijah's example? If the Prophet referred to Khadija as the "most ideal woman," then why aren't more Muslim women following her example of individuality, freedom and ingenuity today?

Khadijah's life-time accomplishments must be leveraged for women's rights and the religious freedom movement. Without her stubborn yet sacrificial spirit, free-thinking, entrepreneurship and generosity, Islam would not have been birthed. As a wealthy and respected woman, she provided Muhammad the platform, visibility and resources to develop his ministry and expand his outreach. Without her empowerment, Islam would not have been sustainable.

After the Prophet's death, Muslims errantly sidelined women for the following 1,300 years. They ignored the enormous economic and creative engine that women provide when they are free to express their gifts and ideas. Rather, Muslims must re-examine Khadija's role in Muhammad's life. As Nabia Abbott shares in *Women and the State in Early Islam*, Khadija was supportive of Muhammad's prophetic mission, always helping in his work, proclaiming his message and belittling any opposition to his prophecies. It was her encouragement that helped Muhammad believe in his mission and spread Islam.[78] Thus, Muslims must expand women's freedom to share their talents just as Khadijah did. They need to learn to support religious liberties which allow women to fulfil their God given purpose and help build thriving economic and peaceful communities.

Islamic Feminism

According to the New World Encyclopedia, "Islamic feminism is concerned with the role of women in Islam. It aims for the full equality of all Muslims, regardless of sex or gender, in public and private life."[79] Islamic feminists promote women's rights, gender equality, and social justice grounded in the Qur'an and other Islamic teachings. "Although rooted in Islam, the movement's pioneers have also utilized secular and European or non-Muslim feminist discourses and recognize the role of Islamic feminism as part of an integrated global feminist movement."[80]

Muslim feminists and reformers encourage the questioning of patriarchal interpretations of Islamic teachings of the Qur'an, Hadith, and Sharia so that women may participate in a more equal and just society. However, for Muslim-born women to experience true women's rights, the first key is the expansion of religious freedom in the Islamic world. Consider the words of Saeed Abdullah,

> ...the ability of a person to believe freely is central to the Qur'anic idea of true belief. Forced conversions to keep an individual bound to a particular religion are condemned in the Qur'an. An understanding of the intersection of Islam and religious freedom must include consideration of religious freedom for Muslims themselves, not least of all in Muslim majority societies. This is because religious freedom is at the heart of belief itself for Muslims.[81]

Abdullah, along with other scholars, argues that for the Muslim world there is a precedent for freedom of belief. The Qur'an reads in *Sura* 2:256, "Let there be no compulsion in religion." This means that

---

[78] Nabia Abbott, *Women and the State in Early Islam* (Chicago, IL: The University of Chicago Press, 1942), 106-109.
[79] "Islamic Feminism," New World Encyclopedia,
http://www.newworldencyclopedia.org/entry/Islamic_feminism.
[80] Ibid.
[81] Abdullah Saeed, *Islam and Belief: At Home with Religious Freedom* (Farmingdale, NY: Minute Men Press, 2017), 7-10.

individuals must not be forced to follow religious teachings and traditions. Faith under force is invalid and ingenuine. Therefore, it is never in the public's interest to force belief on individuals, regardless of gender, and restrict their right to question, explore or fulfil their purpose. Rather, we must work to create space for women to freely form their own beliefs and practices. Like Khadijah, women need the freedom of conscience to express their gifts and talents without fear, discrimination, sexual harassment, or persecution.

Interpreting the Qur'an in Modern Day

Like Christians, Muslims have debated for centuries whether the Qur'an should be interpreted literally or through reason. They have asked, "how should Muslims understand the Qur'an?" "Should Muslims understand the Qur'an through reason or the Hadith?" This fundamental divide among reason-based scholars and literal-based scholars led the Mu'tazilites to argue that the primary method for studying the Qur'an must be led by reason, not a literal reading.

The Mu'tazilites were a Muslim community that started in the 8th century and thrived until the 11th century. Influenced by the Greeks, they had a deeply rationalist view of the world and theology. They argued that the nature of God is accessible though philosophy, logic, and observation. They believed that revelation cannot be contradictory to logic. Therefore, Qur'anic verses that seem to contradict other verses or the state of the world are metaphorical.[82] Interpreting the Qur'an through reason led the Mu'tazilites to argue the following:

1. God is One. Nothing competes with his pre-eminence.
2. The Qur'an cannot be an uncreated entity (it is not eternal like God).
3. God must be just.
4. Therefore, humans must have free will. Otherwise, God would not be just.
5. Because of God's just character, he must punish the sinner and reward the good.
6. However, humans cannot judge others. It is God's role.
7. The task of the believer is to command the right and forbid the wrong.[83]

---

[82] "Who are the Mu'tuzalites?" https://www.quora.com/Who-are-mutazilites.
[83] Peter Riddle, "History of Islamic Discussion and Debate," YouTube, https://www.youtube.com/watch?v=P07ZViI8EeI.

Based on the works of a growing number of scholars, I suggest we encourage today's Muslims to approach their texts through the lens of a just and fair God. Additionally, we must cultivate a correct understanding of the nature of God, one that shapes our relationship with him, ourselves and each other. It is his divine nature that compels us to worship him and obey his life-affirming commandments every day.

Qur'anic View of the Nature of God

Christians can find common ground with Muslims who share similar views about the nature of God. When addressing issues of women's rights and religious freedom, we can refer to Qur'anic passages that elevate the nature of God. There are many verses in the Qur'an, for example, that speak about the nature of God in a way in which Christians and Muslims can agree. Especially important is the idea that God is forgiving and merciful.

Some sample verses in include Q2:255-256; Q5:41, 45; Q7:54; Q11:44, 46; Q32:6-9; Q41:11-10. Many of the verses speak of God's mercy and forgiveness. He is concerned with the welfare of the downtrodden, urging humans to steadfastness and compassion. For example, in *Suras* 90, 92, 93, 106, and 107, the Qur'an shares that the "Lord provides food for the hungry and safety to ward off fear," therefore believers are to avoid greediness, but rather care for the poor and the orphans. For many, these verses show the character of God in that he loves all people regardless of their gender or station in life.

Additionally, many verses in the Qur'an point to the beauty and magnitude of God's creation. In *Sura* 16:68-69, the Bee, we read, "And the Lord inspired the bee, saying, 'Build yourselves houses in the mountains and trees and what people construct. Then feed on all kinds of fruit and follow the ways made easy for you by the Lord. From their bellies comes a drink of different colors in where there is healing for people. There is truly a sign in this for people who think." Like the industrious bee, women are also capable of feeding and healing humanity. But they need the freedom to step outside man-made confines that limit their contribution. Muslims and Christians share many common beliefs about God's character and involvement throughout human history. Together we can celebrate his nature and build common ground as we explore the Scriptures together. We can have hope that, as people encounter God's love, he can do a transforming work in their hearts.

On another positive note, the Qur'an gives proof that the Biblical stories (of Jews and Christians) were circulating in Arabia prior to the 700s. In *Sura* 21, we read, "Command them to remember the prophets Moses, David, Solomon, Job. This is your community." This presents Christians an opportunity to bridge the Qur'an's account of Old Testament stories and to the gospel. More importantly, the Qur'anic accounts create a connection between the Abrahamic faiths. For example, *Sura* 37 writes that Noah cried out to God and was saved, along with his household. Abraham asked for a son who is later offered as sacrifice. Isaac is described as a good prophet. Moses, Aaron, Elijah, and John's stories are recounted too.

Thus, Christians need to engage Muslims in scriptural reasoning. We can encourage Muslims to explore the benefits of the history and significance of women's rights and religious liberty. It is our duty to share the research and biblical texts which show that when women are treated with dignity and equality in conjunction with religious freedom, communities experience greater innovation, peace and prosperity in the long term.

Qur'anic View of Religious Freedom

According to *Women and Religious Freedom*, by Nazila Ghanea, inherent in religious freedom is the right to believe or not believe as one's conscience leads, and live out one's beliefs openly, peacefully, and without fear. Freedom of religion or belief is an expansive right that includes the freedoms of thought, conscience, expression, association, and assembly.[84]

The world is changing, especially as Muslims are increasingly exposed to the ideals of pluralism. Even though they do not discuss it openly, social media is causing the new generation to embrace democratic and human rights ideals like never before. When considering the growing movement of freedom of belief around the globe, there are a number of shared values that Muslims and non-Muslims can support. According to Hassan Usman, "religious faith and practice under coercion is clearly not genuine – this has been

---

[84] Nazila Ghanea "Women and Religious Freedom," University of Oxford, July 2017, http://www.uscirf.gov/sites/default/files/WomenandReligiousFreedom.pdf.

noted by Islamic theologians and jurists over the centuries since the early days of Islam."[85] Usman categorically asserts that faith and non-faith involve active belief or unbelief, rather than a passive state or coercion. "Therefore, it is never in the public interest," shares Usman, "to attempt to force belief and faith on other people and restrict their right to question, criticize and explore."[86]

Similar to their counterparts in the West, many Muslim women value the freedom to choose their own faith perspective and activities. Muslim women want the right to choose their support network and husband. Muslims want the freedom to play sports, travel or drive a car. As for helping business economies, many Muslim women also want the freedom to choose where they work, whether in a boutique, office, bank, theatre, restaurant or hotel.

Many scholars have reported that religious freedom was established by Muslims in the previous millennia and set the bar for most tolerant nations. Muslims were admonished to not only resist persecution, but help protect churches, synagogues and other religious entities. Early Muslims were commanded to respect all houses of worship, including monasteries. In *Sura* 40:22, we read,

> God has the power to protect them… if God did not repel some people by means of others, many monasteries, churches, synagogues and mosques, where God's name is much invoked, would have been destroyed… God controls the outcome of all events.

Namely, God has chosen to protect Christians, Jews and Muslims over the ages, and that includes women and religious minority believers. For without God's protection, many would perish. In the same way, Muslims are to support the religious freedom of outsiders and people of other faith perspectives.

Sura 2:256 says, "there is no compulsion in religion." In conjunction with verse 62, the Qur'an states,

---

[85] Hassan Usama, "No Compulsion in Religion: Islam and Freedom of Belief,"
https://docs.wixstatic.com/ugd/789970_2a2065ac91a04f4dbb95f49fc4aaaaaa.pdf.
[86] Ibid.

The Muslim believer, the Jews, the Christians and the Sabian—
all those who believe in God and the Last Day and do good—
will have their reward with the Lord.

From these passages and others, we see a clear apologetic that Muslims are directed to live respectfully of outsiders. Clearly, the extremist guard is losing step with the spirit of God's peace-promoting message.

As for secular people or people of no faith, there are verses that warn believers to act justly. In *Sura* 80, titled "He Frowned," the Prophet is reproached to not bother with disbelievers. In *Sura* 68, titled "The Pen," Muhammad deals with accusations that he is mad. But God tells him to be patient with the disbelievers. In *Sura* 109, titled "The Disbelievers," the Prophet is instructed to say he has his religion and the disbelievers have their own. In *Sura* 88, the Qur'an reads that it is not the Prophet's job to control, but to remind people. In fact, the Prophet is told to patiently endure disbelievers, ignoring them politely (*Sura* 73). Time and time again, we see throughout the scriptures God's admonishment to love, serve and pray for our neighbors, rather than judging them.

Where Do We Go From Here?

Islamic scholar, Christine Schirrmacher argues, in conjugation with Armin Hasemann, whether religious freedom will be accepted in the future or not is ultimately and unquestionably dependent upon the result of the struggle between radical Islamic forces and progressive forces. It will be determined by the masses' acceptance of confining religion to the private sphere and the extent to which individuals detach from tradition.[87]

However, the huge task of promoting women's rights in conjunction with religious freedom is not a venture that Muslims can accomplish alone. The risks are too dangerous. Extremism is everywhere. Women are punished for speaking out or demanding their universal human rights. Some Muslim women are imprisoned and even killed. Forward thinking Muslim-background people need the support of fellow Christians, Jews, secular people, NGOs,

---

[87] Christine Schirrmacher, *"Let there be no compulsion in Religion (Sura 2:256): Apostasy from Islam as judged by contemporary Islamic Theologians* (Eugene, OR: Wipf and Stock, 2016), 563.

churches, seminaries, celebrities, athletes, and business leaders to help them kick-start the new wave of pluralism and democracy.

Religious freedom, Jennifer Bryson shares, is an antidote to violent Islamic extremism.[88] Crime is down. Innovation is up. Typically, as women earn income, more is invested in education and charitable causes. All people are encouraged to respect the freedoms of others and contribute their whole self to the good of society.

Thus, as the Muslim world has been plagued with warfare, corruption, division and poor economies since 9/11, I believe it is time to expand women's rights and religious freedom globally. This means the right for women in the business world to choose to believe or not believe, to worship or not worship, without the fear of a backlash. Women must be free to decide in their own heart what is right for them personally. Together, we can unleash the power and resourcefulness of women to contribute to economies and the overall well-being of the world.

After all, as most Muslims would concede, true faith is based on free will. The Muslim-majority world can thrive once women are free to share their full potential, leading to creating free, safe, diverse and inclusive communities.

Conclusion

While I have explored the connection between women's rights and religious freedom in Muslim communities, I do not suggest that Christians must embrace Khadija, Islamic Feminism or even the Qur'an to promote peace and freedom. Rather, I seek to make the case that Christians must come along side Muslims in the workplace and society, carefully inquiring what our faith perspectives actually say about women's roles. In fact, I want to challenge Christians to partner with Muslim-background leaders to address core human rights issues while promoting religious freedom for all people. We must recognize that more and more Muslims operate out of the belief that there is no single authoritative understanding of the Qur'an. Many are challenging the subjugation of women at all levels of society. However, extremists make convincing counterarguments to shift the debate back to medieval male-centric norms. Many also

---

[88] Jennifer Bryson, http://arcoftheuniverse.info/muslims-call-religious-freedom-religious-freedom.

disagree among themselves about specific interpretations of the Qur'an, which can lead to divisions within the movement. Thus, the Muslim community needs our support to work toward a more unified understanding of pluralism and religious liberties.

Today, there are many modern examples of Muslim women triumphing in the academic, business, humanitarian and political worlds. Gender inequalities persist in the fabric of every human society. To make a global impact, Muslim women must continue to build bridges with their non-Muslim counterparts (Christian, Jewish, and secular women) to provide a defence of their work. They must focus on universal human rights and avoid the subjectivity of religious arguments.

At a time of change and upheaval within the Muslim world, we can applaud the bold women who articulate a fresh vision of women's rights and religious freedom. Harvard Economist and Nobel Laureate Amartya Sen argues that the combination of gender equality and freedom of belief within a country will result in better lives.

Thus, if religious freedom is an integral part of the "bundled commodity" of human freedoms, religious freedom should be closely associated with "the general betterment of people's lives."[89] The Hudson Institute data confirms the correlation between women's rights and religious freedom – as was put forth in its thesis report.

> The study found that when religious freedom is high, there is less conflict, better health outcomes, higher levels of earned income, and better educational opportunities for women. Moreover, religious freedom is associated with higher overall human development, as measured by the human development index.[90]

The future of the Muslim world and business economies will depend on these leaders' abilities to incorporate human rights into a cultural and religious framework. Hand in hand with Christians around the world, Muslim-background women have an important role to play in helping to advance democracy and pluralism for generations to come.

---

[89] "Religious Freedom and Business Foundation,"
https://religiousfreedomandbusiness.org/price-of-freedom-denied.
[90] Ibid.

Believing that prosperous economies are dependent on creating diverse and inclusive communities, I hope my writings inspire and challenge a new generation of leaders to carefully examine the role of Khadija, Islamic Feminists and the Qur'anic texts that Christians and Muslims can agree on, to expand women's rights and religious freedom so that all people everywhere can fulfil their God-given purpose.

Bibliography

Bryson, Jennifer.
> http://arcoftheuniverse.info/muslims-call-religious-freedomreligious-freedom.

Guillame, A. *The Life of Muhammad.* Pakistan: Oxford University Press, 1982.

Ghanea, Nazila. "Women and Religious Freedom." University of Oxford, July 2017,
> http://www.uscirf.gov/sites/default/files/WomenandReligiousFreedom.pdf.

Grim, Brian, and Jo-Ann Lyon. "Religious Freedom Empowers Women." World Economic Forum Agenda, May 2016,
> https://religiousfreedomandbusiness.org/2/post/2016/05/religious-freedom-empowers-women.html.

Islamic Feminism. New World Encyclopedia,
> http://www.newworldencyclopedia.org/entry/Islamic_feminism.

Marshall, Paul, and Nina Shea. *Silenced: How Apostasy and Blasphemy Codes are Choking Freedom Worldwide.* Oxford: Oxford University Press, 2011.

Religious Freedom and Business Foundation,
> https://religiousfreedomandbusiness.org/price-of-freedom-denied.

Saeed, Abdullah. *Islam and Belief: At Home with Religious Freedom.* Farmingdale, NY: Minute Men Press, 2017.

Schirrmacher, Christine. *"Let There Be No Compulsion in Religion" (Sura 2:256): Apostasy from Islam as Judged by Contemporary Islamic Theologians.* Religious Freedom 4. Eugene, OR: Wipf and Stock, 2016.

Usama, Hassan. "No Compulsion in Religion: Islam and Freedom of Belief," https://docs.wixstatic.com/ugd/789970_2a2065ac91a 04f4dbb95f49fc4aaaaaa.pdf.

Wahid, Kyai Haji Aburrahman. "Foreword: God Needs No Defense." In *Silenced: How Apostasy and Blasphemy Codes are Choking Freedom Worldwide*, by Paul Marshall and Nina Shea, xvii-xxii. Oxford: Oxford University Press, 2011.